Moored to the Continent?
Britain and European Integration

Moored to the Continent?
Britain and European Integration

Edited by
Roger Broad and Virginia Preston

La Grande Bretagne a fait 'les premiers pas dans la voie que,
un jour peut-être, le conduira à s'amarrer au continent'.
*Great Britain has made 'the first moves that, one day perhaps, will
bring it to moor alongside the continent'.*
Charles de Gaulle, 14 January 1963

Institute of Historical Research
University of London

© Institute of Contemporary British History 2001,
individual chapters, the contributors

Cover photograph: Joining the Market, Hulton Archive

Published by:
Institute of Historical Research
University of London
Senate House
London
WC1E 7HU

ISBN: 1871348617 $2172\overline{3}117$

Typeset in 11 point Garamond by the Institute of Contemporary
British History
Printed and bound by Quorn Litho

For Edmund Dell, 1921–1999

Contents

Contributors

BRIVATI, Brian, Reader in History, Kingston University

BROAD, Roger, an official of the European Commission 1964–73 and head of the European Parliament's UK Office 1973–86.

CROWSON, Nicholas J., Lecturer in History, University of Birmingham.

DAVIDSON, Ian, *Financial Times* correspondent, Brussels and Paris, at various times 1962–72; principal foreign affairs commentator 1979–97.

DELL, Rt Hon Edmund, MP for Birkenhead 1964–79, Secretary of State for Trade, 1976–8.

ELLISON, James, Lecturer in European History, Queen Mary, University of London.

JUNKER, Théo, director in the Committees and Delegations Directorate-General, European Parliament.

KAISER, Wolfram, Department of History, University of Portsmouth and Visiting Professor, College of Europe in Bruges, Belgium.

KITZINGER, Uwe, Founding President of Templeton College, Oxford, the first British economist to the Council of Europe in Strasbourg, 1951–6, Cabinet Adviser to Sir Christopher Soames at the European Commission, 1973–5.

MARTINEZ ZARZOSO, Inma, Lecturer in Economics, Universidad Jaime I, Castellon, Spain.

MIDDLEMAS, Keith, Professor Emeritus, University of Sussex.

PRESTON, Virginia, Deputy Director, Institute of Contemporary British History, University of London.

SINCLAIR, P. J. N., Professor of Economics, University of Birmingham and Director, Central Banking Studies, Bank of England.

TURPIN, Colin, Fellow of Clare College, University of Cambridge.

Foreword

The contributions to this volume are updated papers read at a conference organised by the Institute of Contemporary British History to mark the 40th anniversary of the signing of the Rome treaty on 25 March 1957. We are grateful to those who read papers at the conference and prepared them for publication, and those others who contributed to the discussion. Warm thanks are due also for the financial support for the conference arranged by Martyn Bond, former Head of the European Parliament's UK Office, Geoffrey Martin, Head of the Representation of the European Commission in the UK, and Robert Elphick, Secretary-General of the European League for Economic Co-operation.

Roger Broad
Virginia Preston

Cross-Channel or Transatlantic?

Roger Broad

The contributors to this volume implicitly or explicitly offer an indictment of the British political system in the past two generations. Confronted with a fundamental change in national fortunes at the end of the Second World War the political and governmental establishment failed to understand the consequences, and when belatedly it did so, failed to think through the problem to a coherent response.

As Edmund Dell and James Ellison demonstrate, neither the leadership of the two major political parties nor the main figures of the Whitehall mandarinate of the 1940s and 1950s understood how the post-war world was evolving. The major reason for this, these two authors indicate, was attitudes of mind best summed up as arrogance. Blinded by pride in Britain's undoubtedly admirable wartime role in resisting Nazi aggression, the country's leaders refused to admit either to themselves, and even less to the wider public, that the status quo ante bellum could not be re-established. Diplomatically and politically Britain was one of the 'Big Three' in 1945. Economically and militarily this was not the case, as the step-by-step abandonment of imperial authority from the late forties showed. Britain could only maintain even a reduced world role by sitting in the shadow of the United States. The Suez adventure in 1956 posed a choice between being an American satellite and following France and other west European states through economic integration towards political unity (however vaguely and variously defined). The 1945–51 Labour governments had spurned the integration movement on the Continent, which took concrete form without Britain in 1950–2 with the Coal and Steel Community. For all Churchill's rhetoric and criticism of Labour over the ECSC when in opposition, back in office he took no different a line. Eden followed suit and rejected constructive participation in the Messina conference that laid the basis of the European Economic Community, today's European Union. Britain did not chose, and when forced to do so as occasion arose, took the American option.

Apart from the attitude of condescension, Dell and Ellison underline the failure of the establishment to grasp – or openly to admit – that the aim of the continentals was political, not merely economic. If any in high position in Britain did understand this, they did not like what they found and preferred to ignore it. Thus in the late 1940s Ernest Bevin did nothing for Anglo-German reconciliation nor for the more important need, the promotion of Franco-German reconciliation. It was left to these countries alone to find their own solution, and this resulted in the Franco-German leadership in Europe that lasted for the remainder of the 20th century. About the abortive free-trade area negotiations in 1957-8, Ellison records how the Macmillan government envisaged no fundamental change in the country's place in the world. Once again, as in 1950, the continental will would not bend to Britain's demands to have what appeared to be the best (for it) of both worlds: free trade for manufactures within western Europe but little limitation on trade with the Commonwealth and other overseas food suppliers.

An unwillingness to choose

With this background Wolfram Kaiser sees the successive attempts by Britain under the Macmillan and Wilson governments in the 1960s to seek full EEC membership as being characterised by tactical foreign policy manoeuvres and short-term party advantage. Certainly in both cases there was no willingness at the leadership level, and even less among backbench and general opinion in either the Conservative or Labour parties, to accept the consequences of Britain's diminished world position. Macmillan's application, Kaiser concludes, was an element of his transatlantic policy in order to try to achieve leadership in Europe. He sees these aims as incompatible. Wilson, he contends, was 'exclusively motivated by tactical considerations', whether internal or external. This contributor is right to conclude that when de Gaulle resigned in 1969 the British political elite had 'not developed any clearly defined strategic objectives in Europe'.

Uwe Kitzinger takes us through the 1970–2 negotiations and the 1975 referendum. He is convinced that without Edward Heath's commitment to European unification (which he had demonstrated from his earliest days in Parliament) it is doubtful whether the negotiations would have been successful. It was in this period that Labour, back in opposition, fell into the temptation to play the European card for domestic advantage to a degree that undoubtedly threatened national interests (a temptation to which the Conservatives have now in their turn fallen). The extent to which the issue cut across party lines became clear when one quarter of the Parliamentary Labour Party voted for Community membership against the whip, or abstained, and when a few weeks later the Heath government connived with pro-Market Labour MPs to get its entry legislation through Parliament, though narrowly.

The referendum was of course a means to try to reconcile the Labour Party to membership. It failed.

Loss of parliamentary powers

Once inside the Community British constitutional practice was profoundly affected. The European Communities Act of 1972 Colin Turpin describes as 'an unprecedented limitation on Parliament and government'. There is now much more delegated legislation and 'power has drained away from Parliament, some to the institutions of the Union and some of it to the government'. Parliament's own attempts to influence European legislation at a nascent stage Turpin finds impressive but insufficient, in part because it is the government that controls how Parliament scrutinises draft EU legislation. Another major consequence of membership is that British courts have acquired a power of judicial review, which has 'profoundly modified their traditional deference to a sovereign Parliament'. He expresses disquiet at these developments, although pointing (somewhat tentatively) towards potential amelioration to the Union's democratic deficit through greater powers for the European Parliament, more effective participation by national parliaments and the decentralisation of decision-making to member states and to regional and local authorities. On the other hand Turpin notes that individual British citizens have gained important rights through the EU treaties and secondary legislation, notably in the field of sexual equality.

It is not only the British constitutional situation that has become more complex. Keith Middlemas stresses the plurality of the players involved in EU decision-making: governments, ministries, state agencies, regions, industries, financial institutions and unions. The characters and interests of each contribute to the outcome in legislative and administrative forms. The first enlargement of membership in 1973 accelerated progress towards greater intergovernmental activity, and this continues, by no means solely due to British influence. He points up one of several contradictions in British policy in noting how in the eighties the Thatcher government strongly advocated the Single Market, but took a long time to appreciate the corollaries: deeper integration, including movement towards economic and monetary union, stronger interventionist powers for the Commission, increased qualified majority voting and extended jurisdiction by the Court of Justice. Conversely, other corollaries were not all welcomed by enthusiasts for integration in some other countries when faced with structural unemployment, wage cutting, mergers and hostile takeovers and heavy investment in new technologies. Fears of 'Anglo Saxon capitalism' were rife. The comment by a French diplomat during the British entry negotiations that 'Il faut vouloir les conséquences de ce qu'on veut', works both ways.

British membership: profit and loss?

The lack of a clear strategic aim of British membership, whether under Conservative or Labour governments, and the continuing domestic controversy, has meant that a great deal of time, effort and emotion has been devoted to trying to establish whether Britain has 'benefited' from membership. P.J.N. Sinclair and I. Martinez Zarzoso provide substantial statistical detail, concluding that, especially in the first few years of membership, Britain gained economically. But so long as at least half of the Union budget was devoted to agriculture and as successive enlargements have directed more regional aid to the Mediterranean members and Ireland, Britain has been at a financial disadvantage. These contributors see 'no compelling justification' for the CAP. The only mitigating factor is that the USA and Japan have had agricultural markets no more open to competition, although international pressures are now moving towards more open markets. They conclude that Britain paid a small net contribution into the EU budget from its GDP on a factor cost basis, although more than its 'fair' share. But Germany and the Netherlands paid proportionately more. On the other hand, taking GDP on a per caput basis, Théo Junker suggests that Britain's position has been more favourable, at least on occasion paying in less net than any country but Ireland.

However, the concentration in Britain on such financial matters has acted as a displacement activity to escape developing an overall sense of purpose to Britain's participation in the European integration process. In the resultant clamour Britain's positive but necessarily unquantifiable contribution to the EU risks going unremarked. Apart from the pressure for the Single Market cited above, Junker notes the urging of CAP reform, insistence on tighter controls over and more transparency to the budget, the push for sharper European parliamentary scrutiny over legislation and the growing role of precedent in European jurisprudence on the lines of English common law. Resistance to over-regulation at home and advocacy of freer trade abroad have also been marked British traits. Within the monetary union, Sinclair and Zarzozo note the potential constraints on national fiscal policy.

Two divided parties

The lack of fundamental sense of purpose results from disagreement both within and between the governing parties. Over Europe the traditional left/right division did not apply. Within the Conservative Party, as Nicholas Crowson records, discord over Europe contributed to the downfall of three successive leaders – Macmillan, Heath and Thatcher – and caused difficulties for two more – Major and Hague. Several senior ministers resigned office over the issue; lesser figures left the party. For Labour, Brian Brivati recounts, dispute over Europe has been part of the party's search for a wider purpose since the fifties: did 'modernisation' mean seeking new forms of state intervention in the national economy or loosening the state's role nationally and internationally? Even more than with the Conservatives Europe for Labour was a disruptive element and contributed to the Social Democratic breakaway in 1981.

Germany: the strategic issue

Ian Davidson sees Britain's failure as not understanding three fundamental strategic issues before Europe: relations with Russia, the United Sates and Germany. For the foreseeable future Russia is no threat. Relations with the United States have been mostly benign, but the US lurches between wanting to dominate Europe and hinting at withdrawal. The fundamental strategic problem in Europe, Davidson argues, is Germany, once the most dangerous country militarily, now the most powerful economically and (excluding Russia) largest in population. Past attempts to defeat, dominate and dismember it having failed, the only strategic solution was treaty-based integration in the European Union. It is only through collective action that other European states can achieve a satisfactory solution to all three issues. Sitting offshore and with a global history Britain has evaded facing up to the situation. Admittedly, even since the end of the cold war, most Europeans have been reluctant to emerge from under America's wing and to accept responsibility for their own future. Britain has been most hesitant of all, relying on old military and intelligence links with the USA and unwilling to clarify its long-term aims in Europe. So the British have time and again in the past five decades sacrificed opportunities to influence European policy at crucial early stages. They have held back, then chased to catch up, complaining about the decisions reached in its absence. Sitting out the introduction of the euro follows that pattern.

History v. geography

The basis of Britain's European dilemma has been its difficulty in reconciling three centuries of history as a global empire centred on the edge of Europe with the facts of geography. Britain has reverted to its natural position as one among European countries, important and influential within that continent, but of limited importance at world level. The supposed 'special relationship' with the United States, so valuable to some British eyes, and cultural and residual constitutional links with Commonwealth countries, have hindered clear thought about Britain's position and interests in the closing decades of the 20th century. But it should be possible to play football with Europeans and cricket with the Commonwealth – even occasionally to win.

These divided emotions underline that Britain is home for 57 million members of a worldwide language community of over 350 million English mother-tongue speakers, plus another billion and more who live in countries where the language has official or semi-official status. Beyond even that English is unrivalled in use in international trade, finance, transport, communications, science, technology, academic discourse, the internet and culture (using the word generously). In contrast, German can muster nearly 100 million, French some 70 million and Italian barely 60 million true mother-tongue speakers. Apart from French in parts of Africa these tongues are little spoken outside Europe. Spain and Portugal, like Britain, have languages spoken by far more people abroad than at home, but with their imperial days long behind them they do not hanker for the past.

The memories of empire are reinforced because few Britons need to go outside the English-speaking world for television, films, books, plays, and scientific and technological information, so varied is the stock available without the need for translation from or knowledge of another tongue. Only 2 per cent of the 100,000 books published each year in Britain are translations. When they travel the British can usually rely on English being understood. But the effect is culturally limiting. Films and television programmes seen in Britain – whether good, bad and indifferent – are overwhelmingly of English-speaking origin. Foreign-language films provide less than one per cent of cinema revenue. That Tony Blair is the first British prime minister in four decades able to speak another language competently only underlines the insularity of British cultural attitudes.

The illusion of the 'Anglosphere'

The problem for Britain as the 21st century opens is still to decide where its priorities lie. For some Conservatives the answer lies in the 'Anglosphere', increasingly as a off-shore province of north America with its culture fed from Hollywood and its economy directed from Wall Street. It could certainly coast along comfortably, its media and publishing dominated by north American owners who promote their own political agendas without the responsibility of British citizenship and whose interest in the country is primarily commercial. Canadians and Mexicans knows who pays the piper in the North American Free Trade Area. Ironically, it is the traditional home of British nationalism on the right which toys with this concept, submerging Britain into north America. But so far Conservative Eurosceptics have lacked the courage to draw the logical conclusion from their attitudes: outright withdrawal from the European Union and trying to join an Atlantic extension of NAFTA – exchanging a grouping 30 miles from our shores for one 3,000 miles away. Outside the Union Britain could certainly negotiate a trade arrangement, but only on the EU's terms, like the other countries in the residual European Economic Area. And in any trade agreements between the EU and the USA Britain would be a minor element. The essential decisions determining Britain's economic and social – and by extension political – conditions would be taken in its absence from the centres of power. The branch-office/factory elements of the British economy – well known to employees of Ford, BMW, General Motors and Corus – would increase.

The alternative for Britain to such abdication of control over its future is to recognise that it could assert a distinctive national role - though in a challenging and demanding way – through whole-hearted participation in the European Union, learning from its partners while playing a consistent role in the Union's evolution. Its world language and links could be its most valuable contribution to Europe and the wider world. It could help restrain the more isolationist elements in the US, whether of a commercial or a military nature. Conversely, Britain could head off those continentals who still dream of a Europe tightly bound together, protectionist and pugnacious, treating the outside world - especially the USA - as a constant threat. The "Euro-Colbertism" beloved by some in France particularly is hardly compatible with a world of instant communication and persistent technological drive towards global interdependence. The continental preference – which has support from the left to the right - for social cohesion has qualities which, like the Britain's own tradition of individual social and economic initiative, could make a contribution to 21st century Europe. The weaknesses and strengths of both Anglo-Saxon and Rhineland capitalism are now evident, and challenge of the new century will be to forge a synthesis of their strengths.

For the British it comes down to which media photocall they prefer: a prime minister on the lawn of the White House as sole but subordinate companion to an American president, patronised and flattered when US needs require it; or a place in the front rank in a European summit line-up, where he or she takes a full and influential part in the joint decision-making for a giant player in the world economy that is seeking a political role to match?

Britain's Failure Over the Schuman Plan
Edmund Dell

Let me start with seven dates:

- 9 May 1950   announcement of the Schuman Plan
- 2 June 1950   UK rejects participation
- 20 June 1950   Paris negotiations start between the Six
- 18 April 1951   Treaty of Paris
- 25 October 1951   election of the Churchill government
- 10 August 1952   High Authority of the European Coal and Steel Community (ECSC) meets for the first time
- 21 December 1954 Treaty of Association between the ECSC and Britain

Britain's handling of the Schuman Plan is one of the least inspiring stories in the long history of British diplomacy. Yet the Foreign Secretary, Ernest Bevin, was probably the most powerful holder of that office in this century and was served by admiring and experienced officials. He dominated the government of which he was a member, and sat in negotiation, without too great an impression of incongruity, alongside representatives of the two superpowers. Yet his handling of the Schuman Plan announcement demonstrates a depressing failure of understanding and diplomacy. There was nothing wrong with the Schuman Plan that could not have been corrected in negotiation. And there was so much right with it that Britain should have made the effort to participate particularly as it considered itself not just a European power but a global power, a power in other words with pretensions to world leadership.

The leadership of Europe

These were days when people did speak, without the least incongruity, of British leadership in Europe. Oliver Franks was

Provost of The Queen's College, Oxford (1946–8) at the time
that I was a don there. He was serving as chairman of the
Committee for European Economic Co-operation set up to
negotiate Marshall Aid. I remember him saying to me in late 1947
what a pity it was that Britain did not seem interested in the leadership of Europe which was there for the taking. Actually the
Attlee government was interested. The trouble was that Bevin
and the Foreign Office acted as though leadership could be exercised in Europe without effort or imagination. Franks did all he
could from his position as ambassador in Washington to
encourage the Attlee government to understand French motives
in announcing the Plan. He came to regard the signature of the
Paris treaty as a major turning point for Europe.[1] On the other
hand, at the time, even he was thinking only of what he later
called 'country membership' for Britain, that is a somewhat priv-
ileged status for a somewhat distant cousin.[2]

Robert Marjolin was sure that the leadership of Europe was,
after the war, Britain's for the asking. He was in a position to
have a view. Friend and collaborator of Jean Monnet, he became
the first Secretary-General of the Organisation for European
Economic Co-operation. Subsequently he was leader of France's
delegation in the negotiations leading to the Rome treaty and
Vice-President of the European Commission. He saw Britain as
the main European victor in the war, the head of a great
Commonwealth and Empire, the centre of the sterling area.
Britain's capacity to lead was, indeed, overestimated in Europe.
Many, including Marjolin, were somewhat disillusioned by the
1949 sterling devaluation which they interpreted as demonstrating that Britain's economic health was less vibrant than had
at first appeared. The devaluation was not only a blow to Britain's
prestige. It was a source of deep resentment, at least in France,
because of the lack of consultation with Britain's European
friends. It was taken as confirming that Britain was unconcerned
by the effect of policies on western Europe. Nevertheless,
Britain, unlike the French, did have a stable government and the

British economy did seem to be regaining peacetime levels of activity faster than those of its continental neighbours.

In his memoirs, written after his time as Foreign Secretary in 1966–8, George Brown asserted:

> I have always quarrelled with Dean Acheson's much-repeated remark about Britain's having lost an empire and not found a role. We *have* a role: our role is to lead Europe. We are, and have been for eleven centuries since the reign of King Alfred, one of the leaders of Europe. It may be that Britain is destined to become the leader of Europe, of western Europe in the first place, and of as much of Europe as will come together later on.[3]

Long before George Brown wrote these words any chance of British leadership had been sacrificed. First there was the UK's relatively poor economic performance and, perhaps even more important, its conduct of economic policy which made it a frequent supplicant for the assistance of the IMF and foreign central banks; secondly, there was its failure to participate in the Schuman Plan; and, thirdly, there was its failure to participate in the negotiations leading up to the Rome treaty and hence to take part in the creation of the European Economic Community.

Supranationalism

The Attlee government did in a curious way want to be a leader in Europe even in the 1940s. But it was on one condition: that leadership did not involve binding commitments inconsistent with what were seen as the UK's wider responsibilities. Unfortunately for any British leadership ambitions, that criterion was interpreted as ruling out almost any commitment to the kinds of European economic integration sought by its continental allies. Specifically, it ruled out British participation in any purely European supranational institution.

There were three treaties into which the UK did enter with its continental partners. There were the Dunkirk treaty (1947) and the Brussels treaty (1948). But those treaties were essentially about the security of western Europe, including the UK, and they were stepping stones to the North Atlantic treaty (1949) and the creation of the North Atlantic Treaty Organisation (NATO), which committed the USA to the security of western Europe. For the British, there was a world of difference if the Americans were involved. If the Americans were involved, the British were even ready to accept the supranationalism of NATO. But European institutions which did not include the Americans must, if Britain's participation was expected, be intergovernmental. Supranational institutions were objectionable if they just united European countries. If they just united European countries they were clearly steps on the road to a federal Europe and that destination was unacceptable to Britain. But if the UK could sit alongside the USA as a global power, that was different. The trouble was that the western Europeans did want to commence the construction of a new and peaceful Europe and their chosen method included the creation of supranational institutions. There was no intention on either side that the USA should play any direct part in those institutions even though Washington's influence within them might be immense.

Bevin was suspicious that any form of supranationalism confined to Europe would give the Americans a further lever with which to influence or even control British policy. He was ambivalent about the Americans. On the one hand there was gratitude to the Americans for NATO and Marshall Aid. There was pride in sitting alongside the superpower in international institutions and organisations. On the other hand there was resentment of American power and brutality in its relations with the UK. The Americans had been pretty brutal. They had forced on Britain the acceptance of impossible conditions as part of the 1946 American Loan. They had insisted that, if Britain wanted Marshall Aid, it would be as part of Europe. There would be no special Marshall Plan for the UK. They had at first threatened that Britain might have no part in Marshall Aid if it did not abandon imperial preference. They abandoned the threat but it was impossible to forget that it had been made. They had deeply embarrassed the Attlee government in 1949 by making public their belief that the pound should be devalued. They brought pressure on Britain to take the lead in creating a federal Europe. A federal Europe, they thought, would he more prosperous and more capable of defending itself. The pressure was highly unwelcome in London.

Bevin combined his public gratitude to the Americans with private suspicion of their intentions. He knew that they still wanted to get rid of the sterling area and imperial preference. He suspected that their method was to get Britain locked within a federal Europe and by exercising their influence on the federal European government, they would then control Britain.

On 25 April 1950, Ernest Davies, Parliamentary Secretary at the Foreign Office, sent Denis Healey, the Labour Party's International Secretary, a paper headed *The Labour Party and European Co-operation*. Davies' paper was intended to help in the preparation of a statement by the National Executive Committee (NEC) on the subject of European unity. Davies told Healey that, in a minute the previous day, Ernest Bevin had asked that a paragraph should be included in the statement arguing that European federation could increase American influence over British policy. Davies provided Healey with a draft to this effect. It reads as follows:

> A further and perhaps less obvious danger is that if there is any surrender of sovereignty to Europe an avenue of pressure through which the United States could influence Britain, through Europe, to accept its policies is thereby created. The Labour Party in particular is fearful of encroachment upon Britain's independence by the economic and financial power of the United States. All accept the necessity to co-operate with this, but do not want to place themselves in a position to be dominated. If Britain had to accept the majority decisions made in the Council of Europe all the United States need do to impose its will on Britain would be to influence a majority of the European states there represented.[4]

This paragraph did not appear in the NEC's eventual statement *European Unity* but it was indicative of Bevin's line of thought on European supranationalism.

There was in UK government circles immediate hostility to the Schuman Plan because of its supranational aspects. It was accepted that Franco-German reconciliation should be a prime object of British policy and that the Schuman Plan was a major step in that direction. But supranationalism represented an insurmountable obstacle to British participation however desirable the French objective. Schuman had used the word 'federalism' and there was to be a sovereign high authority with powers that would bind national governments. The very thought of a high authority that could bind governments evoked fantasies in London about what such an authority might do. It could shut down steel plants and coal mines without the agreement of national governments. It could undermine the Attlee government's attempt at bringing the commanding heights of the economy under national control. Attlee had not nationalised the coal industry, and was not proposing to nationalise the iron and steel industry, in order to surrender to a sovereign high authority the power to plan them. Stafford Cripps, Chancellor of the Exchequer, disclosed to the French ambassador in London his nightmare that the high authority could even dictate to national governments about their conduct of economic policy.

Some positive aspects of the Schuman Plan

Repelled by its supranationalism, many positive aspects of the Schuman Plan were overlooked. The Schuman Plan was unique among proposals for European economic integration in that it did not impact in any significant way on Britain's perception of itself as a global power – and as the centre of the Commonwealth. Bevin and Attlee prized Britain's global role. Whether that global role made sense for a Britain impoverished by war was a question insufficiently debated. But there was nothing inconsistent between participation in the Schuman Plan and a global role. Indeed it would help with Britain's global role. There would be fewer worries about quarrels in western Europe. Britain would not just be a global power and a Commonwealth power. In addition it would be a leader of Europe. There was nothing inconsistent between participation in the Schuman Plan and being the centre of the Commonwealth. Britain was part of a system of imperial preference. Any minor inconsistencies between imperial preference and participation in the Schuman Plan could have been negotiated away with ease. Britain was banker to the sterling area. There was nothing inconsistent between participation in the Schuman Plan and being banker to the sterling area.

There was to be no bar on public ownership and hence on control of the supposed 'commanding heights' of the economy. The French did not abandon national planning because of the Schuman Plan. The British could not abandon national planning because they had not yet discovered how to do it but, if the discovery was ever made, there would, in practice, be no inconsistency with the Schuman Plan. Even the 'sovereign' high authority was not really an obstacle. Would the participating countries really be prepared to delegate to a purely nominated authority, consisting of nine unelected experts, powers of life and death over their coal and steel industries? Already there were dissensions within the French government about this idea that they had, unwittingly, permitted Schuman and Monnet to ventilate on their behalf. Belgium and the Netherlands were making it quite clear that, in the form proposed, the idea was unacceptable. It was easy enough to foresee that the high authority would emerge from the negotiating conference a very different institution from Jean Monnet's original conception of it.

To observe all this required thought and analysis. But there was a powerful disincentive to serious thought or analysis. It was confidently assumed in London that the Schuman Plan would not happen. Everyone knew that all French ideas for European economic integration, of which there had been many since the end of the war, fell to the ground. There was, therefore, nothing to worry about. Without British participation any negotiations would fail. Monnet came to London after the Schuman announcement, on 9 May 1950, to try to persuade the UK to take part. Sir Roger Makins, the Foreign Office official who was in the lead, was confident that Monnet's visit had simply proved that the French needed British help. The help that the French needed, Makins told Bevin, was advice on how they could get themselves out of the mess they had got themselves into by making the announcement without consultation with Britain. 'We shall have to do what we can to get them out of the mess into which they have landed themselves.'[5] David Bensusan-Butt, an economist who represented the Economic Section of the Cabinet Office on relevant interdepartmental committees was, among civil servants, probably the most enthusiastic for British participation in the Schuman Plan negotiations. This was not for economic reasons. He discounted the economic arguments. He wanted British participation because he saw the importance of Franco-German reconciliation and believed that the Plan would fail without British participation.[6] Butt forgot the Americans who proved capable, when the negotiations did encounter difficulties, of exerting the necessary pressure to ensure their success.

One of the most extraordinary facts about this story is that Schuman was in London for about nine days immediately after the Schuman Plan announcement. He had come primarily for the meeting of the NATO Council. During the whole of that time Bevin and he had no serious discussion about the Plan. Bevin did take the opportunity of Schuman's presence to remonstrate with him about the lack of consultation before the announcement of his Plan and had to be reminded by Dean Acheson, the American Secretary of State, that Britain had not consulted France about the sterling devaluation. And the night before Schuman's departure, they had a perfunctory exchange in which both admitted that they had not given the Plan much, if any, thought.

There other reasons why no serious thought was given to the Schuman Plan. Bevin was ill and quite incapable of doing his job. So was Cripps. This was particularly unfortunate because he was

the only senior minister who, once he had got over his initial
shock, was, even for a moment, prepared to think favourably of
British participation. Bevin felt deep resentment at the lack of
consultation by Schuman before the announcement – after all
that the UK, in his view, had done for France. That resentment
was doubled when, after a nugatory exchange of telegrams
between Paris and London between 25 May and 1 June, the
French sent an ultimatum demanding to know by the following
evening whether Britain would or would not take part in the Paris
negotiations on the Plan. By this time Bevin was back in hospital
which he had left briefly for the meeting of the NATO Council.
Bevin's response, when consulted in the London Clinic, was that
if the UK submitted to an ultimatum on this occasion, it would
only encourage them to do it again.

Access to materials

A powerful reason for avoiding more than the minimum inevitable economic integration with Europe was Britain's confidence
that it enjoyed a significant advantage in its access to Commonwealth raw materials. The longstanding British attitude was set
out in a book published in 1953 by Anthony Crosland and entitled *Britain's Economic Problem*. Ironically, by the time the book was
published, the supposed advantage was disappearing.

Crosland wrote:

> the second half of the twentieth century seems likely to witness
> a reversion to the trend which frightened the nineteenth cen-
> tury from Malthus onwards, of a rate of demand for the earth's
> natural products which is always tending to outstrip their sup-
> ply ... It is not so much absolute shortages that are in prospect
> ... but a steadily rising level of costs as the richest and easiest
> resources are worked out, and as recourse is had to less accessi-
> ble supplies requiring more capital and labour for their extrac-
> tion ... This is the real threat to the world standard of living...[7]

The fear that the price of raw materials was inevitably going to
rise and that the terms of trade would turn permanently against
the developed world, was enhanced by the outbreak of the

Korean war in June 1950 just as the Schuman Plan negotiating conference met in Paris. There then developed a serious shortage of raw materials, largely due to American stock-piling. The shortage was a factor in the British balance of payments crisis in the second half of 1951.

On the basis that the terms of trade were turning permanently against the industrialised countries and in favour of the raw material producing countries, it was possible to develop a thesis which reconciled the interests of Britain with those of the Commonwealth. Thus, as Crosland put it: 'on balance it is better for Britain that the less developed countries should not hasten on with industrial development too eagerly.'[8] Crosland argued that this was not a selfish attitude on the part of Britain because: 'It must be in the interests of the primary-producing countries themselves to arrest the drift of resources into secondary industry, and to concentrate on raising their output of food and raw materials.[9]

Therefore, and here one recognises the authentic voice of Crosland telling the world what is good for it:

> Nobody wants to deprive the Australians of their all-Australian car, or the Indians of their brand new steel-mills. But if the cars and steel can be obtained from Britain, while American demand for Australian dairy produce may rise by 400 per cent and for InPlan bauxite by 300 per cent, it hardly seems sensible to devote too large an investment to the former, and too little to the latter.[10]

Who would want to sacrifice the advantage the UK had through its access to Commonwealth raw materials by joining with continental Europeans and letting them have a share? Continental Europeans were also worried by the shortage of raw materials and by the fear that it might get worse. They were by no means averse to discussing ways of involving the Commonwealth in their plans for European integration. The fact that there might be here a strong negotiating point for the UK in constructing the kind of Europe the UK wanted was ignored. Then it was too late. From 1952 the terms of trade turned in favour of the industrialised world and the UK then had nothing to offer. Raw materials became cheaper not more expensive. By the time Crosland's book was published, it was already nonsense.

Full employment

The greatest fear of the Attlee government and of economists advising it, was that free international trade, and even just economic integration with Europe, would endanger full employment, a major achievement attributed to the government's management skills. After all there was high unemployment in Germany and Italy.

Keynes had recommended ratification of the Bretton Woods agreements on the assumption that the world was now committed to full employment, that no major country would ever again try to export its unemployment, and in particular that the USA would never again try to export its unemployment. Full employment was therefore now consistent with a one-world economic system based on Bretton Woods. Then came the 1948 US recession, the subsequent forced devaluation of sterling, and a real threat to full employment in the UK. From this time on, Labour politicians like Hugh Gaitskell and Douglas Jay, and economists in the Economic Section, were thinking of a two-world economic system. One of these worlds already existed. It was the dollar world or the gold world. The other existed in potential: the sterling world. The idea was that if full employment was threatened by American recessions, it would be guaranteed by discrimination against the dollar. Britain would only be prepared to pay higher prices in the sterling area if it thereby conserved dollars. Gold and dollars would be spent only where there was no alternative, mainly oil expenditure in the dollar area when the USA was the only practicable source of supply. For the rest, trade within the second world should be conducted with the minimum employment of gold and dollars, and on the basis of extended credit. If it was possible to arrange, sterling should be the medium of exchange within this world as it was within the sterling area.

Europe would have a part to play in this second world but only if it eschewed demands for gold and dollars in payment for any export surplus, if it granted extensive credit to its customers among other European countries and, in effect, became part of the sterling area. Unfortunately, Europe would have nothing to do with such ideas. Europeans wanted dollars in payments for their surpluses, not sterling. They too had much that they wished to buy from the USA and, if they carried dollars, there was no part of the world, including the Commonwealth, from which they could not buy. They could buy from the best and cheapest source whatever it happened to be. Sterling, on the other hand, was officially unconvertible and though it could in practice be converted into dollars, it was only at a substantial discount. In Britain, the hate country was little Belgium, which conducted a deflationary economic policy, ran an export surplus with Britain, and demanded payment for the surplus in gold or dollars.

It had been proposed that to encourage trade within Europe at a time of dollar shortage, a European Payments Union (EPU) should be established. The UK did not like the EPU because there were to be 'gold points', that is points at which credit was exhausted and payment had to be made in gold or dollars. There was a feeling that the Europeans really were intolerable not to understand that the UK had the right ideas about how to organise a world of dollar shortage. Unfortunately it was an illusion to imagine, as Gaitskell did, that one could establish a European payments union which denied surplus countries the right to demand settlement in dollars. So these extraordinary ideas on how to safeguard full employment by protecting it within a totally unattainable two-world economic system, helped to push Britain and Europe apart. Britain did in fact enter the EPU but its accession was the result of a great deal of persuasion by the Americans. And the idea that a two-world system might be attainable persisted in Whitehall for some years to be brought out, and dusted down, at times of balance of payments crisis.

Kith and kin

When to all this was added the fact that the continentals were not our kith and kin and that most of them were Catholics, the prospect of a British government noticing that the success of the Schuman Plan was a major British interest and that therefore the UK should help by participating in it was negligible. The case against Europe was summed up in the statement *European Unity* issued by the NEC of the Labour Party:

> Britain is not just a small crowded island off the Western coast of Continental Europe. She is the nerve centre of a world wide Commonwealth which extends into every continent. In every respect except distance we in Britain are closer to our kinsmen in Australia and New Zealand on the far side of the world than we are to Europe. We are closer in language and in origins, in social habits and institutions, in political outlook and in economic interest. The economics of the Commonwealth countries are complementary to that of Britain to a degree which those of Western Europe could never equal. Furthermore Britain is also the banker of the sterling area.

'They don't want us, Callaghan'

Many have argued that the French did not really want British participation or, as an alternative, they did not want British participation in the negotiations but would have liked Britain to be a signatory of the Paris treaty as eventually negotiated. Bevin himself told James Callaghan, a junior Minister who thought the UK should participate, that 'they don't want us, Callaghan'. Callaghan himself believes that to be the case.[11] That was also the view of Kenneth Younger, Minister of State at the Foreign Office who was, nevertheless, a supporter of participation despite the strong advice he was getting from Foreign Office officials. This allegation that the French did not want Britain at the negotiations is important only because it has been employed to defend the reputation of the Foreign Office and Ernest Bevin. It is not surprising that there may have been a certain ambivalence in Paris about British participation. But the probability nevertheless is that the French government did, on balance, want British participation. It also had political problems in gaining popular assent to the Schuman Plan. The Plan envisaged reconciliation with the Germans when the memories of German occupation were still painful. There was uneasiness in Paris about being left tête-à-tête with the Germans. British participation would have eased the political problems of the French government.

Whatever the ambivalence in Paris, the British government had been invited to the negotiations by the French government. It could have accepted. It was true that the French invitation was conditional on the acceptance of the principle of a supranational high authority. Obviously the way in which that high authority was to be established would be a subject for negotiation. Other countries invited to the talks had reservations about the high authority, notably Belgium and the Netherlands. The Netherlands acceptance of the invitation was explicitly conditional. Britain, too, would have had to accept conditionally. Attlee would have had to reserve the position of Parliament. It would never have ratified a high authority in the Monnet image. But nor, probably, would the parliaments of the other contracting powers. The negotiations in Paris resolved the problem of the high authority. It was decided that there should be a Council of Ministers alongside the high authority. The authority, when established, was quite aware that, in any matter of importance, it could not exercise its supranational powers without the assent of the Council of Ministers. There was no question of the high authority shutting pits or steel mills without the agreement of member countries. Indeed the supranational powers of the high authority had in practice to be exercised with such delicacy that it proved more considerate to the national interests of member states than was appropriate.

The allegation that the French did not want Britain is an attempt to conceal a regrettable dishonesty in the British position. The announcement of the Schuman Plan made an immediate, profound, and favourable impression on international public opinion, notably in the USA. Only five years after the end of the war the French were striving for reconciliation with the Federal Republic of Germany, and the Federal Republic had at once agreed to co-operate in the French plan. An embarrassed Attlee government, which had done nothing to promote Franco-German reconciliation, or for that matter Anglo-German reconciliation, wished to tell the world and the Americans that it was seriously considering participation in the Schuman Plan. In its public responses to the Plan, the British government pretended that it was not in principle opposed to supranationalism. It merely wanted to find out how the supranationalism of the Plan would actually operate. If it received satisfactory explanations, it would join in. It was not true. It was not seriously considering participation. It never intended to participate. It was only looking for a plausible excuse. This was not the full extent of the dishonesty.

The NEC statement *European Unity* was published in June 1950. Attlee found publication of the statement very embarrassing. It appeared to contradict the British government's claim that it wanted to participate if a way could be found. In Europe and the USA, the statement was interpreted as implying that the Attlee government should co-operate only with other socialist governments in Europe. So of course it would not participate in the Schuman Plan. Attlee denied that that was government policy whenever the impression created by *European Unity*. He insisted that *European Unity* was a party document not a government document. Indeed Attlee told the American and French ambassadors that he had known nothing of *European Unity* until it was published. He had a very short memory. He had actually taken part in the meeting of the NEC which approved the statement and he had suggested an amendment which had been incorporated.

The British version of the Schuman Plan

If Bevin and the Foreign Office had had their wits about them. and had been concerned to find an approach to Franco-German reconciliation, they could have proposed a European structure that would have met the needs of Britain even more closely than did the Schuman Plan. In the immediate aftermath of the war the French sought the dismemberment of Germany so as to ensure that France would never be invaded again. In particular they wanted the separation of the Ruhr from Germany under some kind of international authority. It was, in other words, an intensification of the policy of the Versailles treaty. French ideas had something in common with the American Morgenthau Plan of 1944. However it rapidly became clear that Washington, with its eye on Moscow, saw Germany as a potential ally not as an erstwhile enemy. The dismemberment of Germany was therefore no longer, for France, a politically viable objective. The alternative was not the dismemberment of Germany but Franco-German reconciliation. It was an alternative that had been advocated by many far-sighted Frenchmen during the war, Frenchmen who had noted the failure of the Versailles policy.

The core of the problem was the Ruhr. The industrial and raw material resources of the Ruhr had provided the motive power of German agression. A condition of Franco-German reconciliation was, therefore, that the Ruhr should be under some kind of international control. An international authority for the Ruhr was in fact established after the war. But there were two problems with it. It lacked powers and so could not satisfy the French. It was overtly discriminatory against Germany and therefore would not be acceptable to Germany as it progressed towards sovereignty. The answer could only be that the coal and steel resources of France as well as Germany should be put under an international authority together with those of any other European countries that wished to join the plan. It did not need great perception to identify this way forward. Such an idea was repeatedly proposed by a variety of leading figures, German, French, American and even British, after the war. Indeed it had been proposed by Adenauer in the 1920s. It was certainly not a revelation. After the Schuman Plan had been announced, the French sociologist and journalist, Raymond Aron, asked the plain rhetorical question: 'One may ask how it is that an idea as banal as this should now be accepted as something vital and new ...'[12] The answer to Aron's question was that this banal idea now had the backing of the French government.

Bevin was always complaining that it was all very well to draw up paper plans for European unity but that in fact the task was very difficult. On 22 January 1948, he found it necessary to tell the House of Commons:

> It is easy enough to draw up a blueprint for a united western Europe and to construct neat-looking plans on paper. While I do not wish to discourage the work done by voluntary political organisations in advocating ambitious schemes of European unit, I must say that it is a much slower and harder job to carry out a practical programme which takes into account the realities which face us, and I am afraid that it will have to be done a step at a time.[13]

The trouble was that, as the years passed, he never came up with any plan of his own which met his specification that it should be practical. Yet the idea of an international authority for European coal and steel was being advocated by a horde of politicians and commentators. All Bevin had to do was to propose a version of the Schuman Plan without its supranational characteristics. After the Schuman Plan had been announced, Britain, inspired by the announcement, produced its own intergovernmental plan with the idea that, when the Schuman Plan negotiations failed, the British plan would take over. So, in the bowels of Whitehall, an intergovernmental version of the Schuman Plan was produced which never saw the light of day because the Schuman Plan negotiations did not collapse. But what had been put together in Whitehall with much labour after the Schuman announcement could equally have been put forward before the Schuman Plan, for example after the formation of the first government of the

Federal Republic of Germany in September 1949. Of course, after the Schuman announcement with its supranationalism and its high authority, such an idea would have looked dull and prosaic. But, if advanced before Schuman, it would have appeared imaginative and forward-looking. It would have proved that there was in London a genuine commitment to European integration, not just words and whinges about other people's ideas.

The Cabinet decides not to participate

The final British decision not to participate in the negotiations that were to take place in Paris occurred at a Cabinet meeting on 2 June. Bevin was still in the London Clinic. Attlee and Cripps were on holiday, Cripps ironically enough in the country home of Maurice Petsche, the French Minister of Finance. Morrison, in charge of the government, had been told of the French ultimatum on the previous evening. He commented: 'It's no good. We cannot do it; the Durham miners won't wear it.' The Durham miners thereby acquired an unwitting place in the demonology of the Schuman Plan. But Morrison may have been mistaken. Sir William Lawther, President of the National Union of Mineworkers and previously General Secretary of the Durham miners, was quoted in the *Manchester Guardian* of 9 June 1950 as favouring participation in the negotiations. There is no doubt that if the government had decided to participate in the Schuman Plan it would have had problems with the unions. But the problems would have yielded to political leadership, just as far greater political problems yielded in France. The Cabinet of 2 June, instead of agreeing to participate, tried a diversionary manoeuvre in the hope of sabotaging the Schuman Plan without appearing to do so. It proposed a meeting of ministers 'at which the question of the most effective and expeditious method of discussion the problems at issue could be examined and settled.'[14] The French at once rejected the British manoeuvre for what it was. They wanted negotiations on their Plan, not discussions about an alternative. They already had the agreement of the Germans to the commencement of the negotiations. That was the key to the success of their Plan. They also had the agreement of Italy and the Benelux countries. Finally they had the warm approval of the USA for the initiative they had taken. The time had come to make progress. Britain, after having been given a full opportunity to participate, had decided to exclude itself.

Having excluded itself from the negotiations, the British government remained sceptical of their success and considered itself wise in its scepticism. Bevin was still in the London Clinic on 30 June, ten days after the start of the negotiations. Difficulties seemed to be emerging among the Six. Bevin was in his most outgoing mood. He told one of his senior officials that the French would come to see that their conditions 'were unacceptable, not only to us, but to others.' He speculated that Schuman might be 'seeking a way out of the impasse.' Therefore, with due reservations and subject to great care, because he did not want to be accused by the French of sabotage, he expressed his gracious willingness to rescue the French from the consequences of their own folly. 'If M. Schuman were prepared to drop his impossible conditions, and so make negotiation possible, but was in such a difficult position that he could not say so openly, Mr Bevin might be prepared to help him out by making suggestions from outside.'[15] But Schuman did not need Bevin's assistance. He was en route to a great diplomatic triumph. No senior Foreign Office official seems to have warned Bevin that the Schuman Plan was likely to succeed, unlike earlier French proposals which had run into the sand. It was too important an idea to be allowed to fail. Unlike earlier French proposals for European economic integration, it brought in the Germans. Even if difficulties did arise among the Six, and they did, the Americans would use every effort to ensure success. Bevin's generous thoughts merely demonstrated a pathetic ignorance of the probabilities, an ignorance entirely shared by Foreign Office officials.

Aftermath

Sir Edward Heath regularly and justly criticises the Attlee government for its failure to participate in the Schuman Plan. There was a debate in the House of Commons on 25 and 26 June 1950 during which Sir Edward made his maiden speech. Churchill and Eden led for the Opposition and argued that the government should have participated in the Schuman Plan negotiations, on the basis of a reservation comparable to that of the Netherlands. Their subsequent conduct showed that they did not mean what they said or they misunderstood what was proposed. The European Coal and Steel Community did not enter into formal existence until 10 August 1952. If the Conservatives had been as enthusiastic for European integration as the speeches from the opposition benches suggested, it was open to the Churchill government, elected on 25 October 1951, to sign the Paris treaty and thus become a participant in the ECSC. The treaty, as negotiated, met every reasonable objection to the Schuman Plan as it had been originally proposed. On the contrary, Churchill stated as a principle that the UK should be friendly but abstinent. The most that the Churchill government was prepared to do was to negotiate a treaty of association with the ECSC. It was done on such minimalist terms as to be meaningless in practice. Even to achieve that, the opposition of the Foreign Office had to be overcome. These are facts that Sir Edward, in his partisan enthusiasm, manages to forget.

Britain's refusal to participate in the Schuman Plan led on to its refusal to participate in the negotiations leading up to the Rome treaty. If Britain had participated in the ECSC, it would have learnt the advantages of European cooperation and the realities of supranationalism as it existed at that time. It would have been much more likely that it would have participated in whatever form of European integration followed from the experience of the ECSC. Such developments, with Britain taking part, would not necessarily have been identical with the Rome treaty. As one of the founding partners, Britain's voice might even have been listened to from time to time. The origins of Britain's European problems are to be found not at Messina but in the abdication of leadership in Europe represented by the myopic reaction of the Attlee and Churchill governments to the Schuman Plan.

Notes

1 Alex Danchev, *Oliver Franks, Founding Father* (Oxford: Clarendon Press, 1993) pp.71, 74-5.
2 O. S. Franks, *Britain and the Tide of World Affairs*, BBC Reith Lectures 1954 (Oxford: Oxford University Press, 1955) pp.43, 45-7.
3 George Brown, *In my way: the political memoirs of Lord George-Brown* (London: Gollancz, 1971) p.209.
4 Ernest Davies papers, British Library of Political and Economic Science.
5 *Documents on British Policy Overseas (DBPO)* series ii, vol i (London: HMSO, 1986) 31.
6 PRO T230/180.
7 C.A.R. Crosland, *Britain's Economic Problem* (London: Jonathan Cape, 1953) pp.77, 81.
8 Op. cit., p.119.
9 Op. cit., pp.163-4.
10 Op. cit, p.164.
11 James Callaghan, *Time and Chance* (London: Collins, 1987) p.79.
12 *Manchester Guardian*, 30 May 1950.
13 HC Debs., 22 January 1948, col. 395.
14 Cmd. 7970/13.
15 *DBPO*, 124.

Britain and the Treaties of Rome, 1955–1959

James Ellison

The period from 1955 to 1959 was a turning point in both European and British postwar history. On 25 March 1957, the Six (Belgium, France, the Federal Republic of Germany, Italy, Luxembourg and the Netherlands) signed the Treaties of Rome establishing the European Economic Community (EEC) and Euratom. Britain was invited to join this movement at the outset but declined to do so. Instead, from 1956 to 1958, it pursued its own policy for economic cooperation which aimed at securing a European free trade area (FTA) around the core of the EEC. When this failed, and prior to Britain's first application for membership of the Community in 1961, the Macmillan government initiated the European Free Trade Association (EFTA) as a counterweight to the EEC. This crucial period has received great retrospective attention and is the focus for specific criticism in the troubled history of Britain's policy towards postwar European integration.

It is the aim of this chapter to examine British policy development from 1955 to 1959. There are three sections. First, the creation of the FTA proposal is analysed leading to the suggestion that it had its origins in negativity towards the Six, but eventually became an attempt to complement their development. Second, the FTA negotiations are examined revealing that policy was set in established foundations. Finally, there is a consideration of Britain's motives for EFTA membership, a course which many in Whitehall advocated months before the failure of the FTA negotiations.

Origins of the free trade area proposal

Britain's response to the Six's plans for a European common market has been the subject of much historical interest. Cautious criticism has come from those who suggest London might have seen the European FTA as 'a genuine substitute for the common market' or 'an attempt to change the European agenda'.[1] More vigorous assessments see harmful intent in the FTA, variously suggesting that it was a 'counter-proposal', a 'spoiling tactic', and an attempt by the Macmillan government to use 'all means in their power to sabotage the Messina powers'.[2] Conversely, very few studies of British policy have attempted to take a more complex view of the development of Plan G, as the FTA was officially known in Whitehall.[3]

In fact, British policy was more sophisticated than has previously been considered, and evolved in response to the progress of the Six from autumn 1955 to the signature of the Rome treaties in March 1957. It developed from being a possible counter-initiative to the Common Market, through being a potential alternative in expectation of the Six's failure in 1956, before maturing into an attempt to complement the EEC.[4] Even then, although the Macmillan government accepted that the EEC would have to be accommodated, there were still those in Britain who maintained a negative attitude towards the Six's ambitions.

The search for a new British initiative in Europe which eventually produced the FTA proposal had its origins in the Eden government's autumn 1955 decision to block the development of the Messina plans. Part of the flawed and ultimately disastrous strategy of attempting to bring the Six's plans under the aegis of the Organisation for European Economic Co-operation (OEEC) was that once there, they would be mollified by a British counter-initiative. This would include proposals for the lowering of tariff barriers and removal of general obstacles to trade which were regarded in London as the motives for the Six's interest in a common market.[5]

Ultimately, this tactic was stillborn as the Six resisted British attempts to draw their project into the OEEC. Nevertheless, the studies of a counter-initiative at this time reveal that the FTA proposal has its genesis in autumn 1955. This was particularly true of the Whitehall department which pioneered the idea of an FTA: the Board of Trade. Officials at the Board were alone in contemplating the success of the Six at this early stage. Unable to influence the more negative attitudes of the Foreign Office and the Treasury, the Board concentrated on developing policy to meet a future European common market. Russell Bretherton, the infamous Under-Secretary who acted as observer on the Spaak Committee, advocated two courses, one of which would loosely form the basis of the later Plan G. On 22 October 1955, Bretherton suggested that Britain could 'refuse to join the Common Market as a European Customs Union, but offer to join with it as a Free Trade Area'.[6]

When Britain's attempt to sideline the Six failed, the counter-initiative studies gained weight from January 1956, especially when championed by Harold Macmillan as Chancellor of the Exchequer and Peter Thorneycroft as President of the Board of Trade. On 6 February, Macmillan directed his Treasury officials that he was anxious 'if possible, for an advance which would be recognised as such'.[7] Yet this did not mean that Macmillan had accepted the development of the Six. There can be no doubt that Plan G in its early form had an offensive complexion as the description of Macmillan's efforts to a meeting of the Cabinet Secretary's Committee in March 1956 reveals:

> The Chancellor of the Exchequer was seeking to evolve a constructive counter-initiative which would demonstrate our willingness to associate ourselves with Europe while at the same time, it was hoped, administering a *coup de grace* to the Messina proposals.[8]

Although different departments had different opinions, during 1956, on the whole Whitehall proceeded on the basis that Plan G would provide a potential alternative to the Common Market in expectation of the Six's failure. When it began to be accepted in autumn 1956 that the Six would, contrary to previous predictions, actually succeed, Plan G matured into its final stage.

In November 1956, officials concluded that it was 'Politically desirable ... to have a Customs Union as a nucleus [of the FTA]'.[9] What 'Politically ... desirable' seems to have reflected was Whitehall's recognition of the European and also American weight behind the Common Market. These decisions reveal officials' acceptance of the impossibility of opposition to the Six's Common Market and the paramount importance of complementing it with a FTA. Yet at the same time, the FTA was only a positive proposal in the sense that Britain had accepted that an anti-Six policy was not feasible and that accommodation and even containment was the best course. Officials concluded that:

> On wider political grounds ... we should prefer there to be a Customs Union, but only provided a free trade area were also set up to include it. It would be politically as well as economically to our disadvantage if a Customs Union were set up without a free trade area, but a combined organisation would be more stable when achieved.[10]

It is significant that whilst officials recommended to ministers that the FTA proposal continued to assume the existence of a Common Market, they also warned that a Common Market *without* an FTA would be to Britain's disadvantage. This argument had been put to ministers in an earlier guise in November 1955, when officials' warnings of the potential effects of a successful Common Market on British economic policy had received little attention. In 1956, it was hoped that the FTA would obviate the need to confront the possibility of submitting to the Six's progress.

Thus, from early 1957, as the Six moved towards the signing of their treaty, the Macmillan government struggled to create a European FTA. What the British proposed was a FTA in industrial goods, excluding agriculture, which would encompass the EEC and the rest of the OEEC.[11] There would be free trade in manufactures within the FTA but, unlike the Common Market, there would be no common external tariff; members would retain national tariff autonomy on imports from third countries. It was the exclusion of agriculture and the lack of a common external tariff which distinguished the FTA most clearly from the Common Market plans.

Plan G was a reactive policy formulated in response to the Six's development when the pervading view in London was doubt about the Common Market ever succeeding. It was also an essentially conservative policy. It was accepted by ministers and officials because it accommodated Britain's varied interests as well as meeting changes in Europe. For the Treasury, existing external economic policy based on multilateral free trade and payments would be unaffected and perhaps strengthened by gaining some control over European cooperation. For the Board of Trade, the FTA would maintain British access to European markets but without a common external tariff, would allow Britain to perpetuate its preferential trade with the Commonwealth. This was particularly important when the first stirrings of Commonwealth interest in reforming the Ottawa Agreements emerged in 1956. The Board recognised that imperial preference had no future but it did not wish to see open season on the tariff when the future of trade with Europe was uncertain.

Plan G, because it left Commonwealth trade inviolate, was also acceptable to the Commonwealth Relations Office and the Colonial Office in Whitehall which feared a weakening of Anglo-Commonwealth ties in relation to a strengthening of ties with Europe. The Ministry of Agriculture, Fisheries and Food was also content with the exclusion of agriculture from the FTA. These factors met the proclivities of Conservative Cabinet ministers such as Lord Salisbury and R.A. Butler who were less enthusiastic about European cooperation than Macmillan and Thorneycroft, and who also argued that the Conservative Party would not swallow concessions to Europe on Commonwealth trade and British agriculture. In fact, when conditioned by these political factors, Plan G was presented to the Cabinet as providing the opportunity of unifying 'the European and Imperial wings of the Conservative Party'.[12]

Ultimately, the FTA was devised with British interests as the priority. The major considerations which led to the rejection of Common Market membership in autumn 1955 remained intact: Britain's extra-European political concerns, its opposition to federalism, and its trade relationship with the Commonwealth.[13] The only advance from this position was that Britain would abandon protection for its industry from European competition. This was a necessary and limited price to pay for maintaining British interests in Europe and elsewhere through meeting the integration of the Six powers in the Common Market. During 1956, the Eden government avoided consultation with the Six over the FTA, not wishing to attract accusations of offering an alternative to their plans, a constant anxiety during the FTA negotiations. As a result, when presented with the inherent British self-interest in the FTA proposal, there were mixed reactions on the Continent. Why the British government thought this would present no difficulty to the creation of a FTA will be discussed in the next section of this chapter.

The free trade area negotiations

At this stage, it is worth briefly describing the economic aims of the Six in the Rome treaties. The EEC was an ambitious arrangement which would not only eliminate tariffs and quotas within the customs union, but also construct a common external tariff. It aimed to achieve free movement of persons, services and capital, to adopt common policies on agriculture and transport, as well as creating a European social fund and a European investment bank. It would achieve these objectives within the supranational framework of a European Community administered by an assembly, a council, a commission and a court of justice.[14] In contrast, apart from the elimination of tariffs and quotas on industrial goods, Britain's FTA would include none of the more wide-ranging commitments of the Rome treaties. Co-ordinated by an intergovernmental managing board within the OEEC and answerable to the Council of Ministers, it was purely a trading arrangement with no pledge to an ever closer union. It is when this basic distinction is drawn that the objections of those within the Six towards Britain securing FTA benefits without making wider commitments is fully understood.

The obvious question in response to these facts is what attraction the British government believed the FTA had for the

Six and other countries of western Europe? There was a belief in Whitehall, based on overestimation of Britain's influence in Europe, that the FTA would be prerequisite to the Six's success. For example, in February 1957, Bretherton argued that in negotiating with the Six, Britain had 'one ace – the realisation on their part that British participation in some form is essential if the Customs Union treaty itself is to be ratified by their Parliaments'.[15] Britain's involvement was expected to be welcomed either as a counterweight to prospective German strength or as a balance to French protectionist economic policy in the Common Market. This was not such an unrealistic expectation given encouragement from within the Six in early 1957. This came from not only Ludwig Erhard, the pro-FTA German Economics Minister; the powerful Quai d'Orsay official, Olivier Wormser, initially suggested that the Common Market's chances would be improved in the National Assembly if matters progressed favourably in the FTA negotiations.[16] The British government's response to this was, however, tinged with a degree of arrogance and a miscalculation of the limitations of its influence in Europe.

When it became clear in spring 1957 that the French, at least, were reluctant to see rapid progress for the FTA, the British government was forced into reconsidering its approach. The strategy for the negotiations which began in October 1957 was to generate enough political will on the Continent in favour of the FTA to overcome 'the real technical difficulties and the many serious political drawbacks for the various countries involved'.[17] These difficulties and drawbacks rested mainly on the fundamental difference in ambition between the Common Market and the FTA. The classic interpretation of this period is that through the FTA proposal, there was 'a real and substantial shift in the British government's attitude towards Europe and the beginning of a questioning of the priorities that had hitherto conditioned all official, and most unofficial, thinking about the United Kingdom's external relations'.[18] It is difficult to sustain this view after analysing British government records during the FTA negotiations in 1957 and 1958. In fact, the FTA was conservatively designed to accommodate the development of the Six and maintain the status quo in Britain's extra-European relations, both political and economic. It was set firmly in traditional British policy foundations which only began to change as a result of the failure of Plan G and the success of the Six in combination with wider historical movements at the end of the 1950s.

Evidence to support this argument may be drawn from the limitations of Britain's flexibility during the FTA negotiations. Although Whitehall recognised that it would have to make concessions to achieve its goal in Europe, and although this represented an advance in British attitudes, at no point did the Macmillan government consider a significant transformation in its fundamental foreign and economic policies. There are three main examples of this. The first is in the aftermath of the Suez crisis with Cabinet rejection of a Foreign Office initiative to develop closer Anglo-European relations. The second is during the summer of 1957 when the Macmillan government first seriously considered moving from their original FTA conception. Finally, the third is the ultimately still-born consideration of a concession on commercial policy.

With the shared experience of American hostility during the Suez crisis of autumn 1956, some in France expected the British to move closer than ever before towards Europe. The reaffirmation of strong Anglo-American relations at the Bermuda conference of March 1957 revealed this to be a forlorn hope. However, the United States' unfriendly diplomacy and stranglehold on Britain's finances during the Suez crisis did lead the Foreign Office to consider closer relations with the Six. On 5 January 1957, the Foreign Secretary, Selwyn Lloyd, submitted a memorandum to the Cabinet entitled 'The Grand Design: Co-operation with Western Europe'.[19] The Grand Design had two main proposals. First, and most radically, Britain would meet the costs of thermo-nuclear arms development through an association with the Six in the non-supranational framework of the Western European Union (WEU). This would lead Britain into an arrangement 'almost as powerful as America and perhaps in friendly rivalry with her'. Second, the Grand Design envisaged a single General Assembly for Europe which would replace existing institutions and include those of the Six.

Suez had been the main inspiration for this. Retrospectively, Lloyd explained his motives: 'Relations between Sir Anthony Eden and President Eisenhower had suffered a severe shock; Sir Anthony distrusted Mr. Dulles; it therefore seemed better to look towards the Continent'.[20] However, the Foreign Office and Macmillan's newly formed Cabinet drew different lessons from Suez. Although the Cabinet concluded that 'the Suez crisis had made it plain that there must be some change in the basis of Anglo-American relations', the strength of these relations were vital to the primary policy of maintaining a special relationship with Washington for foreign, economic and defence policies, specifically the development of a British independent nuclear deterrent.[21] Hence, Lloyd's nuclear proposals were rejected for strategic reasons but also because they were too rich for those, such as Lord Salisbury, who were ideologically opposed to closer relations with the Continent. The Grand Design did become public policy, but only in the form of the proposition for a General Assembly for Europe. When matched with proposals for Anglo-Six non-nuclear defence collaboration, this represented an attempt by the Macmillan government to give the European FTA a politico-defence boost. Confined by the traditional limits of British policy – Anglo-American relations and doubts about increased integration with Europe – these proposals failed to find success. They also revealed London's inability to meet the demands of the Six which in the political field were supranational, and in the defence field were for more than non-nuclear weapons development, especially in France.

The second example of the limitations of Britain's European policy came during the summer and autumn of 1957 when the FTA was delayed for five months by the ratification of the Rome treaties. To generate support for the FTA when the negotiations commenced in October 1957, the Macmillan government prepared two concessions. First, Britain would depart from its original conception of the FTA institution: an intergovernmental managing board. On Macmillan's initiative, London would propose that the FTA be governed by a supranational institution which involved some surrender of national sovereignty through majority voting.[22] What level of supranationality Macmillan had in mind is unclear, however. What is clear is that the European Commission was dismissed as dangerous because it involved a body of international officials having powers of initiative and recommendation over the Council of Ministers.[23] The British hoped to win over those Europeans who attached weight to political cooperation and also restrict the power of the French to veto FTA development. Yet ultimately, what Britain was able to offer was little more than some extension of the OEEC Council of Ministers' terms of reference combined with limited majority voting. In the long-run, this did little to improve the FTA's chances, especially as the French demanded unanimity as a sticking point in the negotiations. Other more pro-British members of the Six were also sceptical of Britain's political concession. The Dutch were 'left breathless' by the comments of Sir David Eccles, President of the Board of Trade, about EEC institutions in July 1957. Describing them as 'irresponsible aggregates' of European civil servants, Eccles clarified his view by arguing that they were 'irresponsible' because 'they were not answerable to the House of Commons'.[24]

The second concession developed by Britain in the summer of 1957 was on agriculture. Here, once again, British policy was constrained by wider policies. Britain wished to limit the FTA to manufactured goods for two reasons. First, there were domestic political commitments to British farmers to sustain the system of guaranteed prices under the 1947 and 1957 Agriculture Acts. This was a vital consideration for maintaining support in the Tory shires. Second, assurances had been given to Commonwealth agricultural exporters that their preferences in the British market (on which reciprocal preferences for British industrial exports in Commonwealth markets relied) would not be affected by the FTA. As an indication of the importance of this trade relationship, in 1956, 50.98 per cent of all British imports of food, beverages and tobacco came from the Commonwealth, and 49.13 per cent of all British exports of manufactured goods went to the Commonwealth.[25]

Britain's solution to the Europeans' desire for inclusion of agriculture in the FTA whilst maintaining domestic and Commonwealth guarantees was to make a presentational concession rather than one of substance. On 8 October 1957, the Cabinet accepted an agriculture agreement which was, as the Prime Minister said, 'little more than an extension and strengthening of existing arrangements within [the] O.E.E.C.'.[26] Britain would agree to a number of proposals such as annual reviews of prices and trade; commodity arrangements; controls on subsidies and a complaints procedure. It would not, however, accept the abolition of tariffs on agricultural trade and thus effectively blocked increased European access to British markets. Although in 1957, the agricultural provisions of the Rome treaties had yet to be completed, and although free trade was not envisaged for any future common agricultural policy, the Six were working towards managed markets in agriculture where domestic producers had precedence over third countries. Britain's agricultural concession thus fell short of European ambitions and the issue remained unsolved at the close of the FTA negotiations.

As the FTA negotiations proceeded from October 1957, it became clear that these limited British concessions would not bring the necessary dividends. Consequently, during the first half of 1958, the Macmillan government moved towards an unprecedented concession on commercial policy to secure the FTA. This provides the third example of the traditional nature of British policy, despite the apparent advance. To recapitulate, the major technical difference between the Common Market and the FTA centred on the fact that the Six envisaged a common external tariff on all goods from third countries and that the British did not. The FTA was designed to gain access to continental markets for British exports whilst sustaining the protection for British agriculture and the system of preferential trade with the

Commonwealth. There would be no concessions on Commonwealth trade or tariff policy. From the beginning, however, this had been inimical to many on the Continent, especially the French, who argued with justification that the British would achieve disproportionate benefits to those enjoyed by their FTA partners. In early 1958, the French formulated these objections in a counter-plan which, amongst others, had two main proposals: first, that external tariff rates on imports into the FTA be harmonised; and second, that the British should share its preferential markets in the Commonwealth (with FTA members selling a negotiated quota of their exports to the Commonwealth at the imperial tariff rate).[27] These propositions were inimical to Britain's FTA concept. By setting the price for their agreement to a FTA on limited external tariff harmonisation and sharing Commonwealth preferences, the French had presented the Macmillan government with a difficult dilemma. It could either make concessions in Commonwealth policy to secure the FTA, or reject French demands and risk the collapse of its European policy. Either course would mean reassessment of Britain's position in world affairs.

Britain's response to this predicament reveals the limitations of its policy towards Europe, but also the extent to which securing a trade relationship with the EEC was considered vital to British interests. There was unanimous agreement in Whitehall that the French proposals to share Commonwealth preferences had to be killed as they involved too extensive a revision of British external economic and, by extension, foreign policy, as well as implying complete revision of the FTA negotiations.[28] Thus, the concession would have to be directed at French demands for external tariff harmonisation.

Defining the origin of goods entering the FTA because of the lack of a common external tariff had always been more than a technical issue. It represented the difference in external economic policy between the French and the British. The French, supported by the Italians and the Belgians, wanted to see some measure of external tariff harmonisation in the FTA to eradicate trade deflection between high and low tariff countries. The British, supported by others in the OEEC, had argued that the problem could be dealt with by certificates of origin with each member state retaining tariff autonomy. In simple terms, what this divergence represented was France's desire to construct a protectionist Europe in which to modernise its economy and Britain's desire to perpetuate the system of preferential trade with the Commonwealth. The issue of origin, therefore, went to the heart of the Anglo-French dispute. Recognising that without progress on the external tariff issue, there would be no progress for the FTA, Whitehall developed a compromise proposal which conceded external tariff harmonisation on machinery, textiles and chemicals, the latter having been specifically demanded by the French, Italians and the Belgians.[29]

This was a distinct advance in British policy which, from the announcement of the FTA proposal, had categorically rejected any external tariff harmonisation.[30] It was a measure of the changing attitudes towards Britain's external economic position that the concession received majority support at both official and ministerial level, with opposition from the Commonwealth Relations Office and the Colonial Office overwhelmed.[31] Nevertheless, the external tariff concession was strictly limited to the promise of negotiation on basic material tariffs and the offer of some harmonisation. Commonwealth free entry would, on the whole, remain untouched. For this reason, the success of Britain's concession was always open to doubt. Ultimately, however, this is a hypothetical consideration as the May 1958 constitutional crisis in France precluded Britain from implementing its origin concession.

What these three examples reveal – the Foreign Office Grand Design, the institutional and agricultural concessions, and the advance on external tariff harmonisation – is that the British government was fully aware of the importance of the Rome treaties for its interests in Europe and elsewhere. What they also indicate is that the government was reluctant to make fundamental alterations in its attitudes towards European integration. This was mostly because the constraints which had influenced the formulation of Plan G – Britain's wider political and economic policies and the boundaries imposed by the Conservative Cabinet – remained unaltered. What had altered were the fortunes of the Six, who throughout the FTA negotiations developed a community of interest and consistently placed the integrity of their achievements above the prospect of securing British involvement. To its credit, the Macmillan government did show some flexibility in the latter stages of the FTA negotiations, eventually agreeing to French demands for sector studies. Yet, ultimately, as long as Britain attempted to maintain its special position in Commonwealth trade whilst also attempting to gain a special position in Europe, its policy was flawed. Whilst the failure of the FTA negotiations had made this clear, in 1959, the British persisted with their aim of a multilateral economic association in Europe.

From FTA to EFTA

With de Gaulle's termination of the FTA negotiations on 14 November 1958, Britain was left without a policy towards European integration. Realisation of this accounts for the frustrated and often hysterical tone of Macmillan's minutes in the second half of 1958, suggesting that Britain withdraw its troops from the Continent, leave the WEU and the North Atlantic Treaty Organisation (NATO) and that generally, 'Fortress Britain might be our reply'.[32] These views were in contrast with the predominantly conciliatory atmosphere within Whitehall. At the Foreign Office, for example, Deputy Under-Secretary Sir Paul Gore Booth warned that 'A nation of shop-keepers living on international trade and finance and importing 50% of its food-stuffs cannot turn itself into a self-supporting fortress'.[33] Similarly, the Treasury advised that measures be taken in Europe to 'reduce the temperature rather than ... increase it by slashing out wildly in all directions'.[34] It was Cabinet acceptance of these arguments in 1959 which brought British membership of EFTA, a trade arrangement with Austria, Denmark, Norway, Portugal, Sweden and Switzerland.

Although ministers only fully turned their attention to the possibility of a non-Six agreement after the failure of the FTA negotiations, officials had decided on such a course months beforehand. Whilst there was much consternation in London at de Gaulle's termination of the FTA negotiations, and at the German and American governments for not intervening on Britain's behalf, there was civil service relief at the opportunity to move to a post-FTA policy. Contrary to the view that the FTA negotiations came close to success, from early 1958 there was growing pessimism in Whitehall about the FTA's chances and consequent interest in an alternative approach to the Scandinavians.[35] For example, on 28 January, the Permanent Secretary of the Treasury, Sir Roger Makins, warned that officials ought 'to reckon seriously with the prospect that the French [would] block an agreement on the Free Trade Area'.[36] Concurrently, Bretherton described the January 1958 Intergovernmental Committee meeting on the FTA as 'profoundly depressing' and suggested that officials turn their attentions to alternative policies.[37] After a brief period of remission in June 1958 caused by the mistaken belief that de Gaulle had taken positive decisions on the FTA, acceptance of the FTA's demise became the dominant opinion in Whitehall.[38]

It had been the Board of Trade which had pioneered the FTA within Whitehall in 1956. Two years later, it was the same department which led policy on its replacement. From January 1958, Board officials developed alternative courses and by March, decided on a Uniscan FTA, comprising Britain, Scandinavia and Switzerland, as the best choice.[39] The Board also received encouragement outside of Whitehall from Scandinavian governments and also from the Federation of British Industries (FBI). During the first half of 1958, Scandinavian governments were increasingly pessimistic about the FTA's chances and encouraged Britain to consider a non-Six arrangement.[40] Scandinavian industrialists were of a similar view and began a process of co-ordination with the FBI which would contribute to the creation of EFTA.[41]

Outside of the Board of Trade, there had been little support for alternative courses. With great political weight attached to the FTA as part of its wider interest in seeing western Europe united, the Foreign Office had dismissed non-Six arrangements and instead pursued cooperation with the Eisenhower administration to influence the OEEC negotiations.[42] The Treasury had also initially rejected the Board's initiative.[43] Regional groupings were inimical to the Treasury's primary policy of world-wide multilateralism and apart from the fact that a non-Six arrangement was thought to be a 'second-best' policy, the Treasury believed it would be premature to consider alternatives until the FTA had reached crisis point.[44] Nevertheless, both the Foreign Office and the Treasury dropped their opposition to a non-Six arrangement as the failure of the FTA became apparent in the second half of 1958. Consequently, in November, officials concluded that agreements with the non-Six 'appeared to be the best, if not indeed the only alternative policy' and proceeded to make this recommendation to ministers.[45]

There were three main arguments in support of a Uniscan FTA. First, it was thought to be a 'viable project in its own right' which was acceptable to British industry offering exporters an opportunity to expand their sales to Scandinavia. Second, it would be a valuable insurance policy against the danger that Scandinavian countries might otherwise be drawn into the orbit of the EEC. Third, officials believed that a Uniscan FTA 'might become a bridge to an association with the Six equivalent to a European Free Trade Area' or at least some form of multilateral European economic cooperation. These arguments no doubt made the Uniscan FTA more saleable at ministerial level, but with the FTA negotiations over and Britain still committed to some form of association with the Six in the long-term, the truth was that ministers had no choice but to pursue the Uniscan course.[46] It was this stark reality which converted previous doubters. Even Sir David Eccles, who had criticised the proposal for being 'a climb down – the engineer's daughter when the general-manager's had said no' now suggested to Macmillan that although it remained second best, 'half a loaf is better than none'.[47] Thus, at critical meetings in December, ministers approved the Uniscan FTA studies but suggested that they remain low key; Britain did not wish to attract accusations of dividing Europe when it had been a vocal defender of OEEC unity over the past three years.[48] With their eyes still on achieving a FTA agreement with the EEC in the long-run, British ministers eventually entered into negotiations with the Scandinavians in early 1959, leading to the creation of the EFTA in November 1959.[49] This, however, was a defensive policy from the beginning and when EFTA failed to provide the stepping-stone to the original FTA concept, the Macmillan government soon lost interest in it and moved towards making an application for membership of the EEC in 1961.

Conclusion

A number of themes dominate the examination of Britain's response to the embryonic development of the Rome treaties. First, attitudes towards the Messina process were essentially negative. This created the attempt to sideline the Six in autumn 1955 and led to the FTA being seen, for a period in 1956, as an alternative to the Common Market in expectation of the Six's failure. Even when Whitehall officially accepted that opposition to the Six was impractical, this was only because of the weight of support for integration on the Continent. Moreover, Britain did not wish to fall out with the Eisenhower administration which had made its preference for Six power unity clear on many occasions.

Second, policy was reactive. From late 1956 it was the Six who were setting the pace in Europe and Britain struggled to ensure that its previous misconception of their chances did not lead to their dominance on the Continent. Hence, the imperative of complementing the EEC with the FTA and the frustration in

London throughout the negotiations as this became increasingly unlikely. Third, the FTA proposal itself was conservative in design. As it was formulated when the predominant view was that the Six would probably fail, there was no emphasis on casting policy with European demands in mind. Instead, the priority was to secure acceptance of Plan G in London and consequently, established attitudes and priorities, together with the predilections of Conservative ministers, dominated policy decisions.

Fourth, it was during the FTA negotiations that the short-comings of Britain's approach towards the Six became apparent. Great weight was attached to overcoming technical problems by diplomatic means. Britain's primary strategy was to gain German support within the Six to influence the French to accept the FTA. But in the long-term, this presumed too much of the Adenauer government, which was committed to France in the Rome treaties, and too little of the French, whose domestic weakness did not prevent them from taking a strong line in the FTA negotiations. As one ex-Foreign Office official commented in retrospect, Britain did not grasp the nature of the Franco-German relationship in its early stages. The Adenauer government may have wanted to see Britain involved in the development of the European Community but although this did 'often result in them saying "no" to the French, [it] didn't result in making the French say "yes".'[50]

Finally, and most significantly, the failure of the FTA and the shortcomings of EFTA perhaps represented the culmination of the Anglo-French dispute about the European order which had first been exposed over the Schuman Plan in 1950–1. Since then, Britain had pursued foreign policies which prioritised extra-European relations, mainly with the United States. It had followed financial policies which aimed to re-establish the former prestige of sterling as an international currency through convertibility. Moreover, it had perpetuated commercial policies based on maintaining preferential trade with the Commonwealth. The FTA was designed to retain this status quo whilst meeting the development of the Six. But by demanding that Britain pay a Commonwealth price to gain access to European markets, France exposed the incongruity in the British attempt to tilt towards Europe whilst otherwise sustaining traditional policies. For Britain, this was a difficult dilemma, yet it was one that always threatened to develop if the Six proved successful in the formation of a European Common Market and if Britain failed to generate political will in favour of a multilateral European economic association. When this occurred at the close of the 1950s, it was the strength of France within the Rome treaties that forced the Macmillan government into a re-evaluation of Britain's place in a changing world.

Notes

1 H.J. Küsters, 'West Germany's Foreign Policy in Western Europe, 1949–58: The Art of the Possible', in C. Wurm (ed.) *Western Europe and Germany* (Oxford: Berg, 1995) pp. 55–85, esp. p. 71; A. Deighton 'Missing the Boat. Britain and Europe 1945–61', *Contemporary Record*, Vol.3, No.3 (Feb. 1990) p. 17.

2 M. Charlton, *The Price of Victory* (London: BBC, 1983) p.198; S. Greenwood, *Britain and European Co-operation Since 1945* (Oxford: Blackwell, 1992) p. 68; R. Lamb, *The Macmillan Years 1957–1963* (London: John Murray, 1995) p. 111. D.W. Urwin, *The Community of Europe* (London: Longman, 1991) p. 93.

3 W. Kaiser, *Using Europe. Abusing the Europeans* (London: Macmillan, 1996) pp.61–87; D. Reynolds, *Britannia Overruled* (London: Longman, 1991) p. 217, J.W. Young, *Britain and European Unity, 1945–1992* (London: Macmillan, 1993) p. 50, are the exceptions.

4 See J.R.V. Ellison, 'Perfidious Albion? Britain, Plan G and European Integration, 1955–1956', *Contemporary British History*, Vol.10, No.4 (Winter 1996) pp.1–34. Also see James Ellison, *Threatening Europe: Britain and the Creation of the European Community, 1955–58* (London: Macmillan, 2000); Martin P. C. Schaad, *Bullying Bonn: Anglo-German Diplomacy on European Integration 1955–61* (London: Macmillan, 2000).

5 On British strategy at this time, S. Burgess & G. Edwards, 'The Six plus One: British policy making and the question of European

economic integration. 1955', *International Affairs*, Vol.64, No.3 (1988) pp.393–413, and J. W. Young, '"The Parting of the Ways"? Britain, the Messina Conference and the Spaak Committee, June-December 1955', M. Dockrill and J.W. Young (eds) *British Foreign Policy 1945–56* (Basingstoke: Macmillan, 1989) pp.197–224. Also, Kaiser, *Using Europe*, pp.28–60. For the counter-initiative ideas, PRO CAB134/1026, MAC(55)45th meeting, 27 Oct. 1955 and PRO CAB134/889, ES(55)8th meeting, 1 Nov. 1955.

6   PRO BT11/5715, Bretherton minute, 22 Oct. 1955.

7   PRO T234/183, Macmillan minute, 6 Feb. 1956.

8   PRO CAB134/1373, AOC(56)2nd meeting, 5 March 1956.

9   PRO CAB134/1238, ES(EI)(56)17th and 18th meetings, 15 Nov. and 22 Nov. 1956 respectively.

10 PRO CAB134/1240, ES(EI)(56)79(Final) 22 Nov. 1956.

11 For the official statement of policy see the government's White Paper: *A European Free Trade Area. United Kingdom Memorandum to the Organisation for European Economic Co-operation*, Cmnd.72 (HMSO, 7 Feb. 1957).

12 PRO CAB129/82, CP(56)192, 28 July 1956.

13 For these arguments, see the Trend Reports, PRO CAB134/1228, EP(55)53–55, 7 Nov. 1955.

14 Principles based on Articles 3 and 4 of the *Treaty Establishing The European Economic Community*, in Sweet and Maxwell's Legal Editorial Staff, *European Community Treaties* (London, 1977) pp.61–138.

15 PRO BT11/5552, Bretherton minute, 25 Feb. 1957. This view was also held in the Treasury, PRO T234/200, Figgures minute, 7 Feb. 1957.

16 PRO FO371/128333/97, Isaacson to Wright, 25 Jan. 1957.

17 PRO CAB129/89, C(57)222, 4 Oct. 1957.

18 M. Camps, *Britain and the European Community 1955–1963* (Princeton: Princeton University Press, 1964) p.509.

19 PRO CAB129/84, CP(57)6, 5 Jan. 1957.

20 PRO PREM11/2998, Lloyd to Macmillan, 15 Feb. 1960.

21 PRO CAB128/30, CM(57)3rd meeting, 8 Jan. 1957.

22 PRO PREM11/2133, Macmillan minute M.333/57, 15 July 1957. Also, see comments in PRO CAB130/123, GEN.580/2nd meeting, 12 July 1957; PRO CAB130/123, GEN.580/3rd meeting, 30 July 1957.

23 PRO CAB130/123, GEN.580/3rd meeting, 30 July 1957.

24 National Archives and Records Administration, College Park, Maryland, USA (NARA) RG59/440.002/7–1557, The Hague to State, 39, 15 July 1957.

25 Central Statistical Office, *Annual Abstract of Statistics*, No. 96, 1959.

26 PRO CAB128/31, CC(57)72nd meeting, 8 Oct. 1957.

27 See Ellison, *Threatening Europe*, pp.177–197.

28 PRO T234/203, Clarke to Lee, 21 March 1958; PRO PREM11/ 2531, Trend to Macmillan, 26 March 1958; PRO FO371/134495/ 308G, Edden minute, 26 March 1958; PRO BT11/5555, Bretherton minute, 26 March 1958; PRO CAB129/92, C(58)67, 26 March 1958; PRO CAB128/32, CC(58)27th meeting, 27 March 1958.

29 See the report attached to PRO CAB129/93, C(58)110, 16 May 1958. For French, Italian and Belgian demands, *Report of the Group of Trade Experts on the definition of origin of goods in the Free Trade Area*, CIG(58)12, 31 Jan. 1958, Cmnd.641, *Negotiations for a European Free Trade Area. Documents Relating to the Negotiations from July, 1956, to December, 1958* (HMSO, Jan. 1959) p.112, para 5.

30 For the original position, see paragraphs 2 and 23 of the FTA White Paper, Cmnd.72. For a more recent explanation of the limits of British policy, PRO CAB129/89, C(57)218 (Annex B, paragraph 7) 4 Oct. 1957.

31 For CRO and CO objections, PRO CAB134/1836, ES(58)8th, 9th and 10th meetings, 2, 7 and 8 May 1958 respectively.

32 PRO PREM11/2315, Macmillan to Lloyd and Amory, 24 June 1958; PRO PREM11/2352, Macmillan to Lloyd, 15 Oct. 1958; PRO PREM11/2532, Macmillan to Lloyd, 26 Oct. 1958.

33 PRO FO371/134545/3, Gore-Booth minute, 17 Oct. 1958.

34 PRO T234/378, Clarke minute, 16 Oct. 1958.

35 Cf. Camps, *Britain*, p.169.

36 PRO T234/374, Makins minute, 28 Jan. 1958.

37 PRO BT11/5554, Bretherton minutes, 17 Jan. and 20 Feb. 1958.

38 PRO CAB134/1837, ES(58)32, 16 July 1958; PRO CAB134/1836, ES(58)13th meeting, 18 July 1958; PRO T234/377, Clarke minute, 21 July 1958.

39 PRO BT11/5648, Bretherton to Lee, 15 Jan. 1958; PRO BT11/ 5648, Golt minute, 7 March 1958; PRO BT11/5648, Bretherton to Cohen, 28 March 1958.

40 PRO T234/375, Figgures minute, 27 Feb. 1958; PRO FO371/
    134493/266, Makins minute, 5 March 1958; PRO BT11/5555,
    Bretherton minute, 17 March 1958.

41 On links between industrial organisations, R.J. Lieber, *British Politics
    and European Unity: Parties, Elites and Pressure Groups* (Berkeley:
    University of California Press, 1970) p.65.

42 PRO FO371/134491/180, Wright minute, 17 Feb. 1958; PRO
    FO371/134492/235, Hoyer Millar and Edden minutes, 14 and 28
    March 1958 respectively.

43 PRO BT11/5648, Clarke to Cohen, 23 Jan. 1958; PRO T234/374,
    Clarke to Makins, 24 Jan. 1958.

44 PRO T234/375, Clarke minute, 10 March 1958; PRO T234/375,
    Rowan to Makins, 13 March 1958; PRO T234/203, Clarke minute,
    1 Apr. 1958.

45 PRO CAB130/132, GEN.613/57th meeting, 18 Nov. 1958; PRO
    CAB130/123, GEN.580/10, 21 Nov. 1958; PRO CAB130/123,
    GEN.580/13, 2 Dec. 1958.

46 See PRO PREM11/2532, Trend to Macmillan, 3 Dec. 1958.

47 PRO PREM11/2531, Eccles to Macmillan, 14 July 1958; PRO
    PREM11/2532, Eccles to Macmillan, 8 Dec. 1958.

48 PRO CAB130/123, GEN.580/10th meeting, 12 Dec. 1958; PRO
    CAB130/154, GEN.670/3rd meeting, 22 Dec. 1958. The Swedish
    and British industrial federations had formulated their proposals
    by this stage, PRO FO371/134519/1137, Hankey to FO, 18 Dec.
    1958.

49 See in general, Camps, *Britain*, pp.210–32; W. Kaiser, 'Challenge to
    the Community: The Creation, Crisis and Consolidation of the
    Free Trade Association, 1958–1972', *Journal of European Integration
    History*, Vol.3, No.1 (1997) pp.7–33; and R. Maurhofer, 'The Quest
    for the Lesser Evil: Britain, Switzerland and the Decision to Create
    EFTA', unpublished paper presented to the Annual Congress of
    the Swiss Political Science Association, Balsthal, 5 November 1999.

50 Comment made by Sir Michael Palliser, interview with author, 20
    Sept. 1995.

Party Games: The British EEC Applications of 1961 and 1967

Wolfram Kaiser

Britain has had long-term problems with what is now the European Union since its accession in 1973. A comparative analysis of the applications to join in 1961 and 1967 will help to clarify British expectations of membership. It will also illuminate the influence of party politics on Britain's European policy. This analysis also explains why the two applications were launched despite the fact that the first was likely to fail and the second certain to be vetoed.

1961: From laggard to leader?

When the Lee committee of senior officials re-examined Britain's European options in the spring of 1960, the six EEC states had just decided to accelerate their timetable for mutual tariff reductions, leading to increased discrimination against British exports. EFTA was unable to adjust its timetable appropriately, which strengthened the view within Whitehall that its economic value was limited and that it was certainly no long-term alternative to a closer relationship with the EEC.[1] To achieve such a closer relationship, the Lee committee initially advocated the compromise solution of 'near-identification'. According to this concept, the EFTA countries would largely accept the regulations of the EEC in a wider economic association and agree to far-reaching tariff harmonisation, without actually acceding to the EEC treaty.[2]

Whatever its institutional form, any future arrangement between Britain and the EEC had to fulfil three main economic functions.[3] First, it had to safeguard equal access to the EEC market for British industrial exports. By the early 1960s the Europeanisation of British trade patterns, already predicted by the economic ministries in 1955, was speeding up. By 1961–2, Britain exported more to western Europe than to the Commonwealth.[4] Within western Europe, the EEC market was greater in volume and generally seen as more dynamic and important than the EFTA market. As a result, the prospect of rising tariff barriers between the EEC and EFTA resulted in increased pressure from British export industries for an early solution to the trade conflict. The Lee report emphasised that

> there is great uneasiness, amounting almost to dismay, among leading industrialists at the prospect of our finding ourselves yoked indefinitely with the Seven and 'cut off' by a tariff barrier from the markets of the Six.[5]

The second economic function of a closer relationship with the EEC was to secure a share in the economic success of the Six. Britain's structural economic problems, which showed in its comparatively lower growth rates and the recurrent sterling crises, created false hopes that association with the EEC market in itself would exert sufficient external pressure for the modernisation of British industry, leading to increased productivity, higher growth rates and greater exports. As Nigel Birch put it in a speech on Europe in the House of Commons in June 1961, Britain needed 'an external stimulus. What we want here is a good shake-up'.[6]

The third economic function of an arrangement with the EEC was to provide a stable political framework for British monetary policy. Since the formal introduction of convertibility at the end of 1958 the focus of sterling policy had shifted to sustaining its stability and its international role as a reserve currency, which was seen as a vital component of Britain's continued claim to world power status. The Treasury and the Bank of England increasingly expected that EEC membership would help them achieve their monetary objectives by increasing confidence in British economic policy in the currency markets. This view was much strengthened when sterling could only be rescued from devaluation in a concerted effort with the EEC states, and especially with the German Bundesbank, in the spring of 1961.[7]

In addition, the Ministry of Agriculture thought by 1961 that participation in a European system of agricultural protection could be advantageous for Britain. Christopher Soames, Minister of Agriculture since July 1960, argued strongly that early EEC entry would allow Britain to influence the shape of the common agricultural policy (CAP) and to expand domestic agricultural production further at the expense of third countries, including the United States. Moreover, the Treasury reckoned that the government could no longer afford the ever-increasing costs of the national support system of deficiency payments. It calculated that participation in the tariff-based agricultural subsidy system envisaged by the EEC could lead to savings in the budget of £220 million annually.[8] By reducing agricultural imports, it would also alleviate Britain's balance of payments problems.

Important as they were, these economic motives were over-shadowed by foreign policy considerations in the decision-making process leading up to the EEC application. By 1961 Macmillan, the Foreign Secretary, Lord Home, and the Foreign Office strongly believed that Britain could only sustain its close relationship with the United States and thus its world power status from within the EEC. However, with notable exceptions like Peter Thorneycroft, the three circles doctrine continued to dominate Conservative thinking on Europe. According to this doctrine, Britain's world power status depended on its key mediating role in the three circles, the Commonwealth, the transatlantic relationship and western Europe. However, decolonisation and the stagnation in Commonwealth trade, the growing political influence of the EEC states, and Britain's rapidly rising trade with western Europe seemed to necessitate a substantial adjustment in the relative weight accorded to the Commonwealth and western Europe. The argument in favour of a greater British role in western Europe was strengthened considerably when the foreign ministers of the Six began to hold regular talks in the autumn of 1959 and when the EEC governments began the so-called Fouchet negotiations on the setting up of a political and defence community in the spring of 1961. Macmillan and the

Foreign Office feared that a more cohesive political unit would be so much stronger economically and militarily than Britain that it would automatically become the principal ally of the United States. A memorandum by the Foreign Office Planning Section concluded in late 1959 that

> At the best we should remain a minor power in an alliance dominated by the United States and the countries of the E.E.C.; at the worst we should sit helplessly in the middle while the two power blocs drifted gradually apart.[9]

From this conservative perspective, EEC entry would fulfil three main foreign policy functions. Firstly, political leadership of the EEC and of a political and defence community would in future serve as the main source of legitimation for Britain's claim to a special international role alongside the two superpowers. In Macmillan's interpretation of Kennedy's emerging 'Grand Design' for the future transatlantic relationship Britain would form the European pillar. The assumption which underlaid the decision-making process leading up to the application was that once inside the Community, Britain would automatically take over. This general expectation was deeply rooted in the political elite's belief in a historical right to leadership deriving from Britain's role in the Second World War and its superior democratic institutions.

Secondly, Macmillan and the Foreign Office expected that to apply for EEC membership would appease the Americans and thus cement what they still regarded as a special relationship. The Kennedy administration wanted the British to join the Community in order to be able to exercise through them greater political control over the future development of the EEC in foreign policy and defence matters. The Americans made this strategic objective quite clear in talks with the British government on several occasions during the spring of 1961, for example during a visit to London by George Ball, Under-Secretary of State for Economic Affairs, in late March[10] and during the encounter between Macmillan and Kennedy one week later.[11] At least for

Macmillan, the EEC application was in the first instance an instrument of British transatlantic policy. Thirdly, Macmillan also believed that to take account of American interests and to adjust British European policy accordingly would secure the general goodwill of the Kennedy administration. This in turn might help Britain to retain American support for its nuclear deterrent.

By 1961 the European issue had become highly politicised. The EEC application was controversial within the Conservative Party. The hard-core opposition to it came mostly from the Empire wing of the party.[12] The sceptics within the Cabinet included Reginald Maudling, who was convinced that the timing of the application was ill-chosen if the objective was to join the Community rather than to provoke another veto by de Gaulle.[13] Rab Butler was also sceptical, but he was mainly concerned with the effects of membership on British agriculture. Butler only assured Macmillan of his personal support for EEC membership during a private dinner in August 1962.[14]

Despite continued opposition and more widespread scepticism within the party, however, all the domestic pressures that mattered for the Conservatives were increasingly in favour of EEC membership at the earliest possible moment. Although for widely differing reasons, a clear and growing majority of the Cabinet and of the Conservative parliamentary party supported EEC entry. Moreoever, this support was especially pronounced among the 1955 and 1959 intake of Conservative MPs.[15] At the time of the application, European opinion among the élite in politics, administration, the media, banking and industry had also shifted dramatically in favour of EEC membership. In the category of 'informed opinion', 70 per cent were in favour, 20 per cent opposed and ten per cent undecided.[16] Among the smaller foreign policy elite, including politicians, diplomats and international managers, an even greater majority was in favour.[17]

By 1961 most newspapers advocated EEC entry, including the *Daily Mirror* which was otherwise close to the Labour Party. Moreover those interests which largely financed the Conservative Party were also strongly in favour. These were the larger export-oriented companies and the City. Most bankers hoped that EEC membership would help to secure British exports to the Six, improve the balance of payments, stabilise sterling and ultimately safeguard London's future as a leading financial centre. Senior representatives of Lazard's, for example, told Conservative politicians and senior officials in April 1961 that the general view in the City was that EEC membership should be sought at the earliest possible moment.[18]

As early as July 1960, TUC representatives had suggested this option to Conservative ministers in a meeting of the Economic Planning Board.[19] Subsequently, more and more individual unions had come out in favour of membership during 1960–1.[20] At its annual conference in 1961 the TUC followed a more pragmatic line, based on the economic issues, which was in sharp contrast to the increasingly anti-European rhetoric of Hugh Gaitskell and the Labour leadership. Thereafter, the majority of the unions continued until 1966–67 to follow European policies which were broadly in line with those of the companies in the respective sectors.

If anything, these domestic pressures for EEC membership had intensified when the Wilson government began to consider a second application in 1966. Under guidance from its strongly pro-European chairman Cecil King the Mirror Group continued to support EEC membership.[21] Among others, Douglas Jay, President of the Board of Trade, was convinced that King's strongly pro-European views were instrumental in bringing about Harold Wilson's conversion to a second application. According to Jay, Wilson hoped to pre-empt a possible campaign by the Mirror Group against his leadership of the Labour Party, based on the failure of his economic policies and on the lack of progress over ending the division of western Europe into the EEC and EFTA, by demonstrating his willingness in principle to join the Community.[22]

After a brief spell of anti-European sentiment after de Gaulle's veto of January 1963 public opinion too was favourably disposed towards membership. Opinion poll data only indicated a decline in support from late 1966, against the background of flagging support for the government. A majority opposed to membership only emerged for the first time after the Cabinet formally agreed to make an application on 2 May 1967.[23] Finally, pressure from interest groups for EEC membership had also increased further. Export-oriented industry and the City were even more committed to membership than in 1961. Moreover, a clear majority of the trade unions also supported membership.

1967: The last temptation

The first EEC application was not least the result of a lack of alternative policies. When the Conservative government first discussed Plan G for a wider west European free trade area in 1956,[24] even Anthony Eden admitted that an alternative trade policy based on the Commonwealth was no longer feasible.[25] The setting up of EFTA after de Gaulle's veto against Plan G was also largely the result of a lack of alternatives. In the words of David Eccles, then President of the Board of Trade, Britain was marrying 'the engineer's daughter when the general manager's had said no'.[26] Thereafter, it soon became obvious that the desired economic association between EFTA and the EEC was unrealistic, primarily because France was opposed to it. It would anyway have been impossible because of American hostility to such an economic solution which would have involved economic discrimination against the United States without political benefits. By 1960–1, any association between the EEC and EFTA would have involved partial tariff harmonisation and other compromises, which would have necessitated a derogation from GATT rules. During his visit to London in November 1959, Douglas Dillon, American Under-Secretary of State, made it abundantly clear that the United States would not support such a derogation.[27] Thus, by the spring of 1961 the choice for the Macmillan government was effectively between doing nothing and applying for EEC membership.

The policy choice of the Wilson government was reduced in a similar way after 1964. The Labour Party had fought the general election on the basis of a foreign and trade policy centred around the Commonwealth.[28] It soon became obvious, however, that the continued Europeanisation of British trade patterns and the ever increasing diversity of the political and trade interests of the other Commonwealth countries made such a policy unrealistic. Moreover, the persistent problems over Rhodesia in 1966–7 also served to illustrate the extent to which Commonwealth problems were now frequently serious political nuisances distracting British governments from the task of obtaining their wider foreign policy objectives. Furthermore, just as the Macmillan government had come to realise the political limits of EFTA in 1960, the Wilson government too became disillusioned with it during the surcharge crisis of 1964–5.[29] During this crisis the other EFTA states, especially the Scandinavians, attacked the Wilson government vociferously over the extension of the import surcharge of 15 per cent to the other EFTA members. Unlike quotas, which Douglas Jay, the President of the Board of Trade, had recommended to reduce imports and thus to stabilise sterling, the import surcharge was illegal under the EFTA treaty.[30]

Subsequently, the Wilson government also re-examined the case for and against some form of loose economic association with the EEC which had already been discussed in the Lee Committee in 1960. In March 1965 a Foreign Office memorandum on EEC association concluded that it

would probably require acceptance of most of the obligations of full membership without a corresponding degree of control. We should appear as second-class citizens and the effect could even be to frustrate rather than promote the achievement of the type of European policies we want.[31]

Moreover, the idea of a transatlantic economic community between the United States, Canada and Britain, suggested by the American Senator Jacob Javits in 1962, was no realistic alternative to closer involvement in Europe. The Foreign Office was under no illusion that 'the Americans are not themselves thinking at all seriously of U.S. association with regional economic groupings'.[32] Thus, as Burke Trend, the Cabinet Secretary, asked rhetorically after outlining the 'very real and very serious' difficulties Britain would have to overcome before it might eventually join the EEC, 'what alternative is open to us?'[33]

In fact, the political and economic rationale behind the second EEC application was very similar to that behind the first, although in the meantime the emphasis had shifted somewhat in favour of the economic arguments, reflecting the ever increasing preoccupation with arresting Britain's relative economic decline.[34] The similarities were at least partly due to the striking continuity in terms of Whitehall personnel dealing with Europe and their official guidance on this issue between 1961 and 1966–7. At the beginning of February 1966 Wilson and the Foreign Secretary, Michael Stewart, agreed that an informal interministerial group of officials should prepare 'a paper on exactly where we now stand' on Europe.[35] This committee was chaired by Eric Roll, a leading British negotiator in Brussels during 1961–3, and it included Sir Con O'Neill, a former ambassador to the EEC, and Frank Figgures, the first Secretary-General of EFTA. Its composition led Thomas Balogh, Wilson's Adviser on Economic Affairs, to complain bitterly in a letter to the Prime Minister that

> You will remember that Sir Con O'Neill made a violently anti-French speech [in The Hague in January 1966[36]] implying advocacy of our entry; Mr. Frank Figgures is one of the greatest protagonists of supra-national institutions. Unless measures are taken to get a balance in the composition of both the ... committee and the papers I fear all this will get out of hand and we shall be confronted with *faits accomplis* [his italics].[37]

The political rationale continued to be very strongly influenced by the Foreign Office which displayed a degree of enthusiasm for EEC membership almost 'bordering on the fanatical'.[38] The Foreign Office experience turned Michael Stewart into an ardent supporter of EEC membership in 1965–6,[39] just as it had strengthened Lord Home's conviction after

1960 that in future it would only be possible from within the EEC to sustain the transatlantic relationship with the United States and thus Britain's world power role.[40]

The key political argument in favour of membership remained virtually unchanged during the 1960s. Just like Macmillan in 1961, George Brown, when he became Foreign Secretary in 1966, believed strongly that once inside the EEC, Britain would automatically assume its political leadership. To Brown, there was no question that Britain was 'destined to become *the* leader of Europe' [his italics], of 'a new European bloc which would have the same power and influence in the world as the old British Commonwealth had in days gone by'.[41] This would also guarantee 'the maintenance of maximum influence with the United States', as it was put in the report which the interministerial group of officials finally submitted to ministers on 5 April 1966.[42] It was this broad political argument that Brown and Stewart put forward in support of membership at the ministerial meeting at Chequers on 22 October 1966 which decided in favour of a tour of the EEC capitals by Wilson and Brown in early 1967.[43] Just as in 1961, this argument was strengthened by continued American support for British EEC membership which President Lyndon B. Johnson reiterated in a letter to Wilson in November 1966.[44] To placate the Labour left, Wilson emphasised Anglo-American differences in foreign policy, especially over Vietnam. He also portrayed his rhetorical drive for a technological and scientific revolution as a means for Britain and western Europe to become more competitive in modern technologies and more independent from the United States. Yet Wilson was basically keen to continue the British role as junior partner of the United States in the Atlantic Alliance.

The economic arguments in favour of membership too were largely unchanged. The officials stressed in their report,

> that as one of the group of advanced industrial countries forming a tariff-free trade area comparable in size with the United States and the USSR, our involvement would act as a catalyst in speeding up the economic expansion of Britain, in bringing

progressive advantages of scale to important industries, and opportunities for specialisation at things we can do better than most. Our involvement would, it is believed, also provide a spur to efficiency and rationalisation generally of a unique and urgent character, bringing results that we should not achieve without it.[45]

Just as the Lee report had done in 1960,[46] the officials stressed that 'it is no part of the economic case to suggest that in membership of the Six there lies an instant panacea or easy relief for present concerns about our economy'.[47] Yet, it became more and more tempting for Labour supporters of EEC membership after the demise of the National Plan in the summer of 1966 to cast such habitual warnings by officials in the winds. As the pressure on sterling continued, they felt the need for a new and stable European framework for economic and monetary policy more strongly, just as the Conservative government had at the time of the 1961 sterling crisis.[48] According to Richard Crossman, the experience of the failure of Labour's nationalist economic policies led Brown and Stewart, but also Wilson and James Callaghan to conclude that 'the attempt to have a socialist national plan for the British Isles' had to be abandoned.[49] Instead, EEC membership in conjunction with Wilson's favourite idea of a technological and scientific revolution was now seen as the best means to revitalise the British economy.[50] This linkage of two policies at least made the public presentation of the economic rationale behind Labour's new European policy different from that of the Macmillan government in 1961.

The arguments against joining the EEC advanced by the opponents of membership in Whitehall, the Cabinet and the Parliamentary Labour Party (PLP) also indicate certain differences in comparison with the debate within the Macmillan government. They were generally more convinced of the lack of competitiveness of British industry. One official paper, for example, which took issue with the generally positive assessment of the likely economic effects of EEC entry in the main report, complained about 'the crude free-trade fallacy that everyone benefits equally from freer trade, ... the basic assumption of the Foreign Office and Board of Trade officials, and some influential officials of the Treasury and the Ministry of Technology'. This view, however, ignored the problem that the British economy did not have enough medium-sized export-oriented companies and, as a result, was not diversified enough, so that it was likely to suffer from increased competition in a common market.[51]

The opponents of joining the EEC also emphasised that at least in the short-term, membership would only aggravate Britain's balance of payments problems because of its net contributions to the budget and of the expected rise in imports from the EEC states. This argument especially suited those in the government who were strictly opposed to a devaluation of sterling which they saw as the likely outcome of EEC entry. During 1966–7 this expectation was confirmed by repeated allusions on the part of French politicians to the necessity of advance monetary adjustment to EEC membership, which was informed by their own experience with combining the introduction of convertibility with a substantial devaluation of the franc before the first intra-EEC tariff reductions in December 1958. The French Finance Minister Michel Debré, for example, made it clear during a meeting with James Callaghan, the Chancellor, in December 1966 that Britain's accession to the EEC would have to be preceeded in the French view by a devaluation of sterling.[52] The argument that EEC entry required prior devaluation was also strengthened when William Armstrong, Joint Permanent Secretary at the Treasury, expressed his belief in such a linkage at the Chequers meeting.[53]

By 1966, the agricultural argument too had shifted. In 1960–1, Butler had emphasised the need to safeguard the interests of British farmers, an important constituency for the Conservative Party which was keen to cultivate the agricultural vote in order to secure marginal seats.[54] In contrast, Jay in 1966 was preoccupied with keeping food prices low, a policy that was broadly in line with Labour Party economic policy at the time of the Attlee governments of 1945–51 and during Gaitskell's leadership.[55]

However, cheap food was only a subsidiary argument in the debate within the Cabinet during 1966–7.[56]

Europe: playing games

British European policy in the 1960s created substantial long-term problems for Britain in Europe. Both EEC applications raised the expectations of the likely political and economic benefits of membership among the elite and in the public to a point where profound disillusionment with the actual effects after Britain's accession was practically guaranteed. Even in 1961 Macmillan's belief that once inside, Britain would automatically assume the leadership of the Community was no longer in line with the reality of the close Franco-German partnership.[57] By 1966–7, in view of Britain's continuing relative economic decline and its obvious lack of clear strategic objectives in Europe it was even more clearly a 'misunderstanding', as the German Social Democrat Foreign Minister Willy Brandt later described it with pronounced British-style understatement.[58] Equally, the desperate hope that EEC membership would provide a magic cure for the British economy conveniently ignored that most of Britain's economic problems were of a structural nature and had to be tackled domestically. Tariffs were not the main obstacle to increased exports and higher growth. Despite relatively rising tariff barriers, Britain's exports to the EEC actually grew at an annual average rate of nine per cent during the 1960s and thus slightly faster than its exports to the other EFTA states.[59]

By provoking the two vetoes by de Gaulle, both applications also contributed to the widespread feeling, especially among the general public, that Britain was not wanted and would not be treated fairly, a feeling that since then has turned into a collective British neurosis over Europe. Neither veto came unexpectedly. The first application was always likely to fail. Macmillan strongly believed that there was only one incentive which could possibly make de Gaulle support British EEC membership. This incentive was a trilateral nuclear deal including the United States which would have involved Anglo-American nuclear assistance to France to speed up the development of the *force de frappe* as a quid pro quo for French support for British EEC membership. However, the Kennedy adminstration refused to give such assistance in the spring of 1961, which destroyed Macmillan's 'Grand Design' entry strategy long before he announced his government's intention to apply for EEC membership on 31 July 1961.[60] Macmillan acknowleged as much in his diaries, describing the European question as 'obviously insoluble'[61] because Britain's interest in sustaining the so-called special relationship with the United States and leading western Europe from within the EEC clearly could not be harmonised.[62] Thereafter, some Conservatives, like Thorneycroft, who became Defence Secretary in 1962, supported a general reorientation of British foreign policy towards France to achieve EEC membership, including the joint development of an underwater missile deterrent for the 1970s. However, Macmillan never seriously considered the French option as it would have brought an end to the close relationship with the United States in defence, security and intelligence matters.[63] At times during the negotiations, Macmillan seems to have hoped that a diplomatic El Alamein in Europe might still allow Britain to join the EEC. His residual hopes were strengthened temporarily when Pierson Dixon, the British Ambassador to Paris, argued in May 1962 that the French President had evidently decided to oppose British membership, but that the superior British negotiators might 'still outwit [him]'.[64] It soon became clear, however, that Dixon had seriously underestimated both the skills of the French negotiators in Brussels and de Gaulle's determination to veto the application, if he so wished.[65]

Unlike the first application, the second was certain to be vetoed, and Wilson was fully aware of this. There were no indications that de Gaulle's policy had changed. In his letter to President Johnson, Wilson acknowledged that 'my own belief is that the General has not changed one iota in his general view of the world or of our own relationship with [the United States]'.[66] On the contrary, leading representatives from other EEC and EFTA governments reiterated their almost uniform view in talks with the British during 1966–7 that as long as de Gaulle was in power in France, there was no chance that another application could possibly succeed. Shortly before the Chequers meeting, George Thomson, Chancellor of the Duchy of Lancaster and Wilson's European emissary, reported that Gerhard Schröder, the anglophile German Foreign Minister, had told him that

> he was sorry to say that his own opinion was rather pessimistic. He based this ... on his assessment of General de Gaulle's overall political concept into which Schroeder [sic] did not think United Kingdom membership of the Common Market fitted. He would be only too happy to be proved wrong.[67]

Schröder had previously advised Michael Stewart that 'we should be deluding ourselves if we thought that the French position had changed in any essential particular since that time [January 1963].[68]

Similarly, Joseph Luns, the equally anglophile Dutch foreign minister, advised Brown during a working dinner on 31 October 1966 that he

> had no illusions as to whether there had been any change in the General's attitude. His terms for British entry were in effect the dismantling of our ties with America. ... While he thought the French might have to give way if the Five ever reached the point of contemplating leaving the Community, forming a new one with us, and re-erecting the tariff barriers against France dismantled under the Treaty of Rome, he had serious doubts whether the Five would ever reach this point.[69]

The Danish government – Britain's closest ally in EFTA and keen to join the Community – entirely shared this view. According to Oliver Wright, the British ambassador to Copenhagen, neither Jens Otto Krag, the Prime Minister, nor Per Hækkerup, the Foreign Minister, 'really believes that the French veto on our membership of the Common Market has in fact been lifted. On the contrary, I think they suspect that the new financial relationship with the United States [to support sterling and the

Bretton Woods system] has double banked the existing veto inspired by the politico-military relationship.'[70] Despite the adverse external circumstances both EEC applications were launched largely as symbolic public statements. Macmillan's main foreign policy objective was to demonstrate to the Kennedy government that he was prepared to join the EEC and that the continued split of western Europe into the EEC and EFTA was entirely due to de Gaulle. After Kennedy's visit to London in June 1961 Macmillan already noted with evident satisfaction that the EEC application was perhaps doomed, but that 'we have at least got a completely new American attitude to our effort and a new understanding'.[71] Macmillan also hoped that in conjunction with other policy innovations, such as economic planning and regional policy, his new European policy would help the Conservatives in the long-term to acquire a modern party image and that it would split the Labour Party.[72] Thus, even a failed application provided significant foreign policy and domestic political benefits.

Both prime ministers, Macmillan and Wilson, were shrewd party politicians. Both were blessed, Macmillan with Edward Heath 1961–3 and Wilson with George Brown 1966–7, with European ministers who were more enthusiastic about 'going into Europe' and unable fully to comprehend their leaders' ulterior tactical motives. In fact, despite the frequent confirmation from other EEC and EFTA capitals that de Gaulle would veto another British application, Brown actually believed in 1966–7 that he could succeed where Heath had failed, namely in out-negotiating the French.[73] The main difference between the two prime ministers was that – whether or not his motives were sound – Macmillan was keen to join the EEC. In contrast, Wilson had never had any strong feelings about Europe.[74] His opposition to the first application was mainly due to internal Labour Party politics, and his interest in Europe in 1966–7 was exclusively motivated by tactical considerations.

Wilson's tactical foreign policy objective in touring the EEC capitals in early 1967 and in announcing his government's decision to apply for membership in May 1967 was further to isolate de Gaulle in the EEC and also within France. He was encouraged by Luns and others to put pressure on de Gaulle by emphasising his government's continued interest in joining the EEC, without attaching too many conditions. At the time, the *Economist* also thought this 'a sound diplomatic investment'.[75] However, few in the EEC were happy with the British decision actually to apply for membership, as they feared another round of time-consuming, fruitless negotiations. Wilson's strategy of European containment was perhaps expressed most elegantly by Michael Palliser, his new Private Secretary for Overseas Affairs. Palliser explained in a private letter to Wright that:

> We ought to ... [make] life thoroughly difficult for the General by explaining to all and sundry how thoroughly willing we are to go in and thereby forcing de Gaulle to find much more explicit reasons than hitherto for keeping us out. This means of course ... playing the German card.[76] ... Most thinking French-men, including Gaullists whether of the Pompidou or Debré variety, want us in as a counter-poise to Germany. So that what is important ... is to make clear to all concerned that we are pre-pared to go in and that, within certain limits, we do not regard all our conditions ... as totally immutable. I believe that if we can take this line with our friends in Europe and at the same time be seen to be pursuing internal policies that conform with it we can both keep up a certain momentum in our relations with Europe and prepare for a post de Gaulle situation where our entry ... can become possible within the reasonably near future; and perhaps even before the next General Election![77]

Yet Wilson's primary tactical objective was clearly of a domestic political nature. In view of the strengthening public support for EEC membership during 1964–6 – a Gallup poll showed 68 per cent in favour and only 14 per cent opposed in October 1966[78] – Wilson hoped that his new European policy would deny Edward Heath, the Conservative leader and a committed supporter of EEC membership, one important policy platform on which to attack the government.[79] More significantly, the application could help to appease Brown and his supporters within the government and the Labour Party[80] and to convey the impression of activity and decisiveness to the electorate after the failure of the government's policy of economic planning. There was no real danger of a serious internal Labour Party split over 'boring our way into Europe', as Barbara Castle called it at a Cabinet meeting in April 1967;[81] at least there was no such threat in the forseeable future, which was all that mattered to Wilson, because the application was certain to be rejected. In fact, de Gaulle, to all intents and purposes, vetoed it immediately after Wilson's announcement at a press conference on 16 May 1967.[82]

The preoccupation with tactical foreign policy manœuvres and short-term party advantage was characteristic of both EEC applications. It is one important reason why the British political elite had still not developed any clearly defined strategic objectives in Europe when de Gaulle finally left French politics and the EEC governments agreed at the summit in The Hague in December 1969 to start negotiations with Britain. Since then, it has become perhaps the most important feature of British European policy, from the 'renegotiation' public relations exercise of the Wilson government in 1974–5 through to the political manœuvring over Europe of both the Conservatives and Labour before and after the 1997 general election.

Notes

1 Wolfram Kaiser, 'Challenge to the Community: The Creation, Crisis and Consolidation of the European Free Trade Association, 1958–1972', *Journal of European Integration History*, Vol. 3, No. 1 (1997) pp.7–33. On the creation of EFTA see also Mikael af Malmborg and Johnny Laursen, 'The Creation of EFTA', in Thorsten B. Olesen (ed.) *Interdependence versus Integration. Denmark, Scandinavia and Western Europe, 1945–1960* (Odense: Odense University Press, 1995) pp.197–212.

2 PRO CAB 134/1819/27, 27 May 1960.

3 On the economic and political motives for the first EEC
   application see in greater detail Wolfram Kaiser, *Using Europe,
   Abusing the Europeans. Britain and European Integration, 1945–63*
   (Basingstoke: Macmillan, 1999 [1996]) chapter 5. For a concise
   interpretation see Wolfram Kaiser, 'From Laggard to Leader? The
   United Kingdom's Decision of 1961 to Apply for EEC
   Membership', in Anne Deighton and Alan S. Milward (eds)
   *Widening, Deepening and Acceleration: the European Economic
   Community, 1957–63* (Baden Baden: Nomos, 1999) pp.257–69. See
   also James Ellison, 'Accepting the Inevitable, Britain and European
   Integration', in Wolfram Kaiser and Gillian Staerck (eds) *British
   Foreign Policy 1955–64. Contracting Options* (Basingstoke: Macmillan,
   2000) pp.171–89.

4 On Britain's changing economic relationships with Europe and the
   Commonwealth/Empire in the late 1950s see also Catherine R.
   Schenk, 'Decolonization and European Economic Integration:
   The Free Trade Area Negotiations, 1956–58', *Journal of Imperial and
   Commonwealth History*, Vol. 24, No. 3 (1996) pp.444–63.

5 PRO CAB 134/1819/27, 27 May 1960.

6 House of Commons Debates, vol. 643, col. 546, 28 June 1961.

7 See also Michael Pinto-Duschinsky, 'From Macmillan to Home,
   1959–64', in Peter Hennessy and Anthony Seldon (eds) *Ruling
   Performance: British Governments from Attlee to Thatcher* (Oxford:
   Blackwell, 1987) p.151.

8 PRO CAB 129/102.I/107, 6 July 1960.

9 PRO PREM 11/2985, Autumn 1959.

10 PRO FO 371/158162/45, 30 March 1961.

11 PRO PREM 11/3311, 6 April 1961.

12 For an analysis of the internal opposition to EEC membership,
   which included Lord Avon, see also David Dutton, 'Anticipating
   Maastricht: The Conservative Party and Britain's first application to
   join the European Community', *Contemporary Record*, Vol. 7, No. 3,
   1993, pp.522–40.

13 See also the otherwise unreliable Richard Lamb, *The Macmillan
   Years. The Emerging Truth* (London: John Murray, 1995) pp.150–1.

14 HMD, 21 August 1962.

15 See in greater detail Nigel Ashford, *The Conservative Party and
   European Integration 1945–1975* (University of Warwick PhD thesis,
   1983) pp.102–4.

16 William Wallace, *The Foreign Policy Process in Britain* (London: Royal Institute of International Affairs, 1975) p.100.

17 Ibid.

18 PRO FO 371/158269/8, 4 May 1961. Heath has confirmed that the majority view of the City was an important additional incentive for the Conservatives to apply for EEC membership. Interview with Edward Heath, 1 April 1993.

19 PRO CAB 134/1815/6th, 4 July 1960.

20 Robert J. Lieber, *British Politics and European Unity. Parties, Elites, and Pressure Groups* (Berkeley: University of California Press, 1970) p.106.

21 Ibid., p.255.

22 Douglas Jay, *Change and Fortune. A Political Record* (London: Hutchinson, 1980) p.367.

23 Cf. James Spence, 'Movements in the Public Mood: 1961–75', in Roger Jowell and Gerald Hoinville (eds) *Britain Into Europe. Public Opinion and the EEC 1961–75* (London: Croom Helm, 1976) pp.18–36.

24 See also James Ellison, *Threatening Europe: Britain and the Creation of the European Community, 1955–58* (Basingstoke: Macmillan, 2000).

25 PRO CAB 128/30.II/66th, 18 September 1956.

26 PRO PREM 11/2531, 14 July 1958. See also Kaiser, 'Challenge to the Community', op.cit.

27 See also Kaiser, *Using Europe*, pp.105–7. On American policy towards European integration during this period see Pascaline Winand, *Eisenhower, Kennedy, and the United States of Europe* (New York: St. Martin's Press, 1993). For an overview of American policy towards European integration since 1945 see Geir Lundestad, *'Empire' by integration: the United States and European integration, 1945–1997* (Oxford: Oxford University Press, 1998).

28 For a brief introduction to Labour's foreign policy during 1964–70 see Chris Wrigley, 'Now you see it, now you don't: Harold Wilson and Labour's foreign policy 1964–70', in R. Coopey, Stephen Fielding and Nick Tiratsoo (eds) *The Wilson Governments 1964–1970* (London: Pinter Publishers, 1993) pp.123–35.

29 Cf. Wolfram Kaiser, 'Successes and Limits of Market Integration: The European Free Trade Association 1963–1969' in Wilfried Loth (ed.) *Crises and Compromises: The European Project 1963–1969* (Baden-Baden: Nomos, 2001) pp. 371–90. For the impact of this

crisis on EFTA cohesion and identity see also Wolfram Kaiser, 'A Better Europe? EFTA, the EFTA Secretariat, and the European Identities of the "Outer Seven", 1958–1972' in Marie-Thérèse Bitsch, Wilfried Loth and Raymond Poidevin (eds) *Institutions européennes et identités européennes* (Brussels: Bruylant, 1998) pp. 165–183. Individual Labour politicians, like Denis Healey, continued to be interested in EFTA as a social democratic alternative to the EEC, which they regarded as dominated by Catholic and conservative forces. See Denis Healey, *The Time of My Life* (London: Michael Joseph, 1989) pp.209–11, 359.

30 Cf. Jay, *Change and Fortune*, pp.298–309. See also James Callaghan, *Time and Change* (London: Collins, 1987) pp.169–72.

31 EFTA-EEC Links – Memorandum by the Foreign Secretary: PRO PREM 13/306, 18 March 1965.

32 Dean (Washington) to Foreign Office, 29 October 1966, PRO PREM 13/909.

33 Trend to Wilson, 28 October 1966, PRO PREM 13/909.

34 On Britain's second EEC application, see also Anne Deighton, 'The Second British Application for Membership of the EEC', in Loth, *Crises and Compromises*, pp.391–405.

35 Wilson to Stewart, 2 February 1966, PRO PREM 13/905.

36 See PRO PREM 13/893.

37 Balogh to Wilson, 10 February 1966, PRO PREM 13/905.

38 Joe Haines, *The Politics of Power* (London: Jonathan Cape, 1977) p.71.

39 Michael Stewart explicitly acknowledges the Foreign Office's influence on his thinking on Europe in his memoirs. See Michael Stewart, *Life and Labour. An Autobiography* (London: Sidgwick & Jackson, 1980) p.146.

40 On Home and Europe see also Kaiser, *Using Europe*, pp.134–5.

41 George Brown, *In My Way. The Political Memoirs of Lord George-Brown* (London: Victor Gollancz, 1971) pp.209–11. See also Peter Paterson, *Tired and Emotional. The Life of Lord George-Brown* (London: Chatto & Windus, 1993).

42 *Future Relations with Europe*, Report by a Group of Officials, 5 April 1966, PRO PREM 13/905.

43 For a summary of the Chequers meeting see Trend to Wilson, 28 October 1966, PRO PREM 13/909. See also RCD, 22 October 1966, quoted in Richard Crossman, *The Diaries of a Cabinet Minister.*

Vol. II: Lord President of the Council and Leader of the House of Commons 1966–68 (London: Hamish Hamilton and Jonathan Cape, 1976) p.82.

44 Johnson to Wilson, 16 November 1966, PRO PREM 13/910 in reply to Wilson to Johnson, 11 November 1966, ibid.

45 *Future Relations with Europe*, op. cit.

46 PRO CAB 134/1819/27, 27 May 1960.

47 *Future Relations with Europe*, op. cit.

48 On the link between the failure of Labour's economic policies and the second EEC application see also Uwe Kitzinger, *The Second Try. Labour and the EEC* (Oxford: Pergamon Press, 1968) p.12.

49 RCD, 30 April 1967, quoted in Crossman, p.355.

50 The ideological link between the second EEC application and the platform Labour and the Scientific Revolution is emphasised in Lynton J. Robins, *The Reluctant Party: Labour and the EEC, 1961–1975* (Ormskirk: G.W. & A. Hesketh, 1979) p.57.

51 Notes on the Report of the Sub-Committee on the Economic Implications of United Kingdom Membership of the European Communities, 1 August 1966, PRO PREM 13/908.

52 Talks Callaghan/Debré, 14 December 1966, PRO PREM 13/826.

53 TBD, 22 October 1966, quoted in Tony Benn, *Out of the Wilderness. Diaries 1963–67* (London: Arrow, 1988) p.480.

54 On the relationship between Conservative party interest and British foreign policy until 1964 see Michael Kandiah, 'British Domestic Politics, the Conservative Party and Foreign Policy-Making', in Kaiser and Staerck, *British Foreign Policy*, pp.61–88.

55 On Gaitskell and Europe see also Brian Brivati, *Gaitskell* (London: Richard Cohen, 1996).

56 RCD, 22 October 1966, quoted in Crossman, *Diaries*, p.83.

57 On the Franco-German partnership see also the perceptive study by Georges-Henri Soutou, *L'Alliance Incertaine. Les rapports politico-stratégiques franco-allemands 1954–1996* (Paris: Fayard, 1996).

58 Willy Brandt, *Erinnerungen* (Zurich: Propyläen, 1989) p.453.

59 'Zehn Jahre EFTA-Handel' ('Ten Years of EFTA Trade'), *EFTA Bulletin*, Vol. 11, No. 4 (1970) p.24.

60 On the perceived linkage between European and nuclear matters see in greater detail Wolfram Kaiser, 'The Bomb and Europe. Britain, France, and the EEC Entry Negotiations 1961–1963', *Journal of European Integration History*, Vol. 1, No. 1, 1995, pp.65–85.

For the wider context of British nuclear policy during this period see the instructive study by Ian Clark, *Nuclear Diplomacy and the Special Relationship. Britain's Deterrent and America, 1957–1962* (Oxford: Clarendon Press, 1994).

61 HMD, 15 June 1961, quoted in Harold Macmillan, *Pointing the Way 1959–1961* (London: Macmillan, 1972) p.374.

62 For Macmillan's assessment see also Macmillan to Caccia, 9 May 1961, PRO PREM 11/3319; HMD, 22 July 1961, quoted in Harold Macmillan, *At the End of the Day 1961–1963* (London: Macmillan, 1973) p.17.

63 On the French option in British foreign policy see Wolfram Kaiser, 'L'option française dans la politique nucléaire et européenne de la Grande-Bretagne, 1957–1963', *Revue d'histoire diplomatique*, Vol. 112, No. 2 (1998) pp.173–204.

64 HMD, 19 May 1962.

65 On the entry negotiations see, from a multilateral perspective, Piers Ludlow, *Dealing with Britain. The Six and the First UK Application to the EEC* (Cambridge: Cambridge University Press, 1997). See also Anne Deighton and Piers Ludlow, '"A conditional application": British management of the first attempt to seek membership of the EEC, 1961–3', in Anne Deighton (ed.) *Building Postwar Europe. National Decision-Makers and European Institutions, 1948–63* (Basingstoke: Macmillan, 1995) pp.107–26; Anne Deighton, 'The United Kingdom Application for EEC Membership, 1961–1963', in Richard T. Griffiths and Stuart Ward (eds) *Courting the Common Market: The First Attempt to Enlarge the European Community 1961–1963* (London: Lothian Foundation Press, 1996) pp.39–58. For an analysis of the most important political and technical problems of the negotiations see still Miriam Camps, *Britain and the European Community 1955–1963* (Oxford: Oxford University Press, 1964).

66 See, for example, either Trend or Palliser to Wilson, 13 September 1966, PRO PREM 13/908 and Wilson to Johnson, 11 November 1966, PRO PREM 11/910.

67 Thomson to Foreign Office, 14 October 1966, PRO PREM 13/908.

68 Talks Schröder/Stewart, 16 March 1966, PRO PREM 13/905.

69 Working dinner: Brown/Luns, 31 October 1966, PRO PREM 13/909.

70 Wright (Copenhagen) to Palliser, 18 October 1966, PRO PREM 13/897.

71 HMD, 11 June 1961.

72 See in greater detail Kaiser, *Using Europe*, pp.146–51.

73 See, for example, talks: Brown/Luns, 31 October 1966, PRO PREM 13/909.

74 Ben Pimlott, *Harold Wilson* (London: HarperCollins, 1992) p.397. This may also explain the scant treatment of Wilson's European policy in Philip Ziegler, *Wilson. The Authorised Life of Lord Wilson of Rievaulx* (London: Weidenfeld & Nicolson, 1993) and Austen Morgan, *Harold Wilson* (London: Pluto Press, 1992). Not surprisingly, Harold Wilson, *The Labour Government 1964–1970: A Personal Record* (London: Weidenfeld and Nicolson, 1971) reveals none of the real motives behind the 1967 application.

75 'Pushing the Door to Europe', *The Economist*, 22 October 1966.

76 Palliser's reference is to the uncertainties of German Ostpolitik and the possibility of German unification which could undermine France's political leadership role in the EEC.

77 Palliser to Wright, 21 October 1966, PRO PREM 13/897.

78 'Six's leading People want Britain to join', *Daily Telegraph*, 24 October 1966.

79 This is stressed in John Young, *Britain and European Unity, 1945–1992* (Basingstoke: Macmillan, 1993) p.89. See also Lieber, *British Politics*, p.263.

80 On intra-Labour Party politics over the EEC application see also Uwe Kitzinger, *Diplomacy and Persuasion. How Britain Joined the Common Market* (London: Thames and Hudson, 1973) p.281 and B. Lapping, *The Labour Government 1964–1970* (Harmondsworth: Penguin, 1970).

81 BCD, 13 April 1967, quoted in Barbara Castle, *The Castle Diaries 1964–70* (London: Weidenfeld and Nicolson, 1984) p.242.

82 Kitzinger, *The Second Try*, Document 24.

Entry and Referendum Revisited

Uwe Kitzinger

This chapter deals essentially with four distinct but interrelated topics:

- the international diplomacy of 1969–72 working towards British adhesion to the Treaty of Rome;
- the persuasion at home in 1971–2 to obtain parliamentary approval for joining the Community;
- the so-called re-negotiation with the Community by the Labour government in 1974–5; and,
- back at home again, the constitutional innovation of a national referendum and the two rival public relations campaigns fought in the weeks leading up to 5 June 1975.

We are – or at least I am – in a slightly odd position in having to cover this period. My *Diplomacy and Persuasion*[1] is an almost 'real time' account that covers 1969 to the middle of 1972. It was written on the basis of intensive interviews on the Continent and in Britain for the most part while the story was still unfolding and was published on 3 January 1973 – the day before Christopher Soames, George Thomson, David Hannay and I flew in a small Heron aircraft to take up our tasks in Brussels. David Butler's and my joint book *The 1975 Referendum*[2] covers the story for 1974–5. It, too, was written very close to the events. Perhaps I should mention that between being involved in writing on these two books, that is from January 1973 until June 1975, as Christopher Soames' adviser – rather unfortunately, as Mary Soames has acknowledged – I was sworn not to keep a diary.

In the absence of the official papers for another few years the chief new sources that have become available since then are the political diaries or autobiographies and various biographies of quite a few of the chief actors. Tony Benn's diary, for example, gives us detailed accounts of who said what both in and out of the Cabinet – in detail indeed so minute that many historians would not want to wade through it all. From continental memoirs it seems clear that Britain's entry and the subsequent story were far from central to continental concerns. I shall concentrate on what these diaries, autobiographies and biographies add – by way of facts missed at the time, by way of anecdote, and by way of perspective. It will be interesting to see how much and what surprises, 30 years after the events, the opening of the official archives then still has to contribute.

Perhaps I should add here a word about one of the difficulties of writing contemporary history in almost 'real time'. Back in 1957 – forty years ago now – when I was working on *German Electoral Politics*[3] I encountered walls of silence in Bonn on certain subjects, notably on money matters – especially on party finance and election expenditure. My way round this was to go to Kiel and to Munich, to Hamburg and to Düsseldorf, to Saarbrücken and other places on the periphery, where lesser mortals were less security-minded and indeed often anxious to have their prowess in fund-raising or their leverage in expenditure recorded for posterity. Extrapolating from an accumulation of partial data that actually covered more than half the waterfront one could first of all get a pretty good idea of the totals. But with that knowledge it was also then not too difficult to judge who at the centre was trying to pull wool over one's eyes and indeed where necessary one could refute those at the centre who tried to palm me off with unrealistic figures and even shame some of them into some approximation of the truth. The 'publish and perish' threats by the Confederation of German Industry that if I divulged these secrets they would ruin my academic career I could at that time treat as silly bombast.

The only real such trouble I had with *Diplomacy and Persuasion* came, interestingly enough, from the Foreign Office. To have my facts double-checked before going to press I sent two of the chapters to the FCO in June 1972. There was an immediate reaction of denials and protests. I was twice summoned to Sir Anthony Royle's office (he was then Under-Secretary of State) and asked to drop entirely at least one of my chapters, that on 'The Campaign in the Country', and to emasculate another, that on 'The Government and the Conservatives'. Not only had I got the facts quite wrong, but even if they had been true they should have remained secret – from which it followed that I must have obtained such facts (if any) as might have borne any relation to the truth under the seal of secrecy and that I could therefore not publish them anyway. There were two topics on which the Foreign Office appeared to be acutely sensitive. First and most ostensibly, there was the Conservative government's anxiety to suppress any mention of its close links with the Labour pro-Marketeers – for their sakes. Second, but perhaps even more, the Foreign Office was anxious to keep under wraps the important role it was then playing in the domestic process of persuasion.[4] Norman Reddaway (then Assistant Under-Secretary of State at the FCO in charge of the Information Research Department and its pro-Market public relations) on both occasions when I was summoned acted as my chief prosecutor. By the time of the second session in Tony Royle's office I was able to prove not only that some of the denials of fact at the first session had been denials of the truth, but also that my informants including the Labour Marketeers (with some of whose leaders I had in any case links of friendship going back to the 1940s and 50s) had given me these facts on the record for publication in the book. Tony Royle at that point paid me some handsome compliments and the publication went ahead. But I seriously doubted that the FCO would ever allow me to go to Brussels as a British member of the Commission staff if the occasion were ever to arise. It speaks well of everyone concerned that when Christopher Soames wanted me to join his *cabinet* I was able to go. (It was this attempt at pressure that lies behind my somewhat histrionic preface ending; 'for me not to publish now would have been to commit *la trahison des clercs'*.)

Diplomacy 1969–72

After two failed attempts to join the Community, both blocked by President de Gaulle, his resignation in 1969 offered the glimmer of a new dawn. Georges Pompidou was elected President under the sign of *'continuité et ouverture'*. At the Hague summit that December Willy Brandt himself supplied at least one cogent argument for France opening the Community to Britain: 'Anyone who fears that the economic weight of the Federal Republic of Germany could work against equilibrium within the Community should support its extension for that very reason.'5 After nailing down the agricultural and financial policies between the Six, the French civil servants made it hard for the British negotiators until May 1971, and it looked a 'Perils of Pauline' story at the time. But once Ted Heath had had his 'very, very good meeting' with Pompidou in Paris that month the pieces of the jigsaw fell into place and even the thorny problem of sterling magically disappeared.

In retrospect one may ask whether British accession to the Rome treaty was not an inevitability. I doubt whether we could ever have been assured of success had de Gaulle been succeeded by someone more intransigent. It is worth recalling that the entry negotiations in 1970 were prepared by the Labour government – before polling day Crispin Tickell wrote the bulk of the opening statement with George Thomson though it was in the event delivered by Anthony Barber. The negotiations thus got off to their start without any delay less than two weeks after the general election which brought Edward Heath to power. Nonetheless one may also doubt if they could have been concluded successfully and received parliamentary approval had Ted Heath not come to power and been since his student days a thoroughly committed 'European', whose maiden speech in 1950 had been on the Schuman Plan.

Persuasion 1971–2

After that May 1971 meeting in Paris the uncertainties lay on the British domestic scene. From early 1970 up to June 1971 the polls – Gallup, Harris, NOP and ORC – showed clear pluralities, indeed mostly majorities, against joining the Community. Even as late as June 1971 ORC showed 55 per cent against, and only 27 per cent in favour.[6] With the idea of a referendum only on the distant horizon at that time, popular opinion was not yet relevant directly: but since accession to the Rome treaty would in practice require parliamentary approval, public opinion and constituency pressures on MPs to vote against it could have become overwhelming.

For the government there thus ensued a double task. First, it had to align or at least neutralise public opinion: and while by the autumn most polls still showed a majority against membership, the numbers in favour had risen almost to level pegging. Second, the Whips had to secure a parliamentary majority. That involved a period of 'nose-counting, arm-twisting, weak knees and stiff upper lips'[7] in the Conservative parliamentary party, and close undercover relations with those Labour MPs whose European convictions took precedence over their loyalty to the decisions of the party conference. Douglas Jay called those convictions 'a religion',[8] and Tony Benn records Charlie Pannell bearing witness to the Parliamentary Labour Party on 19 October: 'Europe is an act of faith ... life has decisions that go to the core of one's being'.[9]

There has recently been an attempt to falsify the record as to the argumentation used both in the 1960s and in the 1970–2 debate, and to claim that the British people were tricked by their politicians and the media into membership of the Community without realising its legal and constitutional implications. That is to ignore a spirited debate which went on for 14 years, from Macmillan's 1961 application until the 1975 referendum itself. For most of that time the anti-Marketeers could be heard loudly, clearly and often stridently, with the *Daily Express* in the vanguard until late 1971. They argued on several fronts. The constitutional argument that Britain and in particular the British Parliament would lose its sovereignty as sole lawmaker was one of the most cogent. Links with the Commonwealth and the USA – Churchill's theory of the 'three circles' – constituted a second. Various economic arguments including the balance of payments effects and the rise in food prices implied by the CAP formed a third cluster of arguments.

As to what effects joining the Community would have on the sovereign powers of the British Parliament, my friend and constant sparring partner on television at the time William Pickles had published his grave warning on that issue already in 1961.[10] (His hobby was listed in *Who's Who* as 'saving Britain and the Common Market from each other's embrace'.) One has only to read Hugh Gaitskell's 1962 speech on Britain's status becoming like that of 'Texas or California' thus ending 'a thousand years of British history',[11] or Enoch Powell's dire and passionate prophecies,[12] Douglas Jay's, Tony Benn's and Peter Shore's speeches or for that matter Roy Jenkins' own memoirs to remember that throughout the 1960s and the first half of the 1970s the big arguments were not just over economics or the technicalities of food prices or harmonisation, but a great deal about Britain's alternative roles in the world whether as an independent loner or as part of a larger unit taking joint decisions, implementing common policies and common rules.

Perhaps the contention is that the constitutional case – though deployed very tellingly by the anti-Marketeers – was not fully and fairly enough explained by successive Labour and Conservative governments themselves. But the Labour government's White Paper of 1967 had already put it squarely:

> The constitutional innovation would lie in the acceptance in advance as part of the law of the United Kingdom of provisions to be made in the future by instruments issued by the Community institutions – a situation for which there is no precedent.[13]

Edward Heath in *The Times* only scraped the surface with his quotations of what was acknowledged in 1970–2 on the

Conservative government side.[14] That whole debate was available for all who were interested to read, and to hear rehearsed on radio and television, almost *ad nauseam.*

The parliamentary crunch came on 28 October 1971 when a five-day debate culminated after nearly 180 speeches in a vote on the principle of joining. There were 356 Ayes, 244 Noes. Free to vote according to their convictions, 41 Conservatives voted against entry or abstained, while despite a three-line whip 69 Labour members voted with the government in favour or abstained. (Their leaders – Roy Jenkins, William Rodgers, Shirley Williams prominent among them – were later to form the backbone of the Social Democratic breakaway from the Labour Party.) In 1972, when the remarkably terse 12–clause bill to translate Community law into British law[15] had to pass its second reading, which was of course made a matter of confidence by the Heath government, it scraped home with a majority of only eight votes. The political editor of *The Times* acknowledged next morning 'I cannot say with certainty that the Government will be able to carry its Common Market legislation'.[16] But 'the mysterious narrow majorities continued without ever falling below four ... the Government could have been defeated twelve times on the bill but for Labour abstentions; and this would have meant the end of the government and the end as well of the Bill'.[17] Thanks to these Labour MPs' abstentions – most of them were about to retire – Britain as well as Ireland and Denmark became full members on 1 January 1973.

The 'Fanfare for Europe' Heath planned to celebrate Britain's accession failed to rouse much enthusiasm except among an elite, and it has to be admitted that the first 14 months of Britain's membership saw little of the progress either in European integration or in Britain for which hopes had been raised. The Labour Party refused to take its seats in the European Parliament. Food prices rose substantially the world over. The Copenhagen summit in December failed to produce the sums required for the regional fund to provide any real counter-weight to the balance of payments effects of the CAP on Britain. Above all the oil shock consequent on the Middle East war showed up a sad lack of solidarity between Community members and their failure to achieve any real agreement on the vital subject of energy, with Heath at the end of 1973 threatening to block progress on energy to obtain a bigger regional fund. By the time the Heath government lost its majority at the February 1974 general election, as Heath's biographer John Campbell puts it: 'Even his proudest achievement seemed to have foundered in acrimony and mistrust ... the European ideal emerged – at least in the short term – badly bruised'.[18]

The so-called renegotiation 1974–5

Stephen George and Sir Roy Denman in their books record the heavy-handed behaviour of the British representatives on the Council of Ministers in the period of early membership under the Heath government, and even more so under the Wilson administration which took over in March 1974 and secured a slender majority in a second general election held in October the same year. At stake still were the issues surrounding Britain's net contribution to the Community budget, the regional fund, the CAP, the plans for economic and monetary union, fishery issues, and – not least – the issue of a common energy policy. It was over the energy issue that Jim Callaghan told Commission President Gaston Thorn that, at the proposed international energy conference, but for the Community Britain would have been represented and his country, Luxembourg, would not. There was the occasion, after the referendum, when Tony Benn deliberately kept his Community colleagues on the Council of Energy Ministers waiting in order to fulfil a constituency Labour Party engagement.[19] Later on John Silkin, no doubt playing to the gallery with an eye on the party leadership, so far ignored his Permanent Secretary Freddy Kearns' advice that the latter was moved in the full Council of Agriculture Ministers to ask for a bowl of water and publicly and literally washed his hands of his minister.[20] These incidents form anecdotal evidence but they are relevant to the atmosphere particularly after the two general elections of 1974.

In 1971 the Labour Party conference had not objected to British entry into the Communities on principle, although Jim Callaghan, in his Southampton speech in May about 'the language of Chaucer, Shakespeare and Milton' was clearly pushing in that direction at a time when many thought he would have liked to oust and succeed Harold Wilson.[21]. From that time on Harold Wilson was, according to one biographer, in 'deadly panic',[22] and said over and over again that had the party conference come out against the Community in principle he would have had to resign.[23] Throughout the Common Market story Harold Wilson felt what the *Daily Mirror* called 'a tethered sacrificial goat' for the sake of party unity making, in Barbara Castle's words 'almost a noble decision to adopt an ignoble role'.[24] On good days he could joke wryly 'I'm at my best in messy middle of the road situations', on bad days he would complain 'I've been wading in shit for three months to allow others to indulge their conscience'.[25] On the one hand he had to cope with Roy Jenkins resigning the deputy leadership in April 1972 in protest at Labour's decision in favour of a referendum (which Roy Jenkins feared would become a weapon against progressive causes in general – 'This constant shifting of the ground I cannot accept'[26]). On the other hand there was Tony Benn, whom even his comrade Barbara Castle felt to be 'a bit mad'[27] and who wore a black armband for a year after the referendum resulted in a 'yes'.[28] Perhaps in my treatment of Harold Wilson's crab-like tactics I did not allow sufficiently for what he must have gone through as a crypto-marketeer crucified by the press but dedicated above all else to keeping his party together,

The objection had been to 'the Tory terms' – no matter that there was a widely published consensus of Labour ex-ministers who had been involved earlier and who certified that the outcome of the Heath government's negotiations fell within what the previous Labour government would itself have accepted. So the way to keep Britain in the Communities and still satisfy the Labour Party had to be a re-negotiation (or at least the appearance of a renegotiation) of the 'Tory terms'.

On 1 April 1974, a month after Labour took office, the new Foreign Secretary, Jim Callaghan, therefore asked for a renegotiation. His biographers Peter Kellner and Christopher Hitchens sum up his confrontational trade union style: rejection of the first offer, followed by drawn-out talks over the points of disagreement, then hard bargaining on details, ending up with the reluctant endorsement of 'the best agreement we could get'; and his June 1974 speech was intended to 'sound differently, depending on where the listener was standing ... for home consumption, April's hard line remained a valid text'.[29]

In fact, however, by June it was understood that neither the Rome treaty nor even the accession treaty were to be amended: to do that would have required another process of ratification in member states. Instead what was negotiated were some supplementary agreements – notably over budgetary matters. There is in fact some reason to argue that it was not actually in Britain's long-term interests to have entered into such precise arrangements in 1975 when the principle had already been adopted in 1972 that were unacceptable situations to arise, 'the very survival of the Community would demand that the institutions find equitable solutions'.[30] When Margaret Thatcher a decade later wanted 'her money back', the very precision of the 'renegotiation' formula rather got in the way.

Reviewing the story of the so-called renegotiation as I tell it in *The 1975 Referendum*, I note two points which I missed, but which are brought out in both Wilson's[31] and Callaghan's[32] memoirs of the period. Helmut Schmidt's brilliant speech to the Labour Party conference in November 1974 is given due weight, as is his visit to Chequers that weekend: but what I (and Stephen George also) missed was that perhaps his most useful contribution that weekend was to stress the need to get France (which was in the chair that half-year) on Britain's side. Helmut Schmidt then and there phoned Giscard d'Estaing to fix a quiet dinner in Paris a few days later between Wilson and Giscard, who had been elected President in May. That lightning visit to Paris in some ways paralleled the meeting between Heath and Pompidou in May 1971, but it appears to have been kept a total secret at the time.[33] It is pleasing that both Wilson and Callaghan pay handsome tributes to the Commission President, Francois-Xavier Ortoli. In Wilson's words: 'in the last difficult hours of the renegotiation arguments he played a decisive role, and it is more than arguable that we should not have succeeded without him'.[34]

The 1975 referendum

The idea of submitting the European Community issue – precisely because of its constitutional implications – to a referendum began to be canvassed already well before Britain joined. Philip Goodhart,[35] Neil Marten, and Enoch Powell raised the issue on the Conservative side. On the Labour side Douglas Jay proposed it in an article in *The Times* on 1 August 1970,[36] and Jim Callaghan at the time called it 'a life-raft into which the whole party may one day have to climb'.[37] With the Labour Party so deeply split, and the leader very much – though covertly – on the side of the minority, the notion of passing the matter over to the people in general by a referendum became a very seductive way out for the party and its leader. In March 1972 Tony Benn chaired a meeting of the NEC, and, in the absence of Wilson, Jenkins and Callaghan, persuaded the NEC in favour. Wilson very quickly fell into line, and in early 1975 the Labour government introduced its Referendum bill into Parliament.

The Cabinet decided that ministers should 'be free to support and speak in favour of a different conclusion in the referendum campaign'[38] – though Barbara Castle remembers Wilson 'outraged when he found out that we antis intended to take it seriously'. He was 'angrier than I have ever known him. "So this is all the loyalty I get!", he snarled'.[39] The story of the campaign has been told pretty fully not only in David Butler's and my book, but also with greater emphasis on tactics and personalities, feints and tergiversations in Tony Benn's, Douglas Jay's, Roy Jenkins's and David Owen's diaries and memoirs. By this time all the best-known party leaders were on the side of the Marketeers[40] while the anti-Marketeers were led by no doubt interesting but rather less powerful characters like Enoch Powell, Neil Marten, Tony Benn, Michael Foot, Douglas Jay, Peter Shore and Jack Jones. Two of the three pamphlets sent to every household, the government's and the pro-Marketeers', urged the voters to plump for 'yes'. The bulk of the press was pro-Market; and the money spent by 'Britain in Europe' and its various allies, supplied by industry, the City, and individuals, was a perhaps tenfold multiple of what the anti-Marketeers could afford. It was no surprise when, on a turnout of 65 per cent, 17.4 million (67 per cent) voted 'yes', 8.4 million (32 per cent) voted 'no'.

This 1975 referendum result was achieved in spite of very clear arguments being deployed again, as in 1970–2, on the loss of British sovereignty that was at stake. It would be tedious to cite all the newsprint and air-time rightly devoted to this issue. Perhaps the most concise evidence for historians about what happened in 1975 is to be found in the leaflet from the National Referendum Campaign which was sent at public expense to every household in the run-up to the 1975 Referendum.[41] Under 'The Right to Rule Ourselves' it argued that the Community:

> sets out by stages to merge Britain with France, Germany, Italy and other countries into a single nation. This will take away from us the right to rule ourselves which we have enjoyed for centuries ... Policies are being decided, rules made, laws enacted and taxes raised, not by our own Parliament elected by the British people, but by the Common Market – often by the unelected Commissioners in Brussels.

And under the caption 'Britain a mere province of the Common Market?' the leaflet goes on:

> The real aim of the Market is, of course, to become a single country in which Britain would be reduced to a mere province ... Unless you want to be ruled more and more by a Continental [sic] Parliament in which Britain would be a small minority, you should vote NO.

As to the results of the referendum I fear I have little to add to the low-key conclusion David Butler and I reached in 1975.

> The verdict of the referendum must be kept in perspective. It was unequivocal but it was also unenthusiastic. Support for membership was wide but it did not run deep … It was a vote for the status quo … not even necessarily a vote of confidence that things would be better in than out; it may have been no more than an expression of fear that things would be worse out than in.

Christopher Soames had put it colourfully: 'This is no time for Britain to consider leaving a Christmas club, let alone the Common Market.' And in the event, as we concluded with what remains an understatement: 'the logic of the argument that Britain needed a strong Community was not carried over into any obvious efforts to speed up the strengthening of the Community.'[42]

Notes

1   Uwe Kitzinger, *Diplomacy and Persuasion* (London: Thames and Hudson, 1973) hereafter referred to as *D&P*; see also Douglas Evans, *While Britain Slept: The Selling of the Common Market* (London: Gollancz, 1975).

2   David Butler and Uwe Kitzinger, *The 1975 Referendum* (London: Macmillan 1976) republished 1996.

3   Uwe Kitzinger, *German Electoral Politics* (Oxford: Oxford University Press, 1960).

4   For a (misleadingly titled) article foreshadowing a study of the domestic role of the Foreign Office Information Research Department see Paul Lashmar and James Oliver, 'How MI5 pushed Britain to join Europe', *The Sunday Telegraph*, 27 April 1997, and subsequently the same authors' *Britain's Secret Propaganda War* (Stroud: Sutton, 1998) pp145 – 151.

5   Willy Brandt, *My Life in Politics* (London: Hamish Hamilton, 1992) p.421.

6   *D&P* contains a chapter with the relevant graphs and breakdowns. This figure comes from p.360.

7   *D&P,* p.168; see also John Campbell, *Edward Heath* (London: Jonathan Cape, 1993).

8   Douglas Jay, *Chance and Fortune* (London: Hutchinson, 1980) p.460. The book is full of good material on the whole issue from the Schuman Plan until the referendum.

9   Tony Benn, *Office without Power* (London: Hutchinson, 1988) p.380.

10 William Pickles, *Not with Europe* (London: Fabian Society 1961) passim. On the other side my book *The Challenge of the Common Market* (Oxford: Blackwells, 1961) started chapter 3 on 'Supranationalism and Sovereignty' with a section headed 'Federalist Strategy', pp.60ff.

11 See Uwe Kitzinger, *The Politics and Economics of European Integration* (New York: Praeger 1963) p.220.

12 Enoch Powell, *Reflections of a Statesman,* Bellew, 1991, reprints some of his speeches on the subject. According to one of his biographers British membership constituted 'a gross affront to his patriotism' – see Humphry Berkeley, *The Odyssey of Enoch Powell* (London: Hamish Hamilton, 1977) p.104. Patrick Cosgrove, *The Lives of Enoch Powell* (London: Bodley Head, 1989) traces his activity as an anti-Marketeer and bluntly states (p.268): 'The kernel of his objection ... was loss of sovereignty'. The story is also told in chapter 9 of Roy Lewis, *Enoch Powell: Principle in Politics* (London: Cassell, 1979) pp.145–166.

13 Cmnd 3301 reprinted in full in Uwe Kitzinger, *The Second Try,* (Oxford: Pergamon, 1968). For the debate at referendum time see below.

14 *The Times,* 18 January 1997.

15 Cf. Geoffrey Howe, *Conflict of Loyalty* (London: Pan, 1994) pp.65–9.

16 February 1972, quoted in *D&P* p.387.

17 Douglas Jay, *Change and Fortune* (London: Hutchinson, 1980) p.469.

18 *Edward Heath – a Biography* (London: Jonathan Cape, 1993) p.560.

19 Stephen George, *An Awkward Partner,* (Oxford: Oxford University Press, 2nd edition 1994) pp.96–7.

20 Roy Denman, *Missed Chances* (London: Cassell, 1996) p.255.

21 see *D&P* pp.300–305. For an insider's parallel view of the issue as a football in intra-party manoeuvres with an eye on the leadership succession by Jim Callaghan, Tony Crosland and Denis Healey see David Owen, *Time to Declare* (London: Joseph, 1991) pp.170–205, where he notes: 'it is quite extraordinary that Jim Callaghan's

autobiography, *Time and Chance*, has no account of his *Non merci beaucoup* speech in Southampton', (p.177) and on the same page, discussing the opposite side, reflects 'I only later discovered that Roy Jenkins was a closet federalist'.

22 Ben Pimlott, *Harold Wilson* (London: HarperCollins, 1992) p.597; see also Austen Morgan, *Harold Wilson* (London: Pluto Press, 1992).

23 Tony Benn, *Office without Power* (London: Hutchinson 1988) p.426.

24 Barbara Castle, *Fighting all the Way* (London: Macmillan, 1993) p. 448.

25 Denis Healey, *Time of My Life*, Michael Joseph, 1989, p.360. Roy Jenkins adds 'while I went around the world with a halo on my head', *A Life at the Centre* (London: Random House 1991) p.319.

26 *D&P* p. 393

27 *Fighting all the Way*, p. 446

28 Tony Benn, *Against the Tide* (London: Hutchinson, 1989) p.578.

29 *Callaghan – The Road to Number Ten* (London: Cassell, 1976) pp.152–5.

30 *The United Kingdom and the European Communities*, Cmnd 4289 (London: HMSO, 1971) para. 96.

31 Harold Wilson, *Final Term* (London: Weidenfeld & Nicolson and Michael Joseph, 1979) pp.88–90.

32 James Callaghan, *Time and Chance* (London: Collins, 1987) pp.312–4.

33 There is also no mention of this dinner arrangement in Nicholas Henderson's five-page account of the German Chancellor's visit, on which Henderson accompanied him (Nicholas Henderson, *Mandarin: the diaries of an ambassador 1969–1982* (London: Weidenfeld & Nicolson 1994), pp.74–79). Henderson was in fact unaware of it until years later – clear evidence of how close to his chest Wilson was playing his cards.

34 *Final Term*, p.9; see also *Time and Chance*, pp.307 and 323.

35 Philip Goodhart, *Referendum*, Stacey, 1971 traces the idea of a national referendum in British politics back to the 1890s.

36 *Change and Fortune*, p.452.

37 *D&P* p.296.

38 *Final Term*, p.99.

39 *Fighting all the Way*, p.474–5. Perhaps one should add the sequel later that night: 'Harold apologised for his earlier rudeness and I

went over and kissed him on the forehead. "Don't I get a kiss?" asked Jim mournfully…'

40 Tony Benn however reports that when Margaret Thatcher was elected leader she told Conservative Central Office to drop their planned tremendous pro-Market campaign – 'this was the price demanded for the support of the anti-Marketeers.' *Against the Tide*, pp. 322–3.

41 All three official leaflets are well worth rereading: they are reprinted as an Appendix in *The 1975 Referendum*; the above passages come from pp. 301 and 303 of the 1996 edition.

42 *The 1975 Referendum*, p.280–1.

From Single Market to Maastricht
Keith Middlemas

Basil Liddell Hart provided the metaphor: the process that ran from the Single Market to Maastricht treaty and beyond resembles an expanding torrent. It replaced the painstakingly slow practice of harmonisation on which the EEC's minimal progress had been based until then and broke through the constraints and restrictive practices so long maintained by its member states. After the Single Market became a certainty (albeit a distant one, by no means completed on the target date of 1 January 1993), it rolled up into one mass of momentum many of the disparate aims set by the Commission during the previous thirty years. But this momentum in economic matters was checked by the same member states' self-interest in political ones at Maastricht, finally to break on a factor largely ignored since the Community's inception: the interests of electorates, media and public opinion.

The Community was not of course a battlefield, rather the site of a many-sided game between players of different status, power and degree of involvement. To answer the questions who set and defended the original constraints, who gave the decisive push, and why the players behaved in one way in the mid 1980s Single Market negotiations, and in another at Maastricht in 1991, one needs to allow for a range of motives from pure self-interest to a measure of collective altruism. Hence my own usage of the device 'competitive symposium' to describe the plurality of governments, ministries, state agencies, regions, industrial, financial and labour players. Such diversity requires the services not only of contemporary historians but economists, political scientists, and the other social sciences; the Community's history is a strong argument in favour of reviving the discipline of political economy.

There is of course no single correct historical version, since each player had reasons which even the collective it belonged to did not know. Permanent players, chiefly governments, had an inner continuity, based on their definition of national interest. What was logical from one home base, however, usually appeared irrational from others, (particularly in the cases of 'semi detached' member states such as Britain, Denmark or Greece). Some of the less studied member states, Portugal and Ireland, like the founder member, the Netherlands, as careful observers have always known, turn out to have been mainstream contenders all along.

In contrast to the governments signing the Single European Act in 1986 from their ten different standpoints,[1] the less frequent or occasional economic players elucidated their interest from a matrix starting within the firm or corporation itself and ending with the global implications for it of trade, technology or investment. Few multinational corporations could stand aside from the growing Single Market (though the majority of financial institutions at first demonstrated a surprising lack of interest); but few of them, five years later, chose to involve themselves collectively in the Maastricht process. The implications of monetary union seemed to have escaped virtually all of them in 1990–91.

Finally it has to be said that, although member states are formally of equal status in the Community/Union, some have much greater informal power than others. Despite the twelve signatories' enthusiasm in 1986, despite the gathering torrent ably channelled by the Commission before and afterwards, it still needed a German-Franco initiative, launched at the Hanover summit in June 1988, to put the Single Market project beyond doubt. For lack of such a decisive move in 1991, the parties at Maastricht slipped out of step, and often out of temper, united only in their determination not to follow every word of the Commission-led agenda.

1973–83: a dismal decade?

The first oil shock, 1973, and the sharp recession which followed, had precipitated a *sauve qui peut* among EC governments which ushered in a decade often seen as stagnant if not actually barren, barely relieved by a slightly more collegiate response to the second oil shock in 1981. Even if the period before 1983 is portrayed in the most optimistic way, it scarcely reflected the hopes that had buoyed up heads of government at the 1970–2 summits, and had attended the entry of Britain (for the first, and until 1997 at least the last time, an active member under the genuinely Europhile government led by Edward Heath) together with Ireland in 1973.

The period witnessed an ingraining of intergovernmental activity, to the Brussels Commission's long-term detriment; in which the main pan-European strands were restricted to national forms of modest industrial restructuring, the *Plan Barre*, the *Modell Deutschland*, the Netherlands experiment, and the evolution of a deutschmark-led European monetary system. In a prevailing climate of government activism, characterised by fish wars, wine wars, the long French-orchestrated exclusion of Spain and Portugal, and endemic conflict between Council of Ministers and Commission, none of the Community's institutions seemed able to provide the stimulus to enable European firms and financial institutions to meet the international challenges of American and Japanese competitors, and the even grander challenge of approaching global markets.

The converse is less often put. During the 1970s, the Commission developed long-planned strategies for the social and regional funds, and a new mode of activity, political cooperation – synonym for foreign affairs – in the aftermath of Helsinki. The European Court of Justice (ECJ) handed down significant judgements, some of them with elements of creative law-making, in cases such as *Kramer* and *Simmenthal* about the Commission's competencies and the direct application of European law. Others followed, *Continental Can* and *Phillip Morris*, crucial to the development of competition policy; and above all *Cassis de Dijon*, with its long-unfolding implications for the mutual recognition of products, subject to national minimum standards. The latter was eventually to put an end to the endless sterile bickering over harmonisation directives and to be a principal harbinger of 1990s liberalisation.

At the same time, and often as the result of the initiatives of individuals such as Etienne Davignon, Willi Claes, and Francois-Xavier Ortoli, relief for industries hard-hit by American and Japanese competition evolved slowly into a more generalised EC industrial policy. What began as cover for beleaguered steel, textiles, defence manufacturing and aerospace industries, and later for consumer electronics, in France, Germany, Belgium, Italy and the Netherlands, took two forms. Both were aimed at inducing change at least cost or political trouble in existing investment and employment, and both were obviously congenial to national governments in their defensive mood.

The first provided support for industrial adjustment and restructuring, directed by the Commission with the Council's agreement: crises cartels, like that for steel in 1980, and the ESPRIT arrangement between the twelve leading information technology companies, demonstrated that something could be done collectively to adjust and restructure, at lesser apparent cost than if member states went their own way.

The second proved far more dramatic and initially unpalatable, save in Britain where similar aims were being pursued by the Thatcher governments, more effectively but in a different way and at much higher social cost. Acting in what it defined as the general European interest, the Commission tried to act as broker between the interests of the larger member states, industrial sectors and the leading multinational corporations, with the general aim of liberalising, deregulating, and diminishing the array of restraints on trade: the voluntary export restrictions, quotas and tariffs, which had attended the first, defensive, opition.

The latter strategy was best put from an industrialist's point of view by Wissi Dekker, on behalf of Philips (Netherlands) in his report *Europe 1990*.[2] According to a Confederation of British Industry paper written at the time,[3] British counterparts showed substantial agreement; their 10 per cent divergence represented a

CBI preference for *positive* adjustment (being influenced by American and prevailing British examples) rather than the *defensive* adjustment envisaged in continental Europe. Here already can be seen the division between what Michel Albert was later to call Anglo-Saxon and Rhineland capitalisms.[4]

The players and the game

Member states

The years 1983–4 mark a conjunction of events and trends without which it is hard to imagine the Single European Act could have come into existence. Two of the most significant concerned France and Germany. The *grand tournant* of March to June 1983 in which, helped by Jaques Delors the Finance Minister, President Mitterrand was forced to accept that no single nation state could run counter to global trends, demonstrated that French governments had not lost their talent for capturing change to French advantage.

Secondly, mutual understanding between Mitterrand and Chancellor Kohl underpinned moves essential before the Single Market could come into final focus.[5] These included solving the British budgetary distribution dispute, starting common agricultural policy reform, and more important, removal of the six year-long French prohibition on Spanish – and by derivation Portuguese – membership. Each had been an obstacle to liberalisation of markets and to the measures of political integration essential to a single market, such as increased majority voting in the Council of Ministers, the evolution of an informal body where national representatives could sift out problems in advance of Council meetings (COREPER), and improved relations between Council and the Commission, even before Delors became its President.

Economic players

Because all this was done in the period when European economies were recovering from the 1981–3 recession, the larger
multinational corporations were freed to became highly effective
players in their own economic interest. They feared on one hand
to lose competitive advantage in international markets if the
Single Market did not develop fully, and hoped on the other that
member states would evolve forms of support which would
allow them to adjust to the transition from 'national champions'
to 'European champions' at their own pace and in their own way.
For the first time in the EC's history, managing directors and
chairman took part, outside the normal framework of trade associations and European sectoral associations such as ACEA (car
producers), EFPIA (pharmaceuticals), EACEM (consumer electronics) and CEFIC (chemicals), or the central employers organisation UNICE. They used their collective influence in Brussels
via less formal bodies such as the European Round Table (ERT),
and in national capitals such as Paris through the association of
large enterprises (AGREF) rather than CNPF.

  Their potential influence, like that of the American Chamber
of Commerce's European Committee with whom they linked in
the campaign, had already been demonstrated in the campaign to
delay, frustrate and eventually destroy the Vredeling Directive
which had attempted to ensure organised workers' access to
corporate decision-making on large companies' supervisory
boards.[6] Now it centred on industrial regeneration, particularly in
the car production, chemicals and consumer electronics sectors
most hard hit by American and Japanese competitors.

The Commission as player

Officials in the Commission's Directorate General III (industry)
had been putting together elements of an industrial adjustment
strategy since at least 1981. The part taken by leading individual
officials such as Paolo Cecchini, Maurice Braun, Charles Carpen-
tier, Riccardo Perissich, and Peter Kline, reinforced the

geographical lozenge-shaped image of a Rhineland core incorporating Benelux, Germany, France and Italy.[7] Their work underpinned the preparations that were accidentally subverted at Athens in December 1984; but which, renewed under France's presidency, influenced the pre-planning for Fontainebleau six months later.

The game

The extent to which each of these three levels of activity was responsible for the Single Market outcome is unlikely to be resolved before all the national as well as Commission archives are opened.[8] It is, however, significant that when Jacques Delors, shortly before taking up the Presidency in January 1985, visited each of the ten member states in turn and put four suggestions for the next stage of European development: (foreign policy and defence, monetary union, institutional reform, or the Single Market) the only favourable majority responses were to the last. From then on, in his 'State of the Community' address to the European Parliament, and in the period before Fontainebleau, Delors built on the conjunction of industrial players, the hesitant confluence of governments, and the increasingly coherent force of Commission planning.[9] Beside him almost inextricably in the early stages, stood Arthur Cockfield, his choice and Margaret Thatcher's for Commissioner in charge of the Single Market initiative.

It helped that 1985–9 were good years for the European economies, and that the exchange rate mechanism (ERM), child of the EMS, but managed by central banks, operated in its classic phase as a deutschmark zone to enhance stability and growth and to reduce inflation; and also that the early years of Gorbachev in the Soviet Union helped massively to reduce tension in the dying days of the cold war. These contextual factors help to explain why all the member states, even the British government which was not in the ERM (but was keener than any other on liberalisation, and to gain advantage by restructuring its economic sectors, including banking, insurance and other financial markets in advance of the change on the Continent) subscribed to the Single Market project. Initially it seemed to British observers something obviously economic in character and generally advantageous; only later (much later in the British case) did the corollaries of deeper integration, monetary union, Commission initiative and competences, majority voting in Council, and ECJ jurisdiction become clear. For ten demonstrably different sets of reasons, all the governments agreed on the Single European Act (SEA) in 1985.

Yet substantive difficulties remained, about how to restructure, how to liberalise, how to increase technological momentum and improve human skills; and nation-states' different approaches were inevitably portrayed in Anglo-Saxon or Rhenish or in some cases Mediterranean colours. In the late 1980s, and even when the Single Market deadline of 1 January 1993 had passed, there remained a high political and electoral price – underlined to the rest of the Community by the British transitional experience: structural unemployment, wage cutting, mergers and hostile takeovers, and the necessity for deep capital investment in new technology, all of which appalled many continental observers. To trades union movements in particular, the loss of jobs which was the inevitable price of restructuring, and the increasing weight in that restructuring of decision-taking by banks and financial institutions, provided a new and frightening demonology.

Such fears grew among trades unions *pari passu* with the numerical decline of their memberships and the concomitant loss of influence which all labour organisations suffered during the 1980s. They were reflected by the administrations of the more *dirigiste* states, above all in France, Italy and Belgium, deeply concerned about the future of their public sector industries and the economic patrimonies established as part of their post-war settlements. They weighed also heavily in Brussels, in some Directorates, and with Delors himself, always a social democrat, as the complex momentum grew.

Achieving the Single Market

The basis of the Single European Market, set out clearly by Arthur Cockfield, was the intention to remove three sets of obstacles: physical (such as frontiers), technical (product standards etc), and fiscal (different rates of VAT and other taxes). Taxation harmonisation he relegated, knowing that it would be unacceptable at that stage. From his point of view, it was more important to maintain the momentum against physical and technical barriers, and to defend progress against member states' backsliding and intergovernmental horse trading. Hence his injunction 'not to overload the boat' and to leave for the next stage of liberalisation the largely state-controlled energy, telecoms, and transport sectors, as well as the whole gamut of competition policy for which DG4 was responsible.[10] (It is significant that among these sectors the electricity directive was only finally passed in 1997, and full telecoms liberalisation not achieved until 1 January 1999.) But the expanding torrent was already widening, and parts of it flowed through areas of the Commission over which Cockfield had no control. Less guarded than Cockfield, Delors had already linked it to social (i.e. employment) policy, regional and environmental improvement, monetary union, institutional reform and political integration.

Delors' first presentation of this wider agenda to the European Parliament in January 1985 could be – and in London often was – dismissed as part of the role of drama in political life. It did not seem unduly important, as the intergovernmental political process moved on from the Single Market plan of action endorsed at Milan (October 1984). British premonitions grew in a different direction – that of encircling Continental states. First, the Franco-German *démarche* of May 1985 (the so called 'treaty of European unity' which finessed Geoffrey Howe's scheme for a Single European Act *without* a new intergovernmental conference or treaty), demonstrated the British government's failure to build alliances. Then at the next meeting, again at Milan, in October 1985, Margaret Thatcher, again having failed to prepare a substantial defence, was out-manoeuvred by Bettino Craxi and Giulio Andreotti into accepting not only an intergovernmental conference, but its corollary, a new treaty incorporating wider qualified majority voting (QMV).[11]

Concealed by these dramatic events, the expanding torrent developing deep in the Commission may not have received sufficient notice at the time, although Geoffrey Howe christened the phenomenon 'hanging baubles on a mobile Christmas tree'.[12] The political game, after all, depended at this stage on member states, and continued to do so, long after each had signed the SEA. To outsiders measuring Brussels' activity by volume and in terms of time spent, the greater part of the Commission's work in the years up to 1992–3 was to ensure that the 285 items of Cockfield's legislation were drafted, agreed, passed, and then successively transposed into member states' national law and finally *implemented*.[13] The work of Delors and his closest cabinet colleagues, to create a more effective bureaucratic machine than even Hallstein had known in the 1960s, and to imbue it with a policy-making ethos, was not immediately obvious.

In December 1985, the Intergovernmental Conference (IGC) resolved, after a remarkably rapid passage, the question of which elements in the Single Market legislation should be resolved by QMV, and how the system of EC funding might help disadvantaged states, in particular Ireland and Greece (but very soon Portugal and a new major player, Spain) to cope with the initial advantage conferred by market deregulation on the more highly developed economies. It also agreed the next stage of parliamentary cooperation, how the more advanced – and highly complicated – process called co-decision should develop between the Council of Ministers and the European Parliament, and under what form of words monetary union would be recognised as an inevitable consequence of the SEA.

None of these was an easy matter. Each formed part of the continuum leading towards Maastricht six years later. All disturbed British Conservative leaders (though not their civil servants in Whitehall to the same degree) but not enough for them to break off, considering the enormous economic gains that were anticipated – and fostered in the public mind not only by Arthur Cockfield's advocacy, but by the Cecchini report.[14] In the end, monetary union featured only in the preamble. But as member states' leaders with memories of the Rome treaty knew, to express sentiments in a text, for later implementation in ripe time, is the Community's main contribution to the practical application of political science.

Conclusion

For a time, the aftermath seemed to demonstrate that the legal formulae were not enough to prevent governments from going their own way. To ensure their *rassemblement* had been an essential part of the Commission's intention from the Single Market's inception. But in the late 1980s, as Cockfield's legislative factory issued the directives, governments made excuses for delay. By 1988, only 91 out of the 285 legislative instruments had been accepted by the Council of Ministers. As in the case of the later treaty of European Unity, it required a Franco-German understanding, set out by Helmut Kohl at the Hanover summit in June 1988, to impose urgency and to achieve what Cockfield called 'irrevocable political acceptance of the Single Market'. By the end of 1992, nearly all 285 had been transposed to each member's national legislation.

Whatever complaints have been raised since about sloth or wilful obstruction in implementing elements of the Single European Market, and even if Cecchini's figures were not entirely borne out, it is hard to deny its success, or its incremental assistance to European firms and financial institutions in meeting to some extent the challenges of global markets and the impact of international competition. In that sense, the Delors-Cockfield project should be compared with the original customs union. That first part of the expanding torrent has since incorporated the entry as active players of the great majority of European financial institutions, and in the later 1990s the former public utilities, now largely privatised. Until the severe recession of 1991–3, it buoyed up a sustained sense of optimism about European capacity to adjust; and it has been probably the principal force behind the surge towards liberalisation and the restructuring of industrial and financial institutions in continental Europe since 1995.

As an immediate legacy, the quality of European governance improved, measured by the speed of transposition of Community law into national law, by implementation of enactments and ultimately by enforcement by national government agencies. Second, the financial sectors, banking, insurance, pension funds and asset management institutions, involved themselves, increasingly sensitive to global market pressures: the stimulus to rationalise reached even sheltered regional and national stock exchanges. At the same time, within the Commission (and to a variable extent in member state systems of government), the barriers between industry, trade policy and competition regulation were eroded. Finally, synoptic thinking in Brussels and national capitals, surfing on the expanding torrent, began to associate restructuring and rationalisation with technological advance and competitiveness, in alliance against the intangible and often highly political barriers that remained, giants to be slain in the harsher 1990s.

These were and are great gains, monumental by comparison with the Single Market's limited beginnings in 1983. The Commission has moved far into liberalisation of telecoms, electricity, gas, air transport and road haulage, into harmonising VAT, and into trade negotiations as GATT evolved into the World Trade Organisation. It has created – usually against entrenched national governments' hostility – a coherent and remarkably powerful competition policy, together with merger and takeover regulation, sustained by a line-up of notable Commissioners at DGIV, Peter Sutherland, Sir Leon Brittan and Karel van Miert, under Mario Monti.

Against that has to be set a persistent mood of pessimism about the socio-economic consequences of change and the erosion of national cultures and identities which still causes resistance by governments, industrial sectors and labour organisations. Opposition to what is often characterised as global flux lies deep in industrial cultures, is entrenched in state sectors and persists below the level of the larger firms, in often moribund national trade associations. Like the fears of 'American business methods' which plagued Britain and France in the 1920s, fear of the unrestricted harshness of 'Anglo Saxon capitalism' which grew after the recession of 1990–3 has been associated increasingly since then with the discipline necessary for monetary union. Restructuring and rationalisation are inevitably associated with increasing unemployment and job insecurity; in the 1990s, unlike the 1920s, they are also associated with deflationary assaults on public spending and its principal costs, the welfare states of Europe and their postwar settlements, and with privatisation of what remains of each nation's long-cherished state sector.

Maastricht

If the period immediately before and after the Single European Act can be designated, in stockbrokers' argot, as a 'sweet spot' in European politics, the conjuncture four years later seems with hindsight positively baleful. A triumph of willpower over political logic, the Maastricht treaty 1991 came at the wrong time: too late in the cycle of member states' economies, too early in terms of their domestic political preparedness. Yet in the run up to it, the climate appeared benign. The Soviet Union's collapse and disintegration, followed by German reunification, enhanced politicians' natural tendency to aggregate coming triumphs before the hard work had been done.

In theory, the Hanover summit 1988 had produced the Council of Ministers' agreements on some of the least tractable problems, with France and Italy on abolishing exchange controls, and with Germany and Britain on recasting the EC budget. Delors had his second term of office confirmed. Meanwhile, in the global arena, the GATT Uruguay round achieved a modest progress despite the high tide of American protectionism under Presidents Reagan and Bush, embodied in the 1987 US Trade Bill.

On the negative side, German reunification 1989–90 aggravated existing feelings in France and Britain about what was already felt to be a novel German assertiveness over political union. It was true that for several years after 1989, the German government cautiously avoided any formal claims to a new status based on increased population and geographical extent. In a gesture later to be criticised by sections of the German media, Kohl asked only for more MEPs after reunification, not the larger weighted vote in the Council of Ministers to which in theory Germany was entitled. Nevertheless the very different responses of President Mitterrand and Margaret Thatcher were deeply to affect their governments' plans for the forthcoming IGC.

Mitterrand, after a period of several months when he seemed unable to make up his mind, accepted Germany's new status but sought to confine German's political, economic and financial potential. Thatcher, on the other hand, whose last two years as Prime Minister were increasingly shadowed by a vision of the Community as a conspiracy between Christian Democrats and Socialists fostered by a politically corrupt Commission, made her views clear at Bruges in September 1988: reunited Germany was a real threat, in contrast to the governments of Italy and France which were merely to be distrusted, their ambitions (at Britain's expense, like those of Brussels) to be obstructed whenever possible.[15] Yet she found herself unable to form alliances capable of resisting the expanding torrent, either in the United States (where President Bush made it clear that new Germany was now the USA's main European coadjutor among the Community) – or indeed at home, being induced to accept ERM entry by a deeply disruptive entente between her Chancellor and Foreign Secretary.[16]

British entry to the ERM in October 1990, at a level set for internal Conservative Party reasons rather than economic logic or in consultation with European partners, was at too high a parity with the deutschmark and probably at the wrong time in the UK's economic cycle.[17] It had its own denouement in September 1992, under her successor John Major, giving Thatcher a sort of vicarious revenge, for it undermined not only the one substantial Maastricht accord, on monetary union, but Major's own subsequent Conservative leadership.

Meanwhile, within a renewed Franco-German understanding, Kohl and Mitterrand came to a tacit agreement: the German government's aims of furthering political union (shared among others by the Netherlands government) would be matched by rapid progress towards the French desideratum of monetary union. Most commentators then and later have assumed that the Mitterrand government's aim was, first, to rebase the EMS on the French franc rather than the deutschmark and secondly to proceed as fast as possible to a monetary union in which the otherwise-dominant deutschmark would disappear.[18] This looked rather different from Paris, Bonn and Milan or Madrid (though the Netherlands government may have shared the former intention). But it followed that the IGC in 1991 would conjoin monetary and political union, the latter to include political cooperation (foreign affairs), home and justice matters and, inevitably (as the French government began to edge back towards European defence cooperation once the cold war ended) Western European Union (WEU) and its role, if any, vis-à-vis NATO.

Because the EC's twelve member states could not possibly share a common attitude, on such a diverse agenda, as they had done in 1985–6, touching as it did each one's national interests, sensibilities and rivalries at every point, there can be no common historiography of the Maastricht IGC's making.[19] It can, however, be said that the non-governmental economic players took little part, even in the separate part of the IGC dealing with EMU, except at second hand, via their industrial peak organisations, and in the case of financial institutions via the European Banking and Insurance Federation, and their national govern-

ments and representatives in Brussels. The main question about
motivation, for contemporary historians, concerns the distinct
roles of the Commission on one hand and the member states on
the other, whose governments rapidly took over the process
once the IGC began. From the Commission's point of view this
represented a distortion of the expanding torrent by political
manoeuvres on the Council and later on the European Council.

The view from Britain, put most lucidly by officials rather
than the politicians who took part,[20] was that in the period often
described as Delors II, an overweening Commission, organised
and directed in a positively Napoleonic bureaucratic way for the
first time since the early Community days, widened the
expanding torrent to include not only EMU and EPU in its
broadest sense, but also the provisions of the Social Chapter to
counter-balance the forces of unchecked economic rationalisation already unleashed even before completion of the Single
Market. To the fury of the Thatcherite persuasion, many of the
1980s gains appeared to be threatened by proposals intended to
safeguard not only full employment on the Continent but already
over-extended European national welfare states, and the powers
and aspirations of other member state governments which were
still far more closely meshed with their parastatal economies than
had been in the case in Britain since the mid-1970s.

It would be easy to show that what seemed then to be a
single-minded defence of Rhineland capitalism differed
according to French, German, Italian or Netherlands conditions.
Yet there were indeed common ideological elements. Strong
traces of those national debates, on the role of the state in the
economy, and the public/private balance, survive today in
France and Italy, to a lesser extent in Germany, and among later
newcomers, in Austria, for example. Conversely they have been
much modified in Sweden and the Netherlands under the 1990s
demographic and political threats to ravage their welfare states
and postwar settlements. Contrary to what British observers then
believed at the time of Maastricht, but under the spur of convergence required for monetary union, nearly all member states had

successfully embraced re-structuring, rationalisation and divestment of state-owned utilities – albeit in a different and sometimes more successful way than the British example.

What is not clear, and cannot be certain until the Commission archives open, is whether in 1990–1 Delors himself and his highly structured cabinet were as overweening as British or Danish commentators thought;[21] or whether in pursuit of the Commission's fundamental duty, they aimed high, in order to orchestrate a consensus which dissenting member state governments might later amend, but not reject entirely. Whichever answer is given, the Commission's planning for the IGC, and the way its proposals were launched with the European Parliament in mind as well as the Council of Ministers, in fact alienated players far better-disposed to its intentions than the British or Danish governments. Delors' approach gave the impression of ignoring the proper rights of member states, of intruding on their national interests, and more practically, of bringing in extraneous pan-European social, if not actively socialist elements, just as the era of rationalisation and restructuring began.

At heart, the dispute about who should take the initiative ran back to the Community's origins and the original late 1950s presumption that the Commission should play a leading role – which member states in turn should welcome as a means of defining and declaring the common European interest. But, coming after twenty-five years of increasing *de facto* intergovernmental practice since de Gaulle's empty chair *démarche*, the ambitious agenda set under Delors II came to be seen as a pre-emptive strike and may even have encouraged governments' natural predisposition to resist. Meanwhile Spain's government complicated the game by engaging in a well co-ordinated, aggressive attempt that lasted until 1993 to win a financially better deal from the new pool of cohesion funds that was intended to offset new members' disadvantages as the Single Market began: one, unlike the earlier British budget claim, in which Portugal and Greece and to an even larger extent Ireland emerged as potential allies.

Two summits point up the chronology: Madrid 1989, when Britain agreed to join the ERM, and the special 'informal' meeting in Rome in October 1990, when Andreotti put Thatcher in baulk for the last time and lit the fuse presaging her fall.[22] There followed the double IGC held at Maastricht over a period of twelve months, starting under the Luxembourg presidency and ending under that of the Netherlands at the end of 1991. The first, lesser known, and relatively tranquil IGC on monetary union (EMU) ran concurrently with the second, on the main elements of political union. Surprisingly, given the complexities of EMU, it was the latter which exhibited all the characteristics of a closed system, run by a *noyau* of insiders driven by a sense of time running out, too secretive, too complex, too hard worked, claustrophobic and cut off from their electorates and publics.

1. EMU

Monetary union, as it had appeared in the previous IGC's preamble, had for a time remained an aspiration, lacking clarity or detail. Huge problems of research and definition remained to be solved, then translated from the economic-financial terminology employed by a small group of professionals into a more general political language. Beyond the complexities of educating the educators, this first IGC had to begin making cautiously public what until then only a tiny elite of central bankers, economists and finance ministers (and not all of these) could claim to understand – and on which by no means even these could agree.

EMU did not, actually, follow from ERM practice as that had been defined within the EMS since the early 1980s. Yet it was generally assumed that the ERM would provide the 'glide path' for EMU.[23] The underlying problem was that EMU embodied political elements and judgements which resisted (and to some extent still resist) the efforts of technicians and governments to remove. Margins of political manoeuvre remained, even in 1997–8, despite creation of the 'stability pact', impeding the search for intellectual clarity and consistency. The years after 1989, as the

Bonn government first unwisely exchanged deutschmarks for ostmarks at par,[24] saw the ERM and the franc fort which was intended to achieve political and moral equality with the deutschmark become a distinctly costly burden in France, in terms of unemployment and deflation. This was followed, inevitably, by much intergovernmental recrimination about German government responsibility for the depth of the recession in 1991–3.

Nevertheless the process was driven by two dominant coalitions, the first at political level between the French and German governments, albeit informally hampered by the Bundesbank deeply opposed to a monetary union created by political fiat, rather than steady accretion of currencies to the deutschmark core; second on the technical level between the Commission's different directorates, ECOFIN and central bankers and their advisers. The central bankers, grouped together in committee with Delors in the chair, had in 1988–89 settled in principle many of the hardest details of EMU: what the new currency should be, its praxis, the rules of membership and the constitution of the forthcoming European central bank (ECB). At the end, led by the governments of France, Germany, Italy and the Netherlands, they even settled the method of transition to the new currency. Crucially however, it was only after the report had been agreed but before it was submitted to ECOFIN, that Delors himself added a three-stage schedule of growing commitment to an irreversible single currency.[25]

It is not certain that the central bankers' committee would have supported the concept of a strict schedule. Neither is it clear whether the outcome should be seen as a triumph for French government interests, keen to envisage a common monetary policy based on a common currency able at last to face the dollar; or as a Franco-German core combination of economic logic and political pragmatism. But the fact that the plan was overtaken first by the consequences of German reunification, and secondly the start of the deep early 1990s recession, meant it could not be construed as was originally intended. This affected the Italian and Belgian governments in particular for both had hoped it would be the means to impose, from above and outside, the fiscal discipline they themselves had failed over many years to establish.

Events after 1991, notably the first breach of the ERM in September 1992 when the pound and the lira were forced out, and the second in August 1993, when global money markets forced governments to abandon the ERM's narrow band of fluctuation, demonstrated that the ERM had not in fact been the glide path that the Maastricht IGC as late as 1991 took for granted. Neither did the timetable, at least until about 1995–6, lead towards convergence; though the remarkable transformation which has since then occurred in Italy, Spain and even Belgium as the final deadline approached, provided a belated justification for it. But the political momentum, based on continued Franco-German understanding, ensured that there would be no reversion to the earlier plan of a clustering of stable currencies around the deutschmark – even though this remained for a long time the Bundesbank's secret hope.

The EMU IGC attracted a minimum of notice while it lasted and aroused virtually no debate even among financial and industrial peak organisations in the EC, let alone in their member firms and institutions. Even national parliaments largely ignored it before the public debacle in 1992, as did all but the financial press. Coherent debate among even the original six member states had to wait until the ERM crises of 1992 and 1993.[26] Yet the potential transfer of nation-states' economic decision-making which was involved in making the ECB independent and responsible both for monetary policy and European-wide interest rates was perfectly clear and had been endorsed, inter alia, by Robin Leigh-Pemberton, Governor of the Bank of England, and Karl-Otto Pöhl of the Bundesbank.[27]

2. Political Union

So many different issues were aired during the political union IGC at Maastricht that quite distinct histories can be written of what the French senior official Pierre de Boissieu was to call the temple with its three pillars. But member state governments, with the exception of the Netherlands, had one thing in common: they rejected transfers of power to the Commission and this outweighed all the treaty's dependent clauses, the new institutions, the additional powers and procedures given to the European Parliament and the one single triumph for the expanding torrent, the Social Chapter. De Boissieu's formula allowed the second pillar, political cooperation (foreign affairs and defence) and the third, home and justice affairs, to remain under governments' control. Only the first, EMU, stood wholly on EU ground. The temple columns, of unequal stature, refuted the Netherlands' presidency's metaphor of a tree growing from its roots to its branches as an organic whole.

The tensions between governments, and between various distinct visions of how the Community ought to work, explain why the treaty's achievements were soon challenged and why its outcomes have rarely matched expectations. They also explain the compromises, vague phraseology and blurred concepts which have since 1991 afflicted not only the sections relating to WEU (where national players' disagreement was endemic) but the Committee of Regions[28] and the Social Chapter.

In the early months, position papers redolent with national self interest proliferated to such an extent that the Luxembourg presidency was forced to issue a 'non-paper' in April 1991 in an attempt to forestall the luxury of dissent. Six months later in the game, the Netherlands' presidency tried to restore primacy to the Commission's original agenda, by embracing the tree metaphor, only to find itself assailed on all sides. The final settlements, much closer to the Luxembourg version, embodied a level of intergovernmental haggling and horsetrading that would have been familiar to participants at Paris in 1919 or Vienna in 1815. The temple formula triumphed.

Quite apart from the fact that the main governmental players had not been prepared beforehand to cede the powers asked for by the Netherlands presidency and the Commission,[29] changes in the external context distorted the original agenda. The Soviet

Union's collapse, the reordering of central and eastern Europe, and the lurch of Yugoslavia towards civil war, forced many European governments to reassess their national interests; just as, over a much longer cycle, the end of the cold war forced their citizens to rethink how their sense of national identity had been constructed since 1945. While EU political cooperation had some successes, particularly under Delors' aegis in the early-stage financing of former Comecon economies, it had virtually none in the Balkans. Indeed, German insistence on the recognition of Croatia may have exacerbated the first stage of Yugoslavia's civil wars.

Many other contingencies, such as defence procurement, state aid in the restructuring of defence-related industries, take-overs, mergers, and (once defence budget-cutting began) the future of employment, hung on member states' adaptation to the cold war's aftermath. In these circumstances, the British were quite unwilling to treat WEU's incorporation to the agenda as seriously as did the French, who saw it as a catalyst for a European third way. Only the vague outlines of a WEU linkage were be allowed to appear in the treaty text, to appease French requirements, while NATO itself was to be maintained unimpaired. Behind these manoeuvrings, embodied in a clause of exceptional opaqueness in the treaty,[30] stood two very different views of NATO and its role in Europe: to British eyes, the United States was still an essential participant, to French ones it represented both a threat and a challenge. In neither country did the authorities speculate publicly on how reunited Germany would fit into the military-industrial or the strategic future.

Deteriorating conditions on the EC's east, south east and southern borders in the late 1980s affected even more seriously the third pillar, the cluster of home and justice matters ranging from crime and drugs to immigration, from prevention of terrorism to passports and identity cards. Certain governments saw themselves by 1991 as standing in the front line. Spain, Italy and France concerned themselves with terrorism and civil disorder in Algeria and Libya, together with the spectre of illegal immigration from all the Mahgreb countries. Germany (and the Scandinavian applicants) concerned themselves with economic migration from a disordered eastern Europe; Austria and again Italy worried about the Balkans, while the Greek government angrily and endlessly contested the customs union with, and the status accorded to Turkey. Others worried about the capacity of Greece or Italy to implement the EC's *cordon sanitaire*, and about the reversal, even in Germany, of postwar asylum traditions induced by extreme right wing demagoguery and xenophobic fears.[31] While the Netherlands' informal tolerance of soft drugs drew increasingly stringent criticism from France, the British insisted on retaining passport controls and resisted cross-border police collaboration.

Because the 12 member states found it so much harder to reach consensus on these political questions than they had on the Single Market treaty, they reverted to the old EEC-EC tradition (last employed in writing the EMU clause in 1986) of putting as much as possible into the text in anodyne, aspirational terms, hoping for full acceptance and implementation at some future date. To win all the signatures, the two British opt-outs on monetary union and the social protocol were granted (and later extended retrospectively to gain the consent of the Danish public after the treaty had been rejected in the first Danish referendum).

A sense that time was running out, and that circumstances after 1991 would be unpropitious, seems to have spurred compromises on one hand[32] and on the other the surge of claims in 1991–3 from Spain and Ireland for better treatment from the cohesion funds before the more prosperous EFTA applicants Finland, Sweden and Austria were admitted.

Acceptance of the treaty on 10 December by the European Council came therefore at a time of open divergence, contrary to all the Commission's hopes, just as the gathering recession emphasised the newly-styled European Union's inherent economic diversity. The EU stood divided between northern and Mediterranean countries, richer and poorer ones, large, medium and small nations, between the core and periphery, between Anglo-Saxon, Rhineland and Mediterranean forms of capitalism. It is hard to sum up without stating baldly that member states ruled the game. Although the Parliament won its very complex codecision procedure and thus acquired a novel, if relatively minor power vis-à-vis the Council and Commission, this happened because the German, Italian, Netherlands, and Belgian governments had too much at stake with their own electorates to permit further delay on the EU's supposed 'democratic deficit'. Meanwhile, in contrast to the remarkable extension of qualified majority voting in the 1986 treaty, QMV was extended only to environmental questions and the Social Protocol. Problems of negotiating national interests, and the trading of real powers as well as formal sovereignty in return for cross-border, pan-European or even global advantage, marked out Maastricht II as fundamentally different from the 1986 IGC. The surprising thing is how easily the Maastricht EMU accord passed, not the failure of hopes for its political union sibling.

Subsequent public reactions to Maastricht II belong to a another discussion. But if the evolution of the expanding torrent from Single European Act to Maastricht is seen as a coherent process, albeit one interrupted and distorted towards 1990, one explanation emerges. The more complex and rebarbative the Maastricht negotiations, the more they became the province of groups of insiders. The longer the process, the more tightly-focused the insiders became, less able to imagine what public repercussions would follow, or even to envisage that there was a need for preparing and educating national publics.[33] Yet the more that government ministers and their officials bargained in a climate hostile to Commission guidance, so that intergovernmentalism became the norm, the more it was likely that many different public reactions would take national, and frequently nationalistic shape. This was so even in the best of the 'good European states' the Netherlands; Maastricht won easy majority approval only where its material advantages were obvious: Spain, Belgium, Italy, Ireland, Portugal, Greece.

Whether or not one argues that the Maastricht treaty represented a triumph of political will over economic and social reality may well depend on the writer's standpoint, and where his or her sense of identity intersects with the line running from locality to nation-state and beyond. Either way, the creation of a European Union based ultimately on a single market and a single currency followed the juridical road begun by the Rome treaty, whose map had at least been sketched by the Commission and whose landmarks were already policed by the European Court of Justice. Consequential cleavages between governments and their publics appear, however, to have been greater since 1992 than in the previous 30 years, and the association between this and the sense of democratic deficit in the EU – on which the Parliament and MEPs have skilfully capitalised when expanding their own powers and status – seems undeniable. Referendums have scarcely solved the problem, and indeed in at least two subsequent member states, Sweden and Austria, the referendums which validated entry in 1994 would hardly have the same results today.

In structural terms, Maastricht advanced the new EU's progress a little towards a new sort of statehood, adding more of a state's essential elements, currency, some policing functions, and the preliminaries of external policy, even security, to the legal-juridical foundations. But it did so without diminishing member states' control of the game, so that other players, notably the Commission, lost momentum. (Of the non-governmental players, only labour movements had a substantial stake in Maastricht II and have been generally disillusioned by the outcome.[34]) The Commission's remarkable level of bureaucratic solidarity could hardly have survived the end of Delors' tenure as President intact, after 1994, because such power is not easily transferable: that it did recover its authority in its own sphere of the consequential provisions of the Single Market, in 1992–3 is a tribute to Delors III. But Brussels' administrative attenuation showed elsewhere in the bad years down to 1995, and Delors' successor, Jacques Santer had to preside over a much more

confederal college of Commissioners and a more embattled
Commission which finally collapsed in indignity and scandal.

Yet of all the criticisms heaped on the Commission, responsibility for Maastricht, far more than with the Single European
Act, lay primarily with member states. Federalism, like the
Cheshire Cat, faded away with the abortive Netherlands draft
treaty, leaving scarcely even the shadow of a smile. Within the
member state array, the Franco-German entente retained its
dynamism for another four or five years, and survived even
Mitterrand's death. Nevertheless the post-cold war soul-
searching that afflicted all the bigger countries, enlarged
Germany, France, even Britain, the Netherlands and Spain,
certainly Italy and Belgium, ensured that national interests would
predominate, accompanied by the slow, frequently checked, but
probably irresistible evolution of a new German exceptionalism.

As a rough distinction, the Single Market and its EMU corollary (though discussed consistently in Brussels in the 1960s and
1970s) emerged as a practical European response to global
economic challenges, in the 1980s from the United States and
Japan; whereas the political union element in Maastricht grew out
of debates about the European idea inherent in the Rome treaty.
The consequences of both are still ever-present. The Single
Market's outcome can be quantified, however, not only in
Cecchini's terms, but in policy decisions and legal judgements
about liberalisation or competition, intangible barriers and
removal of trade restraints. Realms beyond Delors' and Cockfield's aspirations in 1986 are now being liberalised, or are already
open: telecoms, air transport, energy and financial markets.
GATT having given birth to the World Trade Organisation,
Commissioners now negotiate with Washington or Beijing *on
behalf of* the EU.

Non-governmental players, industry, finance, commerce,
which gained unequivocally in all the EU countries, have even
since 1993, frequently found themselves at odds with governments that still seek to maintain bankrupt state-aided sectors or
to uphold intangible barriers to liberalisation. But global change

is on their side, as well as the Single Market and the Commission; it is hard to see a future for protective national economic regimes. Yet the Single Market has itself evolved only a little faster, (albeit much more coherently and consensually) than external forces would have compelled national governments across all Europe. Its greatest long-term political benefit may be to have given time for the leading European industrial nations to evolve their own brand of adjustment, whether in Germany, the Netherlands, or Sweden, and perhaps France, while safeguarding their own visions of how to reform their postwar social and welfare settlements.

This finally touches on the obverse of globalisation, the future of the European nation state. It became fashionable for a time in the early 1990s to see Europe's regions as a counter-weight to obsolescent national political entities. Regions, as polit-ical entities however defined, have indeed benefited substantially since Maastricht. But their increased status derives more from the various crises of national identity following the end of the cold war than from the activities of the loosely hung-together Committee of Regions. The *idea* of regionality has failed to acquire a European dimension or to surpass its national exem-plars. Advocates using the models of Bavaria, North Rhine West-phalia, or Baden-Württemberg to acclaim the (German) federal model of the *Land* as the sub-state ideal, encounter allies of a kind in Catalonia or Northern Italy, Scotland, even Brittany and Languedoc. Yet this line up says more about the internal condi-tion of modern Germany, Spain, Italy, Britain or France than it contributes to the endless debate about subsidiarity, running from supranational organisation, to nation, region, city, or parish.

That being the current state of play, we are left with the Maas-tricht legacy of intergovernmental transcendence, complemented by a Commission whose supranational ethos has been seriously depleted since 1991, but whose status in the Single Market/EMU arena has benefited hugely from the work done by its leading directorates responsible for competition policy, trade, industry, research and technology. If a general conclusion has to be drawn, it must be that the makers of Maastricht, unlike those of the Single Market IGC in 1986, aspired to foster a European identity which was at that time more practicable in an economic than in the political dimension.

Notes

1   I have tried to summarise these, from each national standpoint, in *Orchestrating Europe: the informal politics of European Union 1973–95* (London: Harper Collins 1995) chapter 4, pp.115–135.

2   Dekker was a leading member of the European Round Table and drafted his report under the auspices of ERT but with Philips' backing.

3   CBI Papers, European Committee Minutes, March 1980.

4   Michel Albert: *Capitalism Against Capitalism* (English translation, London: Whurr 1993).

5   As the unfortunate Greek presidency discovered at the Athens summit, December 1984. Even if Andreas Papandreou had not mishandled that event, unblocking the EU logjam at Fontainebleau in June 1985 was to be a triumph reserved for the Franco-German partnership.

6   Their association took vigorous shape initially in resistance to the Vredeling Directive proposed by the Commission on worker participation at board level in all large firms. This campaign required from companies large expenditure and sophisticated opposition techniques at which the Americans were particularly expert.

7   At one point, 15–16 October 1984, these individuals took the initiative and a joint agreement between the French and German economics and industry ministers was fed directly into the steering committee texts for the Athens summit. *Orchestrating Europe*, p.106.

8   For the range of viewpoints, see W. Sandholz and J. Zuysman 'Recasting the European bargain' in *World Politics* XLII, 1 October 1989, pp.95–128; A. Moravcik 'Negotiating the SEA' in *International Organisation*, Vol 45 No 1 Winter 1991, pp.19–56; and Maria Green 'The Politics of Big Business in the Single Market Programme' EC Studies Association 3rd International Conference, May 1993.

9   For Arthur now Lord Cockfield's analysis of these events see *The European Union: creating the Single Market* (London: Wiley Chancery

Law, 1994) for Delors see *Nouveau Concert Européen* (Paris: Editions O Jacob, 1992).

10 Interview with the author, March 1994.

11 It can be argued that Margaret Thatcher was not *so* unwilling to see QMV introduced, having watched appalled the efforts of the Papandreou government to blackmail the European Union in 1983–4, and its failure to conduct properly the Athens summit in December 1984 (I am grateful to Professor Helen Wallace for this insight).

12 Interview with the author, May 1994.

13 In many cases, especially in the financial sector, full implementation is still far from being fulfilled in 1997. The five years since the Act formally took effect have witnessed many convoluted informal and ad hoc negotiations between Commission and governments, and the development of a whole bargaining procedure under the title of *Réunions Pacquets* – a sophisticated form of plea-bargaining in which the Commission takes the view that eventual implementation is better than immediate confrontation.

14 Paolo Cecchini argued that the Single Market would produce not only great but *quantifiable* benefits and demonstrated this with vast statistical backing – even if the figures were massaged to produce the results. He also spelled out what amounted to a supply side shock, followed by a ripple effect bringing a 4 per cent to 7 per cent increase in the Community's GDP, together with trade reciprocity with Japan and the United States, over and above the once for all gain of more than 200 million ecus. The price would be adjustment by labour and management, and a stiffened ERM to inhibit devaluation, which would lead on to EMU. (Introduction to the Cecchini Report, *The European challenge 1992 the benefits of a single market,* UK edition (Aldershot: Wildwood House, 1988).

15 C.f. Margaret Thatcher, *The Downing Street Years* (London: HarperCollins, 1993) pp.136, 708

16 Nigel Lawson, *The View From Number 11* (London: Bantam, 1992) pp.484–6

17 *Orchestrating Europe*, pp.173–5.

18 The history of ERM's evolution into EMU is given in detail by Brian Connolly, *The Rotten Heart of Europe* (London: Faber, 1996)

chaps.1–4. This is the fullest account in English, but its analytical sections reveal a deceptive lack of ambiguity.

19 Recent studies of the Single European Act indicate disagreement about which of the players was most influential in bringing about what all of them desired. At Maastricht however, governments disagreed, often strongly, about aims as basic as cooperation between police forces, drugs policy, border immigration controls, whether membership of the ERM was a necessary preliminary to monetary union, future extension of the Community, and the whole scope of 'political cooperation'. c.f. R Corbett: 'The IGC on Political Union' *Journal of Common Market Studies* (September 1991) pp.261–89 and M J Artis: 'The Maastrict road to Monetary Union', *Journal of Common Market Studies* (September 1992) pp.289–309.

20 C.f. R Corbett: 'The IGC on Political Union' *Journal of Common Market Studies* (September 1991) pp.261–89 and M J Artis: 'The Maastrict road to Monetary Union', *Journal of Common Market Studies*, September 1992, pp.289–309.

21 For Delors' point of view, see *Nouveau Concert Européen*.

22 *Orchestrating Europe*, pp.167–8. *The Downing Street Years*, pp.763–5.

23 This account relies in part on the historical sections of Connolly, *Rotten Heart of Europe*, chapters 1–4.

24 And then borrowed on the international markets rather than via domestic taxation to support former East Germany, at interest rates which drove up those in other member states and worsened the early 1990s recession.

25 The first stage provided that the ERM narrow bands should operate from 1 January 1993; in the second, exchange rates would become nearly rigid, and all central banks were to become as independent as the Bundesbank; in the third and final stage exchange rates would be fixed, a single currency would operate, all others would disappear, and the ECB would take charge. One consequence of this schedule was to make it virtually impossible to float Britain's alternative, the 'hard ecu', and thus to defeat Geoffrey Howe's and Mrs Thatcher's aim of proceeding without an IGC.

26 *Orchestrating Europe*, pp.533–542 discusses these crises at the levels both of central banks and financial media commentators.

27 Karl-Otto Pohl resigned in 1991 in delayed protest at the decision to exchange DM for Ostmarks at par.

28 The Committee of Regions was conceived of as a large body (following on an earlier voluntary association formed in 1985) intended to be representative – as if regions existed generally on the model of the German *Land*. But apart from the federal member states, Germany, Spain, Belgium and Italy, regions as constitutionally-defined entities did not. The concept was further confused by the existence of ancient kingdoms (Scotland, Catalonia), large municipalities and 'city states' such as Strathclyde, Lyon, or Barcelona.

29 If they had, it would not for example have been possible for the German and French heads of government to have negotiated the private deals which allowed John Major to achieve Britain's opt-out on monetary union and the social protocol.

30 After long wrangling between the majority, which was prepared to accept WEU as part of the new union, and the opponents, Britain and Germany, the Italian Foreign Minister de Michelis helped to provide an emollient formula, based on the concept of WEU 'as a bridge' between NATO and the EU. This included the phrase 'an integral part of the EU's development' but only 'insofar as that shall be compatible with NATO'.

31 Asylum admissions to Germany: 1983 70,000, 1989 350,000, 1991 500,000, *before* the impact of Yugoslavia's disintegration.

32 Deletion of 'federal' to please Britain, but inclusion of 'ever closer union'. Inclusion of chapters on education, culture, tourism, youth, public health of no legislative weight whatever.

33 This was amply demonstrated by the contrast between the first and second (far more carefully prepared) referendum in Denmark, and by the immense efforts required from French ministers and their cabinets to persuade the French electors to give even a tiny majority in favour: 51.05 per cent as against 48.95 per cent opposed.

34 The Social Chapter (which was an opt-in of the 11 rather than an agreement to allow Britain to opt out) met its first serious challenge in 1997 when Renault abruptly closed its factory at Vilvoorde in Belgium, apparently without giving any recourse to the Belgian workers.

The Constitutional Impact of British Membership of the European Union

Colin Turpin

The United Kingdom became a member of the European Communities (since incorporated into a European Union) by the Treaty of Accession of 1972. This treaty had of itself no effect on laws or constitutional relationships within the United Kingdom, because no treaty can, according to our legal system, have such internal effects. Legislation was needed to implement the treaty and this was brought about by the European Communities Act 1972. Everything flows from that Act of Parliament: the whole elaborate structure of Community law, the powers of the institutions of the European Union, so far as these impact on our law and constitution, depend upon the European Communities Act. It may be helpful to begin by looking at the main features of this Act.

First of all, it is surely right to characterise it as a 'constitutional' statute, so profound are its effects on such fundamental things as the sovereignty of Parliament, the authority of our courts, the rights of individuals against the state. We must not be misled: the Act is not like the constitutional instruments of states that have written constitutions. It was passed by Parliament in the ordinary way and no special procedures are laid down for its amendment: it is not constitutionally entrenched – even supposing such a thing to be possible in our constitution – against repeal by Parliament in the future. But on the other hand, amendment or repeal of the European Communities Act is subject to constraints of a kind that do not affect the general body of our statute law – so much so, that total repeal, or amendment designed to restrict the application of Community law in the United Kingdom contrary to the Community treaties, is inconceivable while this country remains within the European Union.

In 1996 a bill was introduced in the House of Lords (by Lord Pearson of Rannoch), called the European Communities (Amendment) Bill. A very short bill, the essence of it was in clause 1, which said simply:

> Sections 2 and 3 of, and Schedule 2 to, the European Communities Act 1972 shall cease to have effect.

Sections 2 and 3 of the European Communities Act are the very heart and virtue of the Act: without them, Community law would lose its force in this country. No private member's bill that does this has the slightest prospect of being passed by Parliament; no government will introduce any such bill. Whatever the formal or traditional doctrine of our constitution may say about the sovereignty of Parliament, the reality is that while the United Kingdom remains a member of the European Union, the European Communities Act is effectively unrepealable. Now of course, there are those qualifying words, 'while we remain within the European Union', but if withdrawal from the Union has become, or if it should become, politically inconceivable, then the qualification falls away, and we have an unrepealable statute. That is something novel and distinctive in our constitution. It embodies an unprecedented limitation on Parliament, and on government, in this country.

The effects of the 1972 Act

Turning to the content of the European Communities Act, we find a number of critical provisions.

Section 2(1) enacts that those provisions of Community law – whether in the treaties themselves or in Community legislation – that are intended to have direct, internal effect in the member states, are to have the force of law in the United Kingdom. The relatively unproblematic application of this subsection is to Community Regulations, a form of legislation which, by virtue of Article 249 of the EC treaty, is directly applicable in the member states. But the European Court of Justice has extended this quality of direct internal effectiveness to other elements of

Community law, so that treaty provisions and Community directives (the other main type of Community legislation) can have
direct legal effect in the United Kingdom and can be relied upon
in our courts.

Here then we have a substantial volume of Community law
which flows into the United Kingdom through the gateway of
section 2(1). These laws are not enacted by Parliament (except
once and for all and *en bloc* in 1972) and are not subject to the
normal parliamentary scrutiny of legislation (whether parliamentary or delegated legislation). Parliament cannot repeal or amend
any of these laws and has no effective means of restricting their
application in this country. We have to recognise that in this a
transfer of power has taken place from Parliament to Community institutions, and from Parliament to the executive government of the United Kingdom in so far as it takes part in the
Community legislative process.

While the United Kingdom government does, of course,
participate in Community law-making, its power or influence in
the shaping of Community legislation depends on the circumstances – on its bargaining strength and on whether the particular
legislative instrument can be adopted by qualified majority, as is
increasingly the case. When the European Communities bill was
before Parliament, the government gave assurances that vital
national interests of the United Kingdom could not be over-
ridden because of the Luxembourg compromise of 1966,
requiring a unanimous decision of the Council of Ministers in
such cases. But the Luxembourg compromise was not written
into the treaty. Its status was weak and its application uncertain,
and latterly it has ceased to be of significance in the Council's
decision-making.[1]

We come then to section 2(2) of the European Communities
Act. This is an enabling provision, of very wide scope. It author-
ises ministers to make orders or regulations for the purpose of
implementing Community obligations – essentially, this is for
transposing Community directives into UK law. Now of course,
directives can be transposed instead by Act of Parliament, and

this is the preferred method if the directive relates to matters of particular importance or calls for far-reaching changes in our law. (For instance, Council Directive 96/61/EC on integrated pollution prevention and control was implemented by the Pollution Prevention and Control Act 1999.) But it is the government that decides whether to proceed by primary legislation or by making regulations under section 2(2), and the latter is the course most often taken.

The subsection is unusually wide in three ways:
(i) it is not limited to any particular subject matter: the obligation to be implemented may relate to any matter within Community competence;
(ii) the Act goes on to say that regulations made by Ministers under this subsection may in general do whatever an Act of Parliament can do: in particular, therefore, may repeal or amend existing statutes;
(iii) it is left to the government to decide whether regulations made under the subsection are to be subject to the affirmative vote of both Houses of Parliament or only to the weaker, negative procedure – i.e., subject to annulment by resolution of either House, with no debate guaranteed.

Of course, every delegation by Parliament of legislative competence to ministers shifts the balance of power in favour of the Executive – although often only to a limited degree, in minor, technical matters. But the shift of power in this instance is substantial.

Of crucial significance in the context of this chapter is the principle of the *primacy* of Community law. The EC treaty does not say that Community law must prevail over the national laws of the member states, but this principle is certainly implicit in the treaty. Community law as a system of general and uniform application is nothing if it is not supreme, and that supremacy or primacy has been many times unequivocally declared by the European Court of Justice.[2] We in the United Kingdom had to take it on board, and we find this – for us, novel and revolutionary – principle embedded in section 2(4) of the European

Communities Act. What is said there, in rather circuitous but nevertheless unmistakable terms, is that Acts of Parliament are to be subordinate to European Community law having direct internal effect in the United Kingdom.

UK courts have in a series of cases confronted the dilemma raised by section 2(4), of a 'sovereign' Parliament whose Acts must yet give way to a higher kind of law. In these cases the primacy of Community law over statute has been fully acknowledged by the courts, finding the justification for doing so in the acceptance by Parliament itself, in the European Communities Act, of the overriding authority of Community law. The judicial response is reflected in the words of Hoffmann J. in 1991:

> The Treaty is the supreme law of this country, taking precedence over Acts of Parliament. Our entry into the ... Community meant that (subject to our undoubted but probably theoretical right to withdraw from the Community altogether) Parliament surrendered its sovereign right to legislate contrary to the provisions of the Treaty on the matters of social and economic policy which it regulated.[3]

The acceptance of the primacy of Community law has been the most profound of the constitutional effects of Community membership in the United Kingdom.

There is one further provision of the European Communities Act to be considered: section 3(1). What it says is that United Kingdom courts must decide any question of the meaning or effect of Community law that arises before them in accordance with the principles laid down by the European Court of Justice. The rulings of that court on Community law are conclusive in our courts. While our courts give independent and final judgement on all questions of English law coming before them, where Community law is concerned they are taking part, together with the courts of other member states, in a transnational system of adjudication, at the apex of which is the European Court of Justice.

We can now try to assess the impact of the European Union on our constitutional arrangements, in the light of the progressive integration of the United Kingdom into the Communities since 1972. Let us start with central government.

Central government

Of course government has had to organise itself to handle European Union business, but the administrative arrangements made for this purpose have been by way of adjustments to existing structures, and have not had a broader, constitutional significance.[4] We may simply note that many government departments are involved to a greater or lesser extent in Union business and that a substantial although unascertainable proportion of the time and resources of our reduced civil service is devoted to administrative and policy matters connected with the Union. There is a standing ministerial sub-committee on European issues, with the Foreign Secretary as chairman. There is no Cabinet minister for Europe but a minister of state has responsibility, under the Foreign Secretary, for European Union matters and in the Department of Trade and Industry the Minister for Trade and Competitiveness in Europe is responsible for internal EU issues. The work of government departments relating to the European Union is co-ordinated by a European Secretariat in the Cabinet Office, while advice and co-ordination on European law issues are the responsibility of the European Division of the Treasury Solicitor's Department.[5]

It will be evident that membership of the European Union must place restrictions on the capacity of the government to make and implement policies for the United Kingdom. In the first place, there is a body of Community law in force in the United Kingdom (by virtue of section 2(1) of the European Communities Act, as we have seen), which it is outside domestic competence to amend or repeal. Government policy-making and legislation has to respect the inviolability of this corpus of received law. In addition, Community treaty provisions and directives, binding on member states, oblige the government to further a wide range of Community objectives and limit the scope for independent policy initiatives. One has only to instance the common agricultural policy and the common fisheries policy: most aspects of farming and the conservation of fisheries are regulated in detail by Community rules which are implemented by the Ministry of Agriculture, Fisheries and Food, the other agricultural departments and the Intervention Board.

There are many other areas of policy-making in which government is significantly constrained – required to act or prohibited from acting – by Community law, such as competition policy, state aids to industry, company law (affected by a steady flow of Community directives), equal treatment of men and women in employment and in social security, public purchasing, etc. The tendency is for Community competence to increase. As it is enlarged, the scope for national policy-making is reduced. The Single European Act of 1986 extended competence to a number of areas, among them health and safety at work and environmental policy. The Maastricht treaty of 1992 instituted new competences in fields such as consumer protection, public health and social policy. The Amsterdam treaty of 1997 provided for Community competence to legislate against discrimination based on sex, racial or ethnic origin, religion or belief, disability, age or sexual orientation. Decisions of the European Court of Justice have also contributed to the extension of Community competence.

Within these areas of Community competence the member states are not necessarily excluded from taking action, but national measures must not conflict with Community law and in the event of any such conflict the Community law will prevail. We have also to reckon with the rather imprecise principle of 'pre-emption' or 'the occupied field'. This holds that once the Community has acted in a particular field it becomes out of bounds to the member states, which lose the power of independent action. The restrictive effect of this principle has, however, been mitigated by treaty amendments and decisions of the European Court of Justice.[6] The constraint placed by Community law on national legislative initiatives is alleviated to some extent by the principle of subsidiarity, by which the Community is to legislate only to the extent necessary and to leave as much scope as possible for national decision-making.[7]

Parliament

It might perhaps be thought that a reduction in the scope for action by central government resulting from membership of the European Union is not a matter of direct constitutional significance, as being a transfer of power to an external authority rather than a redistribution of powers within the United Kingdom. But the developments we have been considering have affected the relations between Parliament and government. To the extent that law-making powers have been transferred to institutions of the European Union, Parliament has lost much of its control (capacity for scrutiny and influence) over the making of legislation which has effect in the United Kingdom. Parliament has no direct input into the Union's legislative activity. Instead, it can only seek to influence the United Kingdom government's negotiating position in the Council – a process much less focused and direct than the examination of government bills on the floor of the House and in standing committees.

This brings us to the role of the United Kingdom Parliament in the EU context. The national parliaments like our own, may be seen either as partners or as rivals of the European Parliament in the affairs of the European Union, but the British government is emphatic that 'national parliaments remain the primary focus of democratic legitimacy in the European Union, holding national Ministers in the Council to account'.[8] Proposals to involve the national parliaments directly in Community legislation have come to nothing. Instead, our parliament attempts to exercise an indirect influence through a rigorous scrutiny of Community legislative proposals and the expression, through debates and resolutions, of its judgements on those proposals, in the hope of fortifying or of restraining United Kingdom Ministers in the Council. Each House has a committee for scrutinising draft Community legislation as well as other European Union documents and there are mechanisms for ensuring debate.

Parliament's efforts to get a grip on proposed Community legislation have been impressive, such that all significant proposals are exposed to parliamentary scrutiny and the possibility of debate. The device of the 'scrutiny reserve' is an important feature of this system. In terms of a Commons resolution of 24 October 1990 – in which the government concurred – a minister may not normally give agreement in the Council to a Community legislative proposal until it has cleared scrutiny by the House.[9] An undertaking in similar terms was given by the government to the House of Lords, which adopted its own scrutiny reserve resolution on 6 December 1999.[10] These arrangements do, however, allow the minister to agree to an uncleared proposal in certain circumstances – in particular 'if he decides that for special reasons agreement should be given' – but in that case he must explain his reasons to Parliament.

Although the United Kingdom system of parliamentary scrutiny has its strengths, it cannot be seen as providing adequate democratic control of Community legislation or as assuring the proper accountability of ministers in their role in Community law-making.

In the first place, the imbalance of political power between Parliament and government is as evident here as elsewhere, unless they happen to take the same view about a Community legislative proposal. Where they differ, we will not find ministers pressing Parliament's view rather than their own in the Council. Even if ministers might otherwise be disposed to accommodate Parliament's concerns, they will usually be reluctant to be committed in advance to a particular negotiating position. Unsurprisingly, therefore, the government is careful to retain control of the parliamentary procedures on Community proposals. It is the government that decides whether a proposal recommended by the Commons European Scrutiny Committee for further consideration is debated in standing committee or on the floor of the House, and in the great majority of cases the scrutiny committee's recommendations for debate on the floor have not been accepted. It is the government, again, that decides on the terms of the motion put to the House on any Community proposal that comes before it: the motion may not reflect the view reached by a standing committee which has previously debated the proposal.

Further difficulties for Parliament arise from the intractable nature of the Union's legislative processes. Parliament has sometimes been unable to get relevant documents in good time for scrutiny before proposals are adopted by the Council. As proposals are reconsidered and amended by Community institutions, in a sometimes fast-moving process that is particularly complex in the co-decision procedure (the European Parliament and the Council legislating jointly), they may escape effective scrutiny by Parliament. On the other hand some recent innovations hold the promise of a more effective parliamentary scrutiny. The Treaty of Amsterdam included a protocol on the role of national parliaments which provides that a six-week period must normally elapse between the submission of a legislative proposal by the Commission and its consideration by the Council. Amendments to House of Commons Standing Orders were made in 1998 to improve the flow of information to the Scrutiny Committee.[11]

If we suppose that Parliament has been able properly to consider a Community legislative proposal and further that it has succeeded in persuading the government to take a particular view of it, we must not lose sight of the constraints affecting the government itself, especially when qualified majority voting applies in the Council.

In assessing the effect of Community law-making on the United Kingdom Parliament, we must also take account of the fact that a substantial amount of domestic secondary legislation – law-making by ministers under section 2(2) of the European Communities Act or other statutes – is a product of Community obligations, in particular the need to implement directives. As is well known, parliamentary control of secondary (delegated) legislation is of limited effectiveness, and the growth in the volume of this mode of legislation is cause for concern.

All in all we are driven to the conclusion, when we survey the relations between Parliament and government in the context of the European Union, that power has drained away from Parliament, some of it to the institutions of the Union and some of it to the government.

Two subsidiary points may be made, of some constitutional interest. First, the transfer of Community business from the floor of the House of Commons to European Standing Committees is in line with recent procedural changes, which have shifted much business from the floor to committees. Secondly, the impressive contribution that has been made by the European scrutiny committee of the House of Lords (the Select Committee on the European Union) shows how a second chamber can usefully supplement the scrutiny work – always constrained by shortage of time and personnel – of the House of Commons.

The courts

What has been the impact of the European Union on the role and functioning of the courts in this country? The national courts of the member states are also Community courts, with responsibility – in collaboration with the European Court of Justice – for enforcing Community law. The consequence of this new status and jurisdiction of the British courts has been an enhancement of their power vis-à-vis the executive and Parliament.

We have already seen that our courts have perforce accepted and applied the principle of the primacy of Community law over British law, including Acts of Parliament. Acting on this principle the courts have, in cases of irreconcilable conflict between a statutory provision and a rule of Community law having effect in the United Kingdom, 'disapplied' the statute – robbing it of its effect to the extent of the conflict.[12] In this way our courts have acquired a power of constitutional review, which has profoundly modified their traditional deference to a sovereign Parliament.

While this power is possessed by the courts only where Community rights or obligations are in question and for the purpose of enforcing Community law as initially embraced by Parliament in 1972, we should be alive to the potentialities of this new-found jurisdiction. It has accustomed the courts to operating in a sphere in which the sovereignty of Parliament is in abeyance, and this may colour their response to new challenges that may be raised to the orthodoxy of parliamentary sovereignty. We are on speculative ground, but we may suppose that if a new Bill of Rights were introduced in this country which purported to set limits to the power of Parliament – something formerly regarded as constitutionally unattainable – the judges, already inured to an overriding Community law, might be willing to revise the traditional doctrine of the continuing, unimpeachable sovereignty of Parliament. This question does not, it may be noted, arise in respect of the Human Rights Act 1998, for this Act does not include any mechanism of entrenchment, designed to protect its provisions from repeal or amendment, and does not authorise the courts to override or disregard Acts of Parliament. The Act is respectful of the orthodox principle of parliamentary sovereignty.

In interpreting statutes our courts, again acknowledging their duty to uphold Community law, claim a greater latitude in dealing with the parliamentary text. The first principle of statutory interpretation as practised by the English courts has always been to follow the plain, ordinary or literal meaning of the words of the statute, so seeming to show the greatest deference to the expressed will of Parliament. Only few and strictly limited exceptions to this principle have been admitted. Even when a statute was enacted in order to give effect to treaty obligations assumed by the United Kingdom, the treaty itself could be referred to as an aid to interpretation only if the words of the statute were ambiguous or obscure. Clear statutory language could not be adjusted by the courts even if it contradicted the terms of the treaty.[13]

Our courts have departed from this position when the treaty in question is one of the founding treaties of the European Union. Faced with these treaties, or the secondary Community legislation flowing from them, the courts have resorted to a 'purposive' interpretation of British statutes, in order to ensure the effectiveness of Community law. Now a limited kind of purposive interpretation was already practised by our courts in the domestic context, taking account of the purpose of a statute in resolving obscurity or ambiguity in the wording used, but the courts would not reject the plain or ordinary meaning of a statute in order to give effect to the statutory purpose. Where, on the other hand, legislation is enacted to implement Community law – say, a directive – our courts see it as their duty to interpret the legislation so that it will conform to the terms of the directive, even though this involves a departure from the plain and unambiguous language of the enactment and may require additional words to be read into its provisions. This was done for instance by the House of Lords in the case of *Pickstone* v. *Freemans plc,*[14] in which Lord Oliver said that 'a statute which is passed in order to give effect to the United Kingdom's obligations under the EEC treaty falls into a special category'. Here the courts are reformulating legislation, even Acts of Parliament, albeit to give effect to what they hold to be the true purpose of the enactment.

The question of interpretation is more problematic if an Act falls within the scope of a directive but was not passed in order to implement it: an obvious instance is where the directive is of more recent date than the Act. Even here the courts will, as far as possible, interpret the Act so as to be consistent with the directive. Although it is accepted – for the present at all events – that the courts should not go so far as to distort the meaning of an Act in order to achieve this consistency, they will certainly be prepared to depart from what would be, in a non-Community context, the proper interpretation of the Act.[15]

The increased versatility and boldness that the courts display in the European context is not limited to their treatment of statutes. When reviewing the legality of executive acts – of ministers and other public authorities – the courts ordinarily apply a set of principles or standards that reflect the traditional balance between executive and judiciary, allowing a close scrutiny of the lawfulness of the action that has come under challenge but fencing off from judicial examination those matters that belong properly to the public authority's own judgement and its view of what the public interest requires. When executive action impinges on Community law, however, the courts apply a deeper scrutiny to the decision under challenge: in particular, they invoke the Community legal principle of 'proportionality', that is, that the action taken should go no further than is necessary to achieve the legitimate objective that is being pursued. The application of this test leads a court into a judgement on the reasonableness or merits of executive action, something that goes beyond the limits of traditional review in the domestic context. Again, while the English courts have not yet admitted a general principle that reasons must be given for administrative decisions, the European Court of Justice requires that a public authority must give reasons for a decision affecting Community rights, so that the soundness of the reasons may be challenged in a judicial review.[16]

In these developments we see the courts asserting a widened power of supervision of Acts of Parliament, delegated legislation and executive action, so effecting a change in the traditional balance of powers in the constitution. It is the least democratic branch of the governmental system that has emerged with its powers enhanced. In breaking this new ground, the judges act under the guidance and control of the European Court of Justice, that innovatory and policy-driven court.

The effects of EU membership on the constitution of the United Kingdom, in particular on democratic accountability, the authority of Parliament and the balance of powers between executive, legislature and judiciary, give cause for some disquiet. We find this expressed, for instance, by Nevil Johnson in saying that

the EU can operate and survive only on the basis of continuous (and often private) bargaining and negotiation among member states. This is very hard to reconcile with responsible government and public accountability as understood within the British political tradition.[17]

To what may seem a rather bleak assessment it is, of course, possible to oppose a vision of something different and more democratic. This is a vision of the European Union as a dynamic polity, which is still in an evolutionary phase, and supposes that law and policy-making in the Union will be brought progressively under greater democratic control. Through a strengthening of the European Parliament, a more effective participation of national parliaments and a decentralisation of decision-making to member states, regions and local authorities, the democratic deficit may be overcome and accountability be restored. This certainly should be our goal, although opinions will differ as to whether it is achievable.

The citizen

I have been dwelling on institutional effects of EU membership in the United Kingdom, but there is, of course, another perspective – that of the individual citizen. British citizens are now also citizens of the European Union, and as such have the right to take up residence in any other member country in order to engage in economic activity and may vote in local government and European elections in whichever is their chosen country of residence. Individual citizens of the United Kingdom enjoy a range of important rights conferred on them by the treaties and secondary legislation. Notable among these are the right to equal pay for equal work as between men and women and the right to equal treatment of the sexes in employment and social security provision. Community rules have been a significant element in the development of sex equality law in this country.

Besides the rights that are expressly conferred on individuals by the treaties and secondary legislation, individual rights are also embedded in the general principles of Community law elaborated by the European Court of Justice. That court has created a body of fundamental rights which it has derived from the European Convention on Human Rights (to which all the member states of the Union are parties) and from principles that are common to the constitutional traditions of the member states. These rights include, for instance, the right to property, the right of access to judicial remedies, freedom of expression, and the right to privacy and respect for family life.[18]

The existence of these rights in the Community legal order operates as a restraint not only on the Community institutions themselves – that may perhaps be regarded as their primary application – but also on the member states when acting in the field of Community law. Accordingly, when they implement Community rules, member states are bound to take account of the fundamental rights recognised by Community law. This development was seen as part of a process of 'infiltration' of a Bill of Rights into the law of the United Kingdom,[19] but the rights guaranteed by the European Convention have since been directly incorporated into our law by the Human Rights Act 1998.

In conclusion it may be said that the flexibility of our unwritten constitution has been of some value in the United Kingdom's response to the challenges of European Union membership, but it may also allow for a progressive change in our arrangements which is both unremarked and profound. We have yet to see whether the constitution will hold up well, as a strong protection of the democratic values, as we continue to take our part in the European experiment.

Notes

1   A qualified version of the Luxembourg compromise was adopted in a few specific instances in the Treaty of Amsterdam: see in particular the new Art. 11(2) of the EC treaty.

2   The principle was first clearly established by the European Court of Justice in the case of *Costa* v. *ENEL*, Case 6/64 [1964] ECR 585.

3   *Stoke-on-Trent City Council* v. *B&Q plc* [1991] Ch. 48.

4   Simon Bulmer and Martin Burch remark that 'The new challenges posed by EC/EU membership have simply been absorbed into the existing institutions, and into the characteristic methods, procedures and culture of Whitehall', 'Organising for Europe', *Public Administration*, 76 (1998) pp.601–28 at p.613.

5   On the European Division see Terence Daintith and Alan Page, *The Executive in the Constitution* (New York: Oxford University Press, 1999), pp 316-319.

6   See Damian Chalmers, *European Union Law*, vol. I (Aldershot: Ashgate, 1998) pp.239–54.

7   See Article 5 of the EC Treaty and the Protocol on the Application of the Principles of Subsidiarity and Proportionality annexed to the Treaty.

8   *A Partnership of Nations*, Cm. 3181 (1996), para. 33. The Select Committee on European Legislation (the European Scrutiny Committee) is committed to the same view: 27th Report, HC 51–xxvii of 1995–6, para.11.

9   CJ vol. 246 (1989–90) p. 646. The scrutiny reserve resolution was reaffirmed with revisions on 17 November 1998: CJ vol. 254 (1997–98) p. 812.

10 HL Deb. vol. 607, cols 1019–20.

11 HC Deb. vol. 319, cols 803–4 (17 November 1998). But cf. HC Deb vol. 340 cols 236–58WH (8 December 1999).

12 See the *Factortame* cases: *R. v. Secretary of State for Transport, ex parte Factortame Ltd* [1990] 2 A.C. 85, [1991] 1 A.C. 603, [1992] Q.B. 680 and *R. v. Secretary of State for Employment, ex parte Equal Opportunities Commission* [1995] 1 A.C. 1.

13 *Salomon v. Commissioners of Customs and Excise* [1967] 2 Q.B. 116.

14 [1989] A.C. 66. See also *Litster v. Forth Dry Dock and Engineering Co. Ltd.* [1990] 1 A.C. 546.

15 See *Webb v. EMO Air Cargo (UK) Ltd* [1993] 1 W.L.R. 49; *Webb v. EMO Air Cargo (UK) Ltd (No.2)* [1995] 1 W.L.R. 1454.

16 See F.G. Jacobs, 'Public Law – The Impact of Europe', [1999] *Public Law*, 232, pp.235–6.

17 Ian Holliday, Andrew Gamble and Geraint Parry (eds), *Fundamentals in British Politics* (New York: St Martin's Press, 1999) pp.69–70.

18 Article 6(2) of the Maastricht treaty confirms the obligation of the European Union to respect fundamental rights as guaranteed by the European Convention.

19 See Lord Browne-Wilkinson, 'The Infiltration of a Bill of Rights', [1992] *Public Law* 397.

Transfers, Trade, Food and Growth: Britain and the European Union over 40 Years

P.J.N. Sinclair and I. Martinez Zarzoso

This chapter begins, in section 1, by examining the history of the European Union (EU) and Britain's relationship with it. The particular focus here is on the evolving economic policy issues and the outcomes, especially for new members' rates of growth after accession in the enlargement phase that began in the early 1970s. Members' net contributions to the EU budget are analysed in section 2. Section 3 probes the question of how transfers seem to have affected the members that paid and received them. In section 4, attention switches to the common agricultural policy (CAP), which has always represented the largest element of the EU's outlays (and, until recently. amounted to over half of it). Section 5 presents some econometric analysis of the impact of accession on new members' growth rates, and section 6 concludes.

1. Issues and outcomes

The second half of the 20th century has witnessed a huge transformation in Britain's economic relationships with continental Europe.

The 1950s saw the formation of the EU's parent institutions, the European Coal and Steel Community (1953) and the European Economic Community and Euratom (1957). Britain chose to absent itself from these developments. For the UK it seemed preferable to concentrate upon its existing links with the Commonwealth, its special relationship with the United States, and its role in GATT and other international institutions in helping to promote world-wide reductions in tariff barriers. Britain saw the ECSC and the EEC as instruments of self-help for western Europe's most war-shattered economies. The two defeated belligerents, (West) Germany and Italy, were linking arms with the three Benelux countries, already in customs union, and France. Britain could view this process with benign detachment.

By the early 1960s, much had changed. The old white Commonwealth was metamorphosing into a 'dignified' institution of negligible economic and political significance. Britain's share of its imports was crumbling. The black empire disappeared. Suez and the Cambridge spy-ring scandal exposed serious rifts in Anglo-American relations. Britain's world power status was at an end. More importantly, Britain's rate of economic growth, historically respectable as it might be, was barely half that of the EEC-Six economies. West Germany overtook the UK in GDP per head in 1960, and France was to follow shortly. Britain entered a free trade association with most of the rest of non-communist Europe to compensate for the trade barrier handicaps its exporters were now facing in the EEC. In 1961 Macmillan announced his government's intention to apply for EEC membership, after a discreet two-year campaign of persuasion within the Conservative Party. The application was finally vetoed by President de Gaulle in 1963. Three years later Wilson's Labour government tried again, and was again rebuffed. Within the EEC, the 1960s witnessed the creation of the CAP (1961), the elimination of the last internal tariffs (1963), a protracted period of rapid growth in GDP and internal trade, and later, the financial strains, not least for the CAP, induced by the German revaluation and French devaluation of 1969.

With de Gaulle's departure, the 1970s witnessed the first wave of enlargements for the European Communities: the accession of Britain, Denmark and Ireland in 1973, confirmed by Britain's referendum two years later after Labour's 'renegotiation' of the entry terms achieved under Heath. The break-up of the Bretton Woods exchange rate system in August 1971 was swiftly followed, in March 1972, by a precursor to the European exchange rate mechanism (ERM) – a network of narrowed bands for EC currencies around their new Smithsonian parities. This 'snake in the tunnel' mechanism lasted for seven years, surviving the 1974 oil shock, periodic parity changes, a game of hopscotch for the French franc (which kept jumping in and out) and the early, undignified exits of sterling (June 1972) and the Italian lira. It was revised and relaunched in the form of the ERM in March 1979; in one of its last acts, Callaghan's Labour government opted to keep sterling floating freely, a decision confirmed by Thatcher on entering office two months later. The decade ended with the first direct elections to the European Parliament.

The 1980s saw further EC enlargements; Greece (1981), Portugal and Spain (1986). All three had shed non-democratic regimes and displayed some measure of convergence in their (still much lower) levels of GDP per head. Within the EC, there were budget crises for the CAP as agricultural production outpaced and swamped domestic demand, under the influence of high foodstuff prices. A complex new quota system limited the cost of agricultural intervention for dairy products, and Thatcher deployed the threat of British veto to prevent increases in the real prices of agricultural products. Agriculture began to account for a diminishing share of total European Commission outlays, with the slack absorbed by rapid increases in the Regional and Social Funds. Extreme pressure from the Greek government under Papandreou forced the EC into huge transfers to Greece, and that precedent led to large net flows to Spain and Portugal after their accession a little later.

The 1980s ended with rapid progress towards completing the integration of the Single Market (agreed in 1987, to be implemented by 1 January 1993): intra-EC non-tariff barriers were swept away, standards harmonised by mutual recognition and amendment, public procurement opened to all EC firms, and the principles of free internal movement of labour and capital were at last applied rigorously throughout the community.

After a decade of structural and microeconomic reforms, attention switched back, in the 1990s as it had in the 1970s, to exchange rate, macroeconomic and monetary issues. Proposals for economic and monetary union (EMU), which had proved abortive when first aired in 1976, were vigorously revived in the run-up to the Maastricht conference in 1991 (which also coined the name European Union). It was universally agreed that the retention of separate national currencies, even when the exchange rates between them could be kept in narrow bands with infrequent parity revisions, led to costs of currency conversion that could represent as much as 1 per cent of national income. Real resources were devoted to exchanging national monies, resources that could be redeployed to better use. Separate national currencies discouraged intra-EC trade somewhat, particularly for smaller firms that found hedging against exchange risk difficult or expensive to obtain. There would be gains from pooling foreign exchange reserves and removing monetary hurdles to the free movement of capital.

Monetary union would be difficult, however, if participating countries had histories of large exchange rate fluctuation or major discrepancies in interest rates or inflation. The enterprise could flounder if some countries had large levels of public debt or budget deficits, because these could undermine the credibility of commitment to low inflation. The Maastricht treaty therefore enshrined these observations in the form of minimal criteria that aspiring participants in EMU would have to satisfy.

From Britain's standpoint, EMU was always a contentious issue. It was the financial markets' awareness of the Heath government's commitment to a policy of rapid, independent monetary and fiscal reflation that led to the speculative pressures that forced sterling out of the snake in June 1972. The petro-currency character of sterling in the early 1980s helped to push it first up, then down against the main continental currencies in the early and mid-1980s. The asymmetric shocks of world oil price swings, coupled with independent monetary policy targets, were responsible for this. Germany's reunification boom in 1990–2, at a time of severe UK recession, created a marked discrepancy in optimal interest rate policies between these two countries, and paved the way to Black (or Golden) Wednesday, 16 September 1992, and the undignified end to sterling's ill-fated 22–month experiment of full participation in the ERM. Sceptics noted the success Britain enjoyed in reversing the recession after 1992. The advantages of lower interest rates and a more competitive exchange rate for sterling – without the feared accompaniment of increased inflation – led to sharp rises in GDP and falling unemployment, against the continental trend.

Asymmetric shocks affected Britain quite differently from Germany in the 1980s and early 1990s. Under EMU, a common monetary policy would have been enforced, one which could never have satisfied both countries' needs. Perhaps asymmetric shocks of this magnitude would be less likely in the future; but the main lesson of September 1992 seemed to be that for Britain, expulsion from a German-dominated currency system was a blessed release.

In the longer run, the key issue would be whether EU countries do best to tax money, for that is essentially when inflation policy consists of, at similar rates.[1] If the answer is yes, the saving in currency conversion costs suggests that EMU would be beneficial. But if EU countries' optimal inflation rates diverge, EMU would involve compromises that could not suit everyone. Furthermore, a country exposed to recession stemming from an excessively uncompetitive exchange rate would be deprived of the key two instruments most able to rectify its position – the option to devalue, and the option to cut interest rates unilaterally. Even the freedom to employ fiscal policy to combat rising unemployment would be circumscribed, because a European central bank might treat a beleaguered national government rather like a local council, cap its spending, and limit its policy options.

What effect, if any, does membership appear to have on a country's growth rate? Table 1 presents some statistics that may help us gain an impression of this.

In the 1960s, France and Italy record rapid growth, averaging just over 5.5 per cent per year. The EC area as a whole, including Germany and the Benelux countries, grows just over 5.1 per cent annually. This compares favourably with the US (3.8 per cent) and the size-weighted average for the other nine countries that were to join the EU later. But this last statistic is depressed by the sluggish growth record of the UK in this decade; the other eight, as a group, also grew at slightly over 5 per cent. Most of them, like Britain, were experiencing the benefits of trade liberalisation through EFTA at this time.

In the 1970s, growth rates fell everywhere except Ireland, where macroeconomic performance remained strong after accession in 1973. Growth in Denmark fell somewhat faster than the average for the EU-15, both in the 1971–80 decade as a whole and the sub-period 1974–80. In Britain, growth in 1974–80 was a mere 1.4 per cent, but the absolute fall in comparison to 1961–70 (1.5 per cent) was smaller than for the EU-15 as a whole (2.6 per cent). The uneven ebb and flow of the business cycle is just one of several factors that makes it hazardous to draw firm inferences here. But we can say that there is some indication that EU accession could have been favourable for growth in Ireland and the UK, and probably unfavourable for Denmark, in the transition years after accession.

For the countries that joined the EU in the 1980s, the picture is more complex. In Greece, growth collapses after accession, to an average annual rate of 1.6 per cent in the first decade of membership. This is the slowest growth of all countries included in Table 1 for the period. But growth in Greece was on a declining trend; if anything it fell a little less between 1971–80 to 1981–90 than in the previous decade. Macroeconomic perform-ance in Greece in the 1980s may have suffered from idiosyncratic domestic fiscal and monetary policies, which lurched between inordinate expansion and severe squeeze. Portugal and Spain are notable for rapid declines in annual growth during the first six years of EU membership, but rates of growth at the start of this transition period (1986–92) were exceptionally fast, both by international and historical standards. The boost to growth came early. The Iberian growth burst in 1985–9 occurred despite a generally disinflationary monetary and exchange rate policy stance; it was accompanied, particularly in the Spanish case, by high levels of unemployment.

Table 1 Average Annual Growth in real GDP

	1961-7	1971-8	1981-9	1987	1988	1989	1990	1991	1992	1993	1994	1995
Austria	4.7	3.6	2.1	1.7	4.1	3.8	4.2	2.8	2	0.4	3	1.8
Belgium	4.9	3.2	1.9	2.1	4.9	3.4	3.7	1.6	1.7	-1.4	2.3	1.9
Denmark	4.5	2.2	2	0.3	1.2	0.6	1.4	1.3	0.2	1.5	4.4	2.8
Finland	4.8	3.4	3.1	4.1	4.9	5.7	0	-7.1	-3.6	-1.2	4.4	4.2
France	5.6	3.3	2.4	2.3	4.5	4.3	2.5	0.8	1.2	-1.3	2.8	2.2
Germany	4.4	2.7	2.2	1.5	3.7	3.6	5.7	5	2.2	-1.1	2.9	1.9
Greece	7.6	4.7	1.6	-0.5	4.5	3.8	0	3.1	0.4	-1	1.5	2
Ireland	4.2	4.7	3.6	4.7	4.3	6.1	7.8	2.6	4.6	3.7	7.3	10.7
Italy	5.7	3.6	2.2	3.1	3.9	2.9	2.2	1.1	0.6	-1.2	2.1	3
Luxembourg	3.5	2.6	3.6	2.9	5.7	6.7	3.2	3.1	1.9	0	3.3	3.4
Netherlands	5.1	3	2.2	1.4	2.6	4.7	4.1	2.3	2	0.8	3.4	2.1
Portugal	6.4	4.7	2.9	6.4	4.9	4.9	4.6	2.3	1.8	0.3	0.8	2.3
Spain	7.3	3.5	3	5.6	5.2	4.7	3.7	2.3	0.7	-1.2	2.1	2.8
Sweden	4.6	2	2	3.1	2.3	2.4	1.4	-1.1	-1.4	-2.2	2.6	3
UK	2.9	2	2.6	4.8	5	2.2	0.4	-2	-0.5	2.2	3.8	2.4
EU-15	4.8	3	2.4	2.9	4.2	3.5	2.9	1.5	1	-0.5	2.8	2.4
Japan	10.5	4.5	4	4.2	6.2	4.8	5.1	4	1.1	0.1	0.5	0.8
USA	3.8	2.7	2.7	3.1	3.9	2.7	1.2	-0.5	2.5	3.4	4.1	2

In order to gain a more precise indication of how EU membership and EU accession affects the dynamics of real national income, we have conducted a number of econometric regressions. Some results are presented in Table 4. The main conclusion is that there is little evidence of any significant growth impact arising from EU membership. Section 5 explores these issues further, in an econometric framework.

2. Net contributions to the EU budget

As Table 2 reveals, the UK's net contribution to the EU fluctuates year from year. But it has displayed very little trend. Between 1976 and 1995 it averaged just under one third of 1 per cent of UK GDP at factor cost (0.32 per cent). Its average value slipped from 0.31 per cent to 0.28 per cent from the first quinquennium to the second, then climbed to 0.36 per cent in the third before falling back to 0.34 per cent in the fourth. It exceeded half of 1 per cent of GDP in only four years (1979, 1987 and 1995).

The scale of Britain's net contribution was held down from the early and mid 1980s as a result of CAP changes, particularly the adoption of milk quotas and the Thatcher-inspired ban on raising real food prices, and, more importantly, Germany's generous agreement to assume a large slice of the payments for which Britain would otherwise have been liable. What Britain gained here was approximately offset by her share of the cost of the large and continuing transfers to Greece, Portugal and Spain.

It is important to ask how much of the UK's net contribution can be treated as a reasonable share of the central expenditures. Much of what the EU receives from national governments is paid back to them, in aggregate, chiefly through the operation of the CAP and the regional, social and other funds. But something has to be withheld, to defray administrative a and other costs. Let us call these costs 'the residuum' and suppose that they were levied on member countries in proportion to GDP. This provides one benchmark for calculation of a fair club fee for EU membership.

What did the residuum cost in 1995? In 1995, identified payments made by the EU to national member authorities accounted for nearly 86 per cent of total receipts from them. The balance, amounting to £7.8 billion, is the residuum that year. Almost half of this figure consisted of 'miscellaneous' payments to member states not categorised by destination in the Court of Auditors' Annual Report.

On the basis of the 1995 figures, Britain's fair club fee would have been almost £1.2 billion, representing some 0.19 per cent of its GDP at factor cost that year. This suggests that Britain's average *excess* net contribution to the EU was only 0.13 per cent of GDP. More than half her long-term average net contribution could be treated as a fair share of central expenditures for the EU.

Suppose we take an earlier year, 1985. In 1985 the EU collected almost 26.1 billion ecus from its members and paid out nearly 24.7 billion. The residuum that year was 1.426 billion ecus, only 5.5 per cent of total contributions. On a pay-in-proportion-to-GDP basis, Britain's 'fair club fee' in 1985 would have been 268 million ecus, less than 0.06 per cent of its GDP that year. On the 1985 figures, therefore, Britain's average *excess* net contribution to the EU would be over 0.26 per cent of GDP.

Most of the difference between the 1995 and 1985 residua stems from the markedly lower figure for 'miscellaneous' (uncategorised) payments by the EU. They were less than 40 million ecus in the earlier year, as against almost 4.8 billion a decade later. It is possible that the ending of border formalities with the completion of the Single Market by 1993 has made it harder to determine the nationality of recipients of CAP intervention payments. Or there may have been changes in accounting conventions. Miscellaneous payments were negligible until the mid-1980s, but trebled in 1985, doubling again in both 1987 and 1988, with a thirty-fold increase between 1988 and 1991 (across the mysterious years 1989 and 1990 for which they were not reported). In 1994 they accounted for no less than 10 per cent of total EU receipts from member governments, recording their first appreciable fall – over one third – in 1995.

The EU accounts make it hard, therefore, to determine what 'fair club fees' would be. Perhaps the simplest procedure is to calculate the long-term average level of the residuum on the charitable assumption that 'miscellaneous payments', heavily swollen as they have become in later years, do in fact represent justifiable central expenditure to which members should contribute. For the 20 years 1976–95 as a whole, the residuum averages at just over 8.5 per cent of total EU receipts, interpolating for the missing years 1989 and 1990. With the UK accounting for one sixth of EU GDP on average over this period, a fair club fee for Britain averages at 0.11 per cent of its GDP. This suggests that about one third of Britain's actual net contributions in these two decades are a fair club fee, and the balance – 0.21 per cent – is to be treated as *excess* net contributions.

What makes Britain an excess net contributor? There are two main reasons. One is the fact that the share of GDP generated by agriculture in the UK is barely half the EU average. The largest share in the EU budget is devoted to agricultural support through the European Agriculture Guidance and Guarantee Fund (EAGGF). This accounted for over two-thirds of Community outlays in the mid-1970s, and is still almost one-half. If the true level of agricultural support is calculated by comparing internal with international prices for *all* supported production – in accordance with the principles prescribed in Little and Mirrlees[2] – agriculture's true share of the EU's properly constructed budget is probably over 80 per cent even now.

The second factor is Britain's lack of qualification for much of the regional and social fund outlays. GDP per head in Britain is close to the EU average, and much less subject to regional variations than in most other countries. Unemployment is now below the EU average, and surprisingly uniform between British regions. The UK government has also been reluctant to co-finance some investment projects to which the EU might otherwise have contributed. Lastly, the lion's share of the cohesion

funds has gone, understandably, to the three relatively poor
countries that joined in the 1980s, Greece, Portugal and Spain.

Table 2: UK contributions to and receipts from the EU

	Millions ECUs, current prices			Net contributions	
	Contributions	Receipts	Net contributions	£million 1995 prices	as % of UK GDP at factor cost
1995	9252	4531	4721	3913	0.65
1994	6418	5259	1159	920	0.16
1993	7627	4501	3126	2521	0.45
1992	6702	4315	2387	1883	0.34
1991	4736	4070	666	524	0.09
1990	6534	*3798	*2736	2320	0.41
1989	6568	*3526	*3042	2622	0.46
1988	5324	3254	2070	1834	0.33
1987	5728	3122	2607	2537	0.51
1986	4825	3387	1438	1488	0.30
1985	5090	3107	1983	1848	0.38
1984	5430	4030	1400	1380	0.30
1983	5084	4084	1001	1034	0.22
1982	5116	3962	1154	1287	0.29
1981	3877	3125	753	848	0.19
1980	3168	1803	1365	1640	0.37
1979	3026	1541	1485	2491	0.57
1978	2325	1481	845	1686	0.40
1977	1578	1490	88	185	0.04
1976	1250	994	256	624	0.15

Source: For first three columns: Court of Auditors' Annual Report to
European Commission, various issues (supplemented by authors'
interpolation for 1990 and 1989 data for column 2, which were
excluded from these reports). For columns 4 and 5: authors'
calculations.

Britain is indeed a net contributor to the EU budget. But it is important to stress that her net contributions are considerably lighter than Germany's or the Netherlands, in relation to national income or population. Table 3 presents net contributions for each of the 15 member countries, as proportions of GDP, for the years 1993–5. In the case of the three new members which joined on 1 January 1995, data relate to 1995 only.

Table 3: Net contributions as percentages of GDP, 1993–1995 (annual average); actual and excess

	Actual	Excess	
		definition (a)	definition (b)
Austria	(1995) 0.58	0.39	0.47
Belgium	0.10	-0.11	-0.01
Denmark	-0.24	-0.45	-0.35
Finland	(1995) 0.14	-0.05	0.03
France	0.17	-0.04	0.06
Germany	0.83	0.62	0.75
Greece	-5.06	-5.27	-5.17
Ireland	-4.31	-4.52	-4.42
Italy	0.16	-0.05	0.05
Luxembourg	-1.23	-1.44	-1.34
Netherlands	0.64	0.43	0.53
Portugal	-3.65	-3.86	-3.76
Spain	-2.61	-2.82	-2.72
Sweden	(1995) 0.45	0.26	0.34
UK	0.34	0.13	0.23

Definition (a): on 1993–5 average calculation of the fair club fee (1995 for Austria, Finland and Sweden). Definition (b): on 1976–95 average calculation of the fair club fee (0.11% of GDP).

Source: Calculated from data in Table 2, and with assumption in text.

Germany's net contribution averages at 0.83 per cent of GDP. For the Netherlands, the comparable figure is 0.64 per cent. Austria and Sweden come next. Britain ranks fifth by this criterion (or third among the EU 12), followed after a gap by France, Italy, Finland and Belgium.

There are six countries which are net recipients. Denmark's net contribution is the smallest (0.24 per cent of GDP). Luxembourg, is the only founder member of the original EEC to be a net beneficiary, gaining almost 1.25 per cent of its GDP from transfers. This is clearly an instance of where it pays to be small: Luxembourg is strongly over-represented in the European Commission and Parliament. There have been years when Luxembourg was a net contributor, but few, and only on a very modest scale. In addition, Luxembourg, like Belgium, benefits substantially from expenditure resulting from accommodating EU institutions.

The real gains from the EU include Spain, where net receipts account for over 2.5 per cent of GDP, and Portugal, Ireland and Greece, for whom net receipts are considerably larger. Greece tops the list when net receipts are expressed as a proportion of national income; on a per head basis, the greatest beneficiary is Ireland. EU transfers have averaged to Ireland 578 ecus, or £459 per caput in 1995 prices in these years. British net contributions per head are less than one tenth of this.

The second column subtracts the 'fair club fee' from net contribution/GDP ratios. This fee we found to be 0.19 per cent in 1995, when miscellaneous transfers, not categorised by country, are deemed part of central EU expenditures. For 1993–5, the average fair club fee rises to 0.21 per cent of GDP. After these subtractions we arrive at the 'excess' net contributions. It is noteworthy that Britain's excess net contributions are less than one third of the Netherlands', and barely a fifth of Germany's. Excess net contributions go negative for Belgium, Finland, France and Italy. For Greece, excess net contributions fall to over –5.25 per cent of GDP.

The pattern of net contributions and receipts is correlated imperfectly with income per head. Greece, the largest beneficiary on a GDP ratio basis, is the EU's poorest member: at current prices a and exchange rates, GDP per head there was only 63 per cent of the EU average in 1995. But Ireland's GDP per person was only 5.5 per cent below the EU average, and it gains most per head. Portugal and Spain receive less on either definition and are considerably poorer, with GDP per head 27 per cent and 23.5 per cent below the EU average. Most incongruous of all, the EU's two richest countries, Denmark and Luxembourg, are net beneficiaries. The discrepancy is greater for Luxembourg, where GDP per head is a full 67 per cent above the EU mean.

3. Transfers

Membership of the European Union involves nations in the payment of budget contributions, in the receipt of transfers. Transfers come partly in the form of payments to agricultural producers. These will be passed back, in the long run, to the owners of land. Then there have been regional and social fund transfers, paid in the main to poorer new members since the mid-1980s. Our analysis of transfers below will apply to these.

How will a transfer affect the transferor's net income? Suppose the transfer is a fixed sum, x, and that the transferor chooses how hard or long to work (let this be the key influence on output). There are many possibilities here.

If the marginal disutility of labour (MDL) is constant, and the marginal utility of consumption (MUC) is declining, net income will not change. The transferor simply works harder or longer to pay for the transfer. On the other hand, if MUC is constant and MDL is increasing (you value leisure more at the margin the less you have), work stays the same, and net income drops by the size of the transfer, x. More often perhaps we would encounter an intermediate case where MUC declined and MDL increased. Then work would rise a bit, and net income (consumption) would fall a bit; but net income would drop by less than x.

In the long run, capital stocks can vary. Production depends on capital as well as labour. But in simple cases where people choose paths for labour, capital and consumption over an infinite horizon, and the rate of interest is eventually pinned down by the rate at which initial consumption is discounted (the model of Ramsey[3]), we find that labour, capital and gross output all have to change in the same proportion in the end. If the transfer is recurrent, labour, capital and gross output all go up, typically to cover at least some of the transfer. It will usually be true that labour goes up more in the short run than in the long run, and that, in the transition, the economy's growth rate will be boosted more by the additional investment than it is retarded by the slipping supply of labour.

So we can summarise likely repercussions thus. When the transfers start to be paid, assuming that they are not expected previously, consumption drops and labour rises, quite substantially. Then labour probably falls back gently, and consumption and capital climb, and growth is increased (although by a diminishing extent as time proceeds). Eventually we reach the long run, where labour, capital and gross output are all higher than in the initial position, and consumption lower, but the fall in consumption is less than x.

The picture changes if x, the recurrent transfer, is not a lump sum. The worst long-run result obtains if some part of x is levied by taxing income from capital (net of investment). Then long-run capital is liable to fall, and, if it does, long-run consumption will fall, too, by more than x. In an endogenous growth set-up, any tax on capital income has the added disadvantage of cutting the long-run growth rate, too. These effects should not happen, however, if as in the case of national contributions to the EU, transfers are largely collected through added tax. This is a tax on (most elements of) consumption, and will not exert the insidious capital-eroding effect of a tax that falls partly on capital income, although it does create some additional costs.

There is another possible aspect to transfers, too. This is the possible change in the relative price of goods. Suppose two countries A and B are trading two goods which are given in supply, and A is exporting good 1 and importing good 2. A then makes a transfer to B. What happens to the terms of trade for A, that is the relative price of good 1 in terms of good 2? The so-called 'orthodox presumption' here[4] was that the transferor, A, would the suffer the additional burden of a terms of trade deterioration (this is what Keynes once argued in the context of German war reparations after the First World War). Jones demonstrated, however, that this could easily be wrong, and that in simple cases, at least, the opposite could be expected.[5]

When examining the question of Germany's reparations to France after Versailles, Keynes asked whether these would impose a secondary burden on Germany. He argued that to sell enough exports to balance its payments, it would suffer a terms of trade deterioration. The prices of Germany's exports would have to fall in terms of its importables to persuade foreigners to buy them. There would be a real exchange rate depreciation, and the burden of the transfer would be augmented by an additional welfare loss on German residents in aggregate. Keynes's 'classical' position, that the transferor be likelier than not to bear a secondary burden in the form of worsened terms of trade, was supported by Samuelson in later work.[6]

Jones' attack on the Keynes-Samuelson presumption that the donor's terms of trade worsen ran as follows. If nothing is known about countries' supply or endowment patterns, it becomes likelier than not that a country has a higher average propensity to spend upon the class of goods it imports than the country to which the transfer is sent. With average and marginal propensities to spend positively correlated, Jones argued, the chances are that world demand patterns tilt in favour of what the transferor exports. The presence of non-traded goods may qualify, but will not generally overturn that presumption.

In the case of Britain and the EU, it seems likely that the way British taxpayers spend an extra pound is very similar to that of the Irish, Greek and Iberian beneficiaries of the UK's net contributions to the EU. The main exception relates to non-traded goods. British non-traded goods should fall in price somewhat with these transfers while non-traded goods in the recipient countries go up. With similar cross-elasticities of demand and supply between the two sets of non-traded goods on the one side, and the various exportables and importables on the other, there should be no appreciable effect on Britain's terms of trade. We therefore conclude that the 'secondary burden' hypothesis is at best an unproved possibility, and probably quite fallacious.

Indeed, there are compensating factors pointing in the opposite direction. The rise in the price of oil and increasing exploitation of North Sea resources seems to have exacerbated the appreciation of sterling in the early 1980s, with adverse effects on profits, production and jobs in the UK's non-oil manufacturing sector. The phenomenon is known as 'the Dutch disease' and referred initially to the unexpected squeeze on much of the Netherlands' industrial sector in the wake of large sales of high-priced natural gas to Germany in the later 1970s.

For Iberia, Greece and Ireland, EU largesse is not unlike discovering valuable mineral resources. Their governments could have been tempted to increase expenditure excessively, and build up large debts; their workers may have experienced a reduced incentive to work, in anticipation of receiving higher transfers themselves; the stimulus to accumulate capital there could have been stunted. So the legacy of EU transfers could have included reductions in aggregate supply, bloated public sector debt, and mounting unemployment. Reduced rates of economic growth in Greece after 1981, and in Ireland for much of the 1980s, accord well with this idea; so, too, do the serious public sector debt problems these countries were exper-iencing by the late 1980s, and the massive increases in unemployment in Spain and Ireland (where it is still far above the EU average).

In Britain's case, the commitment to make contributions to the EU would act like losing some of the income stream associated with North Sea oil: government has to tighten its belt, domestic workers anticipate a reduced flow of transfer income stimulating greater labour force participation, and wealth-holders redouble their efforts to augment their capital in the face of this unwelcome development. If there is any truth in this argument, the transfer payments to the EU will have exerted some secondary beneficial consequences that mitigated some of their adverse effects.

To set against this 'silver lining', however, is the fact that the UK's net contributions to the EU are levied in a distortionary fashion – via value added tax. This induces an inevitable secondary burden in various forms: a damaging diversion of spending and production patterns towards less heavily taxed goods and services. and a further wedge driven between workers' and employers' perceptions of the trade-off between leisure and certain products. At their current annual average rate of some £2.2 billion, terminating these transfers would permit a 0.6 per cent cut in the standard rate of VAT, from 17.5 per cent to 16.9 per cent. Equally, recipients of EU transfers could, in principle, use (much of) them to reduce their distortionary taxes, with secondary benefits.

4. The common agricultural policy

This section explores five of the principal consequences of the CAP:

(i) The CAP taxes food for consumers.
This could be justified if the consumption of agricultural products did damage to third parties (an 'externality' argument) or hurt their consumer in some unexpected way (the 'demerit good' argument). Such arguments apply to tobacco and alcohol. The problem is – unless overeating is to be treated as a grave social ill to be discouraged – that they do not extend to food. An alternative argument in favour could be based on income distribution grounds. The problem is – unless you actually wish to aggravate inequality – that food occupies a noticeably larger share of the budgets of poor families than rich ones.

(ii) The CAP increases the rent on land, at the expense of other factors of production.
We might justify this on efficiency considerations – the ground that land is especially elastic in supply, or geographically mobile.

The problem is, the opposite is true. Instead, we could argue that the owners of land are particularly deserving or unfortunate. Leaving aside the fact that EU states have systems of progressive income taxation and transfers to the poorest to alleviate some of the unfairnesses of a market economy, the problem is that land-owners tend to be richer than the average.

(iii) The CAP typically levies tariffs in food imported from the rest of the world.

Two arguments might be offered in support here. One would be that the EU is a large player in international markets, able to cut the world price of food it imports from other areas, and, purely in its own interest, would gain from import tariffs on food. Unfortunately this argument will not work, because the CAP raises EU food prices so much that the EU is generally a net exporter! It might also be argued that making food cheaper in the third world, something the CAP certainly achieves, helps relieve poverty there. The trouble is, most of the third world's poorest are farmers, apt to suffer at least as much as they benefit from lower food prices. Furthermore there are plenty of other, better ways of helping the world's poorest.

(iv) The CAP creates free trade in food within the EU, and prevents national governments from distortionary interference.

This is true. But such benefits as this creates are reduced, and quite likely more than offset, by the fact of distortionary interference by the EU authorities, and the absence of free trade in food between the EU and the rest of the world.

(v) The CAP obtains approximate self-sufficiency in temperate-zone food-stuffs for the EU, and this helps improve the union's external balance of payments.

Again, this is correct. These could be laudable achievements in the exceptional conditions of war. In normal peacetime circum-stances, they are clearly detrimental. In practice, 'improving the balance of payments' means increasing the real exchange rate, and squeezing output, profits and jobs in other traded sectors, including export industries where the EU has a comparative advantage. On self-sufficiency, just one European country adhered to that aim for many decades until 1991: Albania. Furthermore, as Sachs and Warner[7] and Proudman and Redding[8] have convincingly demonstrated, closed economies grew systematically and significantly more slowly than open ones, particularly when initial GDP per head is low.

The CAP has some additional effects, too (which are explored, for example, in Brenton *et al.*[9] and Heffernan and Sinclair[10]). These are also, in the main, adverse. But there are two mitigating factors. One is that Japan and the United States also apply policies of supporting domestic agriculture, which operate in different ways but appear to waste resources on no less a scale. The second is that budgetary and international pressures have been leading recently, and will continue to lead, to reforms in the CAP which should greatly reduce its adverse effects.

5. The growth effects of membership of the EU

This section is devoted to exploring the effects that membership of the European Union appears to have had. We are concerned with the investigation of annual growth rates of OECD countries from 1963 to 1993. In addition to the transfers, the European Union has eliminated internal trade barriers. Some trade is diverted from non-members to partners, with ambiguous and quite likely adverse effects. But trade is created with partners, too, and here the welfare effects will clearly be positive. The total effect on welfare and short-run real income can go either way, but the evidence is that, at least for most EU members, and certainly for their manufacturing sectors, there is net gain.

When it comes to growth, trade liberalisation can be expected to exert a variety of effects. In a traditional model of economic growth, such as Solow's,[11] first, some of the gains to short-run real income – if gains there be – should get invested, and added to the capital stock. This must raise the growth rate (temporarily). Then there are likely changes in the prices of capital goods. If they drop, the boost to growth is reinforced. If the distribution of income shifts in favour of those who save a relatively high share of their incomes, there is a second reinforcing effect on growth. These points give us an overall presumption that trade liberalisations which deliver net benefits in the short run should be favourable for the growth rate, too. But the growth effects, while long-lasting, do not go on for ever in a traditional model. Little by little they fade, and within perhaps a century or so, they are all but gone.

In an endogenous growth model (such as those of Romer[12] or Aghion and Howitt[13]) the growth effects of trade policy changes can last for ever. Technological progress could speed up permanently if inventors' productivity is enhanced by access to foreign knowledge, for example, or the value of the discoveries is raised because new goods created as a result of them are sold in a wider range of markets. But not all trade liberalisations are good for growth: Grossman and Helpman[14] show cases where they are not. And the evidence is not all clear-cut. Levine and Renelt,[15] for instance, find that faster growth is associated with a higher investment share in national income, and also that economies more open to trade tend to invest more, but the direct link between trade and openness is very weak. However, somewhat more encouraging evidence of a generally positive empirical openness-growth link is provided, among others, by Proudman and Redding.[16]

Our econometric inquiry began by regressing OECD countries' annual growth rates of real GDP against country-specific constants and a dummy variable, DE. DE takes a value of one if the country is a member of the EU that year, and zero otherwise. The regression equation is:

$$G_{it} = k_i + aDE + u_{it} \qquad\qquad (A)$$

Here, G_{it} is the growth rate of GDP in country i in year t, k_i the constant specific to country i and u_{it} a residual. The estimated value of a is -0.0138 and its associated t-statistic, -3.47, is highly significant. Taken at face value, this result suggests that EU membership exerts a small but well-determined negative effect on a country's rate of growth. This finding is obtained in a 'WITHIN' fixed effects procedure. The diagnostics for the equation are rather disappointing, however (with a poor fit and a regression standard error of 0.0252, for example).

The regression was repeated with a lagged dependent variable as an additional regressor:

$$G_{it} = k_i + aDE + bG_{it-1} + u_{it} \qquad (B)$$

Some improvement was registered. The standard error for the regression fell to 0.0237. The coefficient b is positive and highly significant (0.352, t ratio 7.4). The estimated value of a is still negative, but smaller (-0.0073) and less significant (t ratio -2.37).

An alternative modification to (A) replaced G_{it-1} by the initial level of GDP per head in US dollars for country i in 1962 (Y_i):

$$G_{it} = k_i + aDE + cY_i + u_{it} \qquad (C)$$

In (C), which was conducted by ordinary least squares (OLS), a was only -0.00398, with a barely significant t ratio of -1.97. The estimated value of c was -0.0104, and strongly significant (t ratio -4.26). The regression standard error was slightly larger than (B), however.

The next step was to regress growth rates on their previous values, the EU membership dummy, and starting level of GDP per head:

$$G_{it} = k_i + aDE + bG_{it-1} + cY_i + u_{it} \qquad (D)$$

Here, both b and c were significant, with estimated values of 0.392 and -0.0062 and t ratios of 8.4 and -2.86 respectively. The coefficient on DE, at -0.002, was now insignificant. The standard error of this regression, 0.0237, was an improvement on all previous regressions. The inference to be drawn from (D) is that EU membership does not exert a significant dampening effect on growth, if the previous year's growth, and country's initial income per head are taken into account.

One matter for concern at this point is that all OECD countries were displaying slower growth after 1973, which was when the EU grew, by stages, from its original six to 12 in 1986 (and

15 in 1995). So could the impression of an adverse growth effect on new members merely reflect worldwide trends occurring then?

A natural way to correct for this possible phenomenon is to introduce time-dummies. So we reran (D) on panel data with a dummy variable for each of the years 1964 onwards, using OLS. The regression was:

$$G_{it} = k_i + aDE + bG_{it-1} + cY_i + X + u_{it} \qquad (E)$$

Here,

$$X = d_{1964}D_{1964} + d_{1965}D_{1965} + d_{1966}D_{1966} \ldots + d_{1993}D_{1993}$$

The time dummies turned out negative, and most were significant. The estimated values of b and c here are 0.28 and -0.0074, with t ratios of 7.11 and -3.89. The regression standard error at 0.0197, and the corrected R_2 at 0.43, indicate substantial improvement in fit. Most interesting of all, the estimated value of a is now *positive*. Although too small to be significant, this suggests that, after allowance for individual year effects, EU membership exerts, if anything, a slight positive impact on growth rates for countries that join it.

Could the growth rate effects of EU membership be *transitional* rather than permanent and could they differ country by country? To explore these possibilities, we conducted the WITHIN fixed effects regression:

$$G_{it} = k_i + a_iT_i + bG_{it-1} + X + u_{it} \qquad (F)$$

Here, T is a dummy variable, which takes a value of unity for each of the six new members for the first full seven years after its accession, and zero otherwise. We chose a period of seven years because this is the period over which tariffs against EU partners are eliminated. The term in the initial level of GDP per head was omitted after it had been found that its significance had dropped. (F) was statistically easily the most successful of our regressions. The regression standard error was 0.0193, and the corrected R^2 climbed to 0.453. The estimated value of b was 0.179, with t ratio 4.28, and many of the year dummies remained significant. The estimated values of the transitional dummies for the six new members were as follows:

Table 4: Values of transitional dummies

Country	Estimated value of transitional dummy	t ratio
Denmark	0.0021	0.262
Great Britain	0.0143	1.780
Greece	-0.0199	-2.623
Ireland	0.0165	2.061
Portugal	0.0056	0.646
Spain	0.0131	1.515

One thing this set of results indicates is that EU accession seems to have had a significantly negative temporary impact on the growth rate of Greece. Under threat of veto, Greece had obtained generous transfers from the EU, which as we saw in section 2, could have triggered repercussions on the part of those supplying labour and capital in that economy; and the very sharp increases in Greek government spending which the EU transfers went some way to financing may well have had growth-impeding consequences as well.

For the other five countries to join the EU after its inception, what temporary growth effects accession brought appear to have been positive. For Denmark and Portugal, the size of the effect was quite insignificant. For Spain, it was approaching significance; for Ireland, it was clearly significant, and for Britain, the temporary boost to growth was significant at the 10 per cent level. In other words, there is a probability of 90 per cent that EU accession raised Britain's growth rate in the following seven years, above what it would have been otherwise.

The conclusion of this section is, therefore, that when allowance is made for the tendency of one year's growth to be affected by special factors affecting all countries that year, and influenced by autoregression (carry-over effects from the previous year's growth), new members of the EU usually benefited from a temporary boost to their growth rate for seven years or so. Greece is the only exception, and special factors appear to have been at work there. Of the five countries to received some fillip to growth, significant or insignificant, Ireland and Britain appear to have gained most. In Britain's case, the size of this gain, compounded over the seven years of transition, and augmented by the removal of autoregression, amounts to about 1.2 per cent of GDP in the long run. It is possible that this is an underestimate, because the growth-enhancing effects of EU accession could well have lingered on after the seven years of transition.

6. Conclusions

As with all institutions, the Communities that have been brought together into the EU have had wide-ranging and complex effects, some undeniably positive and others certainly less so.

Probably the most unfavourable overall effects stem from the CAP, for which no compelling justification can be offered. It reduces aggregate real income and it induces wasteful overproduction of many foodstuffs; it represents a regressive tax that bears most heavily on the poor; and it really only benefits landowners in the long run. For Britain, a crowded island lacking comparative advantage in agricultural products, it is singularly harmful (but would have been far more harmful, were it not for Britain's rebate). The only good news here is that the CAP is not noticeably more damaging than the other systems of agricultural support at work, for example, in the United States and Japan; that the CAP share in EU spending has had a downward trend, and that pressure from the international community should see further reductions in the distortions that the CAP imposes in the years ahead.

Britain is a net contributor to the EU, but on a smaller scale, relative to GDP, than Germany or the Netherlands. The UK's net contribution has yo-yoed year by year, but shown no trend, to date, as a proportion of GDP. The scale of net transfers has been less than it would have been, but for the rebate, and there are grounds for thinking that its impact on output is lower than appears at first glance.

The elimination of trade barriers between Britain and the rest of the EU in the 1970s appears to have delivered a temporary boost to Britain's growth rate, adding perhaps three times as much to national income in the long run as what has been lost through net transfers. Ireland and Spain seem to have experienced similar growth-enhancing effects from EU accession. Our econometric analysis suggests that only Greece suffered in this regard after EU accession, and a likely explanation for this lies in the unwisdom of her macroeconomic policies conducted at that time.

Notes

1 P. Sinclair, 'Optimum Inflation, Taxation and Monetary Arrangements in the Open Economy', in J. Borkatoi and C. Milner (eds), *International Trade and Labour Markets* (Basingstoke: Macmillan, 1997).

2 I. Little and J. Mirrlees, *Project Appraisal and Planning for Developing Countries* (London: Heinemann, 1968).

3 F. Ramsey, 'A Mathematical Model of Saving', *Economic Journal* (1928) pp.543–9.

4 P. Samuelson, 'The Transfer Problem and Transport Costs: the terms of trade when impediments are absent', *Economic Journal* (1952) pp.278–304.

5 R. W. Jones, 'The Transfer Problem Reconsidered', *Economica* (1970) pp.178–93.

6 Samuelson, op.cit.

7 J. Sachs and A. Warner, 'Economic Reform and the Process of Global Integration', *Brookings Papers on Economic Activity* (1995).

8 J. Proudman and S. Redding, *Openness and Growth* (London: Bank of England, 1998).

9 P. Brenton, H. Scott and P. Sinclair, *International Trade* (Oxford: Oxford University Press, 1997).

10 S. Heffernan and P. Sinclair, *Modern International Economics* (Oxford: Blackwell, 1990).

11 R. Solow, 'A Contribution to the Theory of Economic Growth', *Quarterly Journal of Economics* (1956) pp.65–94.
12 P. Romer, 'Endogenous Technological Change', *Journal of Political Economy* (1990) S pp.71–102.
13 P. Aghion and P. Howitt, 'A Model of Growth through Creative Destruction', *Econometrica* (1992) pp.323–51.
14 G. Grossman and E. Helpman, *Innovation and Growth in the Global Economy* (Boston: MIT Press, 1991).
15 R. Levine and D. Renelt, 'A Sensitivity Analysis of Cross-Country Growth Regressions', *American Economic Review* (1992) pp.942–63.
16 Proudman and Redding, op. cit.

The Conservatives and Europe since 1945

N.J. Crowson

In the years following the end of the Second World War, as Britain sought to readjust its world role to a new international climate, the European dimension has taken on ever-greater proportions. For the Conservative Party the European issue has presented a dilemma: on the one hand it has provided timely political opportunities and on the other has been a matter capable of inflicting seismic damage to unity, leaders and policy. At best it could be argued that party policy towards Europe has been schizophrenic. As victor in eight of the 14 general elections since 1945 the Conservative Party has been faced with a series of critical decisions regarding Britain's European role: from Churchill's Zurich speech, through Macmillan's first application for EC membership, to Heath's final admission in 1973 and endorsement in the 1975 referendum, through Thatcher's signature of the Single European Act and Major's opt-outs at Maastricht to Hague's denial of the viability of a single currency. The purpose of this chapter is to present an overview of the Conservative Party's vision of Europe during the past 50 years. As a consequence it is evident that there are clearly identifiable themes throughout this period with regard to foreign and economic policy, sovereignty, agriculture and intra-party dispute. As a result this chapter will divide into three sections. Part one will examine Conservative visions of Britain's world role; part two will explore attitudes to economic and political union; and part three will consider the impact of Europe on intra-party politics. Academic analysis of the Conservatives and Europe has been approached from two perspectives. Firstly, using the European issue to discern Conservative governments' views of Britain's world role and the actual mechanics of attempts to join the EEC. Secondly, using Europe as a means of examining the politics of the party, such as the mechanics for policy making, rebellion and control to list a few examples.[1] This chapter is intended as a wider examination of the party from those in the parliamentary party through to the activists in the constituencies.

Europe has proved one of the most contentious, and persistent, issues for the Conservative Party since 1945. Using 1945 as a starting point is rather arbitrary and has been chosen because it represents a convenient chronological point with the ending of the Second World War. Clearly the post-war European order was being debated from the outbreak of war in 1939, while notions of European unity had been discussed during the inter-war years and have a lineage that can be taken back even further. Britain's relationship and cooperation with the Continent since 1945 has arisen in direct correlation to her diminishing world power status and the break-up of the Empire. For the party this has proved a conundrum. Should Britain have sought to foster improved political and economic relations with the Common-wealth? Should she seek to optimise the 'special relationship' with America? Or should Britain wholeheartedly embrace the European movement? These have been, and continue to be, central questions for the Conservative Party.

Visions of Britain's world role

Historians will commit a cardinal error if they examine Conserv-ative attitudes to Europe from a purely European perspective. Throughout the discussions Coanservatives have perceived the viability of participating in Europe in the wider context of the impact this would have upon Britain's world role. Of course circumstances have altered drastically since 1945. When Churchill led the party he still viewed Britain in terms of being one of the Big Three; by the time Thatcher took office Britain had been relegated to the sidelines. Nevertheless with both leaders the response they adopted towards Europe was moti-vated by the desire to maintain and improve Britain's world standing. For Thatcher that meant seeking to revive the special relationship with the United States. However, it was on terms whereby Britain was very much the junior partner and for her last summit with Bush it was apparent that the Americans now gave Germany greater priority. Throughout the post-war years Britain has sought to balance the demands of Europe, the Empire and Commonwealth and America.

Addressing the 1948 Llandudno party conference Churchill spoke of three circles: the Commonwealth, Europe and the English-speaking nations (Churchill-speak for America). He argued that Britain was the common denominator between the circles and this provided Britain with a unique opportunity to forge a role for herself. Although one recent analysis of contemporary Conservative attitudes rejected this as a valid model this denial has been based upon a fundamental failure to contextualise the model.[2] If the evolution of Conservative attitudes over the past 50 years is examined it is evident these three circles have provided the basic premise for most interpretations of the role Britain must adopt. The circles and their inter-relationships are dynamic. Over time the relative importance of each fluctuates. Individual Conservatives may lay greater emphasis upon the significance of Britain's relationship with one or other of the circles. Since the mid-1970s the relevance of the Commonwealth may have appeared to wane, yet Major still felt it necessary in his 1994 Leiden speech to refer to the importance of Britain's relationship with her Commonwealth in making Britain a power of importance. At the same time he urged a more flexible European Union. As will become apparent in the course of this chapter the Churchillian circles model is a useful, if somewhat crude, means of broadly defining Conservative attitudes during the last half century.

Economic and political union

In the political arena perceptions can be more significant than substance. This is especially true of the European debate. Europe is all about myths for Conservatives. One of the earliest was the idea that Churchill was a Euro-enthusiast. As a successful war leader Churchill retained his reputation for being an international statesman of significance despite being relegated to leader of the opposition from June 1945. Having no wish to retire from the international limelight Churchill made a number of significant speeches in the immediate post-war years. From his 1946 Zurich and Fulton speeches and because of his support for the Council of Europe and advocacy of a European army came the belief that should a Churchill-led Conservative administration return to office it would take an active role in European affairs. The 1951–2 administration quashed that belief.[3] What is clear for the period to 1951 is that the Conservative leadership advocated the European ideal based upon a dual rationale. Firstly it was a suitable tactic with which to attack and criticise the Labour Party; secondly, a united western Europe would provide a buttress against communism. The electoral tool of advocating a pro-European stance was evident in 1962 following Hugh Gaitskell's declared opposition to the EC and again in the early 1980s, as the Conservatives were able to look on gleefully as the Labour Party fractured over its stance on continued EC membership. Perhaps in defence of Churchill a word of caution should be sounded. This regards hindsight. It must be remembered that when Churchill spoke of a united Europe the contemporary understanding of words like 'united' and 'federation' was much less specific and more generalised than the connotations these words would have in the 1990s.[4]

Churchill did leave one important legacy. His involvement in the creation in 1949 of the Council of Europe introduced a whole generation of Conservatives to the concept of closer European cooperation. The Council became a form of adult education for a whole generation of young parliamentarians. Many, such as Duncan Sandys and Peter Thorneycroft, who had seen service as 'Tory Strasbourgers', were to become involved in later British attempts to join the EEC. However, this phenomenon was not restricted to parliamentarians; party activists were able to join delegations sent to attend European conferences. The rationale of party managers was simple: it enabled members to make contacts and observe leading European figures first hand. The political benefits where illustrated, as one internal party document noted, when

> the Council, partly because of British Conservative tenacity, had shown a resilience which promised better things for the pan-European ideal, and encouraged our own members in their enthusiastic but realistic interest.[5]

Yet in real terms the value the party placed upon this approach was indicated by its allocation of a mere £750 for the budgetary year 1954–5 which was hardly 'an excessive amount for a great imperial party to spend on its external relations' especially when compared with Labour's £10,500 for 1952 and £4,600 for 1953.[6]

The division of opinion between the three circles was clearly evident during Churchill's leadership. The Empire lobby remained a core element of the party. Herbert Williams, Member for Exeter, denounced his leadership's supposed pro-European stance in 1948. He likened it to a Colorado beetle that would undermine Britain's future trade. His answer was imperial preference.[7] As Empire transformed into Commonwealth the ideas for preference did not disappear.[8] Proponents, who included the likes of Neil Marten, Derek Walker-Smith, Robin Turton and Harmar Nicholls, sought to explore the possibility for evolving some form of North Atlantic free-trade area – this would involve some or all of the EFTA nations, the former Dominions (Australia, Canada, New Zealand, South Africa), the USA and perhaps Japan.[9] Even into the 1970s some of the Conservative anti-Marketeers continued opposing EC membership upon the grounds that it would discriminate against Commonwealth and Dominion markets.

The emphasis of research on the Conservatives and Europe has naturally been towards the period the party was in office. It has been suggested that the significance of Europe declined whilst the party was in opposition.[10] Yet periods in opposition are formative times as a party seeks to evolve in order to regain the electorate's confidence. When an overview of the 1960s is made it is clear that the public disputes characterised by the formation of the Anti-Common Market League (1961) and the set-piece debates of conference in 1961–2 and the general bickering of 1962, receded once in opposition from 1964. But behind the scenes the European debate was far from dead. The anticipated veto of de Gaulle for Labour's EC application spurred the party into action. The period 1967–70 was clearly a fertile time in terms of evolution of attitudes: the Conservative Research Department convened a policy research committee in late 1967 to enable the exchange of ideas 'in order to study the various possible relationships open to Britain while full membership of the EC remains denied to us'. This Committee on Europe comprised both pro- and sceptical Conservatives. Its initial brief was to consider three aspects:

- The feasibility of a North Atlantic Free Trade Area;
- Britain's association with the EC (understood in the broadest sense to mean any possible relationship with the Community other than early full membership);
- Any other relationships worth considering (either European or non-European).[11]

This was not the only committee examining these areas: the Commonwealth and Europe group chaired by William Gorell-Barnes was also at work, having first met in May 1966. Its remit was 'a study of the question of whether or not association with the EC was a possible alternative, if full membership were refused.'[12] Significantly the influence of these committees was restricted by the agreement:

> that it was not for it to question the party's continuing commitment to Europe. This was and would remain official party policy and the majority of the Committee supported this unhesitatingly. If ever this policy were to be questioned, it could only be done in the full foreign affairs committee.[13]

Papers presented to the Committee on Europe had titles ranging from 'Next step after the veto' by Jock Bruce-Gardyne; 'The New Zealand economy and the Common Market' by Tufton Beamish; 'Other ways into Europe' and 'Other relationships' by Gordon Pears; and a paper by Nicholas Ridley outlining tactics for achieving the objective of EC membership. Indeed the motivation behind these committees, at least from the perspective of the party leadership, was to help facilitate British admission to the EC at the earliest date possible. Some pro-European Conservatives were worried that elements 'want to re-open the whole question of whether we should join the Community.'[14] At the same time other Conservatives sought to marry the conflicting interpretations by floating the 'vision' of a European community that included some African nations as 'associate members' along with the Mediterranean nations, Spain, Portugal, Greece, Turkey and Cyprus.[15] Evidently Conservative preference for the concept of widening not deepening the Community has a historical pedigree. The Committee on Europe illustrates a significant feature; namely the relative cooperation between the pro- and anti-Europe factions of the party during the late 1960s and early 1970s.[16] This juxtaposes with the situation during the Major years where the debate was far more polarised and the Eurosceptics perceived as beyond the pale.

However, while parliamentarians were actually benefiting from debate and discussion before Britain's admission to the EC in 1973, many party activists felt isolated and ill-informed.[17] It was not a new problem. It had been a complaint from the time of Macmillan's first entry application. Chelmsford Association's chairman expressed in June 1961 'general concern' and observed 'that the facts were wanted and that so far none had been published.'[18] The National Union general purposes committee observed in May 1962 the general bafflement over EC entry in the constituencies.[19] The following year the party chairman urged that the 'latent xenophobia and jingoism' amongst the party 'should be firmly discouraged.'[20] Part of the problem rested with the inability of activists to accept that Britain's 'world power' status was declining, and clearly many envisaged Britain in terms of Churchill's three circles.[21] The sceptical tendency of the activist has been prominent in terms of the resolutions forwarded to conference. For example, of the 43 motions received on the EC in 1961, only five voiced outright support. A recent survey of conference motions between 1992 and 1995

points to a resurgence of Eurosceptical motions.[22] As if to vali-
date this analysis when the whip was withdrawn from the nine
Maastricht rebels polls suggested that they had the support of the
Conservative electorate.[23] Whilst this loyalty may be explained
on grounds of incumbency it is clear that those constituencies
that have been represented by an anti-Marketeer MP at one time
or another, such as Sir Henry Legge-Bourke (Isle of Ely), Neil
Marten (Banbury), Simon Digby (West Dorset) or Ronald Bell
(South Buckinghamshire), have clearly discussed the matter with
greater frequency, become aware of the issues and in some
instances have been indoctrinated with the sceptical argument.[24]

Concerns about the implications for fishing and agriculture
have been apparent from the beginning of suggestions about
economic union. In 1948 the party chairman, Lord Woolton,
warned Churchill that Conservatives were

> disturbed in their minds as to whether a customs union would
> imperil our ability to protect our industries and agriculture
> from undue competition from European sources.[25]

In Essex, one constituency agent reported the 'concern amongst
agriculturists and particularly horticulturists in the constituency'
to rumours that Britain would apply for membership of the
EC.[26] One of those Conservatives initially opposed to joining
Europe and favourable to imperial preference was Legge-
Bourke. In part his initial opposition arose from a fear that the
agricultural policies of the Six would ruin his Ely constituency
with its reliance on horticulture and agriculture.[27] Rab Butler's
initial opposition in 1961 was based upon his concerns that entry
was not compatible with the needs of Britain's farmers. Butler
represented the rural constituency of Saffron Walden, and he
only changed his mind after a national speaking tour during 1962
convinced him that the farming fraternity was not as hostile as he
had been led to believe. Indeed when de Gaulle vetoed Britain's
first application the parliamentary group on the Common
Market, chaired by Bill Deedes, was quick to point out that

> a large number of intelligent farmers were very disappointed by
> our exclusion from the Common Market and were not in

agreement with the attitude taken by the National Farmer's Union. This was an asset which must not be wasted.[28]

However, the doubts about the disadvantages of membership of the Community for agriculture and fishing have never been fully dispelled for Conservatives. When Thatcher became Prime Minister in 1979 one of her opening objectives was to renegotiate the UK contribution to the EC budget. Generally her successful, if protracted, campaign to reform the CAP received widespread support.[29] More recently there has been the vocal opposition of the Eurosceptic elements of the parliamentary party to the issue of fish quotas, whilst the BSE scare and subsequent European ban on British beef did little to endear the European Commission to the rural Conservative activist.

The sovereignty aspect of closer British cooperation in Europe has always been a concern to Conservatives. It was an issue that was widely debated and understood. This dispels a myth that the Eurosceptics of the 1990s successfully perpetrated. It has been one of their core arguments that the British people were denied the opportunity in 1975 to consider the sovereignty issue and that more generally successive British governments have hidden the loss of sovereignty implicit in closer European cooperation. Yet it is clear that from the time of NATO's formation in 1949 it was agreed that this supra-national organisation had usurped British sovereignty, whilst dependence upon American nuclear technology hardly helped matters. In 1960 Winchester local Conservatives heard one member of the Bow Group favourable to joining the EC declare 'our sovereignty has gone ... and it does us no good to hang on to the trappings of sovereignty.'[30] Whilst another European advocate, Irene Ward MP told an audience at Whitely Bay in 1962:

> If we went into Europe, our sovereign rights would not be altered ... a certain amount of our right to make our own decisions was destroyed when we joined the United Nations. We shall have first class representation on any controlling body in Europe – we run no greater risk than we do at present.'[31]

During the 1975 referendum campaign literature from the 'Yes to Europe' Conservative Campaign sent to the constituencies specifically sought to answer the sovereignty issue.[32] In recent years the extension of qualified majority voting, the single currency debate and a central European bank, and concerns about the possibility of a Maastricht treaty version II have kept Conservative fears about sovereignty alive. A survey of party activists in 1992 found 68 per cent of the sample agreeing that sovereignty was being lost to Europe. Yet a contradiction arose with 67 per cent agreeing that Britain should remain within the European exchange rate mechanism. This aspect of the loss of sovereignty clearly not being opposed by the majority![33]

The debates about economic and political union in recent years have produced an unusual phenomenon. The work of Baker, Gamble and Ludlam has identified two axes that split across the traditional left/right Conservative divisions. The first axis is sovereignty/interdependence, which is the division between Britain's place in the world and the nature and extent of European integration. The second axis is extended government/ limited government, which covers the range of opinions from those who favour interventionist government through to advocates of a de-regulated free market economy.[34] The Maastricht rebels clearly lacked ideological cohesion. For example, Teddy Taylor rejected European interference in favour of economic independence; Bill Cash was opposed on constitutional grounds arguing that it would lead to a loss of sovereignty from Westminster; whilst others, like Nick Budgen, as neo-liberal Thatcherites foresaw problems with the potential loss of independent monetary policy making.[35]

Intra-party unity

For the Conservatives the European issue resembles a tornado danger zone. The ability of a twister to suddenly emerge and leave a trail of destruction is a hazard of the political terrain. The European issue has played a role in the downfall of Macmillan,

Heath and Thatcher caused considerable problems for Major and has hampered Hague. Many of the senior ministerial resignations of the last period of Conservative government have been over matters European: Michael Heseltine (1986), Nigel Lawson (1989), Nicholas Ridley (1990), Geoffrey Howe (1990), and Derek Heathcoat-Amory (1996). Since assuming the leadership in 1997 Hague has lost two shadow ministers (Ian Taylor and David Curry) on Europe, while the issue has caused the defection of Kidderminster's MP, Peter Temple Morris, to Labour in November 1997 and East Midlands MEP Bill Newton Dunn to the Liberal Democrats in November 2000. That Europe is a contentious issue for the party is not in doubt. The ratification of the Maastricht treaty illustrated the deep passions liable to be aroused. It had been demonstrated in 1971 when 39 Conservative MPs rebelled against Heath on the vote as to whether to accept the principle of joining the EC – and throughout the ratification process when the government's majorities were regularly reduced to three or four. The potential divisions had been revealed as early as 1950 when Enoch Powell and Legge-Bourke, amongst others, disregarded the party whip over the Schuman Plan parliamentary vote.

The division of opinion in the party has been evident on a number of levels: the use of early day motions (EDMs); parliamentary questions; cross-voting or abstentions in divisions; and through the activities of single-issue groups with their associated publications or media exposure. Since the Anti-Common Market League formed in 1961 Conservative MPs have been involved in at least 80 ginger groups on Europe.[36] Names such as the Bruges Group; No Turning Back; European Foundation; European Research Group; Positive Europeans; 92 Group; Fresh Starters; the Conservative Group for Europe and the European Movement are familiar to the corridors and smoking rooms of Westminster. In recent years the Eurosceptical groups have succeeded the best in getting their message across to the media. Indeed media exposure (or lack of) was one of the main lessons the 'No' campaign drew in its post-mortem of the 1975 European referendum campaign. In defeat the 'No' campaigners saw themselves as latter day anti-appeasers battling against the misguided majority: 'the men of Munich are now dishonoured, and Winston Churchill – the outstanding leader of the minority at that time – has been abundantly vindicated.'[37] During Major's reign the sceptics succeeded in creating political mayhem for the party leadership. There was Lord Tebbit's anti-Maastricht conference speech, 6 October 1992, which received a standing ovation from some sections of the audience, and added petrol to the volatile ratification process of the Treaty through the House of Commons. Kenneth Baker's 1995 EDM attacking the single currency secured 107 signatures. At the same time activities were conducted in less public arenas. This was illustrated with the 1995 challenge to Sir Marcus Fox remaining as chairman of the 1922 committee that was launched because of his pro-Major stance. Fox had angered sceptics by acting as a conduit for Major's threats of electoral disaster should he lose the November 1994 vote on the Community budget increases, which Major felt obliged to make a vote of confidence. Major's eventual public response to these repeated challenges was to withdraw the whip from eight rebel MPs (Sir Richard Body resigned the whip in solidarity) on 28 November 1994; yet this merely provided a focus for the Eurosceptic tendency and eventually Major was obliged humiliatingly to reinstate the whip on 24 April 1995.[38]

The pro-European elements of the party, via the Conservative Group for Europe and the Positive European group, sought only to counter the Maastricht rebels by parliamentary actions.[39] They failed to organise a public equivalent to the Maastricht Referendum Campaign, launched on 5 July 1992. Only belatedly in 1994 did leading pro-Europeanists (Lords Whitelaw and Howe, Kenneth Clarke and David Hunt) help create the Action Centre for Europe (ACE). The media fight-back by the Europeanists was restricted to a series of letters to *The Independent* signed by senior party figures, such as Edward Heath, Geoffrey Howe, Douglas Hurd and William Whitelaw.[40] In their first letter the authors sought to sound a clarion call for Britain to return to the

Churchillian vision of a positive, internationalist Europe. For them 'the tragedy of Churchill's Zurich speech was that, for too long, it did not inform Britain's post-war policy. We have sought to distance ourselves from Europe rather than decisively to shape it ... We have been working to catch up ever since.'[41] The rationale for choosing *The Independent*, which at a glance hardly appears natural Conservative territory, is unclear. Perhaps the answer rests in the desire to take the debate to a wider non-Conservative audience, and the sympathetic editorship of Andrew Marr. At the same time *The Daily Telegraph* had excluded itself for its constant vilification of Major's leadership and predominance of Eurosceptical views. For some pro-Europe sections of the party the position was intolerable, and in the case of Emma Nicholson it led her to defect, on 29 December 1995, to the Liberal Democrats, specifically citing the anti-European stance of the party leadership.

One historian has suggested expectations of unity mean that a minor policy debate amongst Conservatives generates as much media scrutiny as a major row in the Labour Party.[42] Yet the European issue, particularly since the passage of the Maastricht bill, has proved itself to be a major policy row. Several explanations can be offered for the importance of the Europe debate. Firstly it questions Britain's role in the world economy. This has historical antecedents for the party. The split over Corn Law repeal (1846) and later Tariff Reform (1906) highlight the potency, and dangers, of such debates for the party. Secondly, the very idea of European integration challenges traditional Conservative assumptions about sovereignty. The party has consistently presented itself as the party of the Union, the constitution and the Empire. Thirdly, the economics involved question ideological assumptions about economic intervention and monetary policies.[43] Both the later points cross-cut the traditional left-right divisions in the party. Anti-marketeers tend to be located on the right of the party and federalists on the left. The current debate about a single currency has split the previously united Thatcherite free-market grouping. Consequently those who supported EC membership and the Single European Act but are opposed to European monetary union on the grounds that it challenges nationhood and independence, such as Thatcher, Lord Tebbit and Lord Parkinson have found themselves opposed by former Thatcherite allies who see the EMU as an opportunity to enhance the free market. To these Conservatives, such as Ken Clarke, Geoffrey Howe, Leon Brittan and Tim Renton, further integration is the necessary response to the interdependence of the European economies.[44] This makes talk of an irrevocable party split premature. Major's government did not witness a growth in more widespread factionalism over non-European issues by a disgruntled right. The rebellions over VAT on fuel and the pit closure programme appealed more to the left and the involvement of the Euro-rebels was only marginal. It was clear that as soon as the debate returned to domestic issues the usual left/right or wet/dry divisions emerged. At the same time, given the narrowness of Major's majority the Euro-rebels were faced with a problem that if they ousted Major's government it would probably result in a Labour government pledged to even more support for Europe.

The European issue also offers a perspective on the MP/constituency activist relationship. The deselection of George Gardiner by his Reigate Association directly arose over his criticism of Major's European policy. Gardiner then committed the ultimate sacrilege by defecting to Goldsmith's Referendum Party on 8 March 1997 and unsuccessfully contesting the seat in the May 1997 general election against the official Conservative candidate.[45] Although generally the Maastricht rebels, and especially the whipless MPs of 1994–5, kept the support of their local associations, it became clear in the aftermath of Major's successful defence of his leadership in June 1995 that activists, no doubt conscious of the imminence of a general election, had come to expect greater displays of loyalty.[46] At the same time the apparent scepticism of many at the grassroots appeared to continue. A poll by *The Sunday Times* of 100 constituency chairpersons in the run-up to the 1997 election found that when asked to name one action Major could take to help win the election, 12 suggested 'say no' to a single currency and a further eight felt more clarity or a referendum on Europe would improve matters.[47] The experiences of Gardiner in Reigate were nothing new; in previous decades anti-Market MPs have experienced problems with their local associations, as Marten found in 1971–3 with Banbury, but none were actually deselected. Deselection is normally an option of last resort, and one that more often than not results as much from personality problems as political disputes. The latter usually provides the rationale, and cover, for the deselection. These MP/association spats also raise questions about MPs' accountability to their association and their freedom of action. These issues have been rumbling on behind the scenes for most of the century. Since the local associations retain the right of selection, many activists expect their candidate to be answerable to their views, at times in preference to the wider collective view of the party.[48]

The future?

A return to opposition for the Conservatives in May 1997 and the election of a new leader, William Hague, provided an opportunity for the party to reflect upon its European policy. This has resulted with an increasingly Eurosceptic stance. The luxury of opposition has provided opportunities to harass the Labour government and has meant that the Conservatives do not have to make the decision about joining the single currency. Given the diversity of opinion and animosity the issue raises for Conservatives this is perhaps a stroke of fortune. In fact Europe is once more being used as an electoral tool with Hague's decision to rule out Britain joining the single currency for ten years resting upon a deliberate desire to create 'clear blue water' between Labour and the Conservatives. Hague quickly sought his party's endorsement of this stance with a referendum in September 1998.[49]

Nevertheless European tensions clearly remain in the party. The leader of the Conservative MEPs expressed concerns in the autumn of 1997 that former members of the Referendum Party were infiltrating the party's activist base. A breakaway pro-European Conservative Party unsuccessfully contested the 1999 European elections and resulted in the expulsions of former MPs, Julian Critchley and Tim Rathbone. Pro-Europeans have appeared on the same platform as Labour ministers for the re-launch of the 'Britain in Europe' campaign. Meanwhile pro-European MPs, such as Ian Taylor, have been threatened with deselection by their constituency associations, unsuccessfully in his case. In February 2000 Hague began his 'Keep the Pound' campaign with a nationwide tour speaking from the back of a truck. The fragility of the situation was clearly illustrated by the row in November 2000 over the Blair government's plans to commit British troops to Europe's Rapid Reaction Force: plans that were condemned roundly by the Conservative leadership but which provoked counter-attacks from pro-Europeans like Howe and Hurd. The current leadership appears confident that a sceptical European stance will prove the Conservative electoral trump card at the next election. This still remains a risky strategy when it is clear that the electorate is less concerned about the European debate than the level of taxation and state of the NHS and the party's ability to deliver in these areas.[50] Time will only reveal whether Hague succeeds where Major failed and tames the European twister.

Notes

The author wishes to acknowledge the financial support of the Nuffield Foundation, which facilitated the research at a constituency level for this ongoing project.

1   For example: W. Kaiser, *Using Europe and Abusing the Europeans* (Basingstoke: Macmillan, 1996); S. George and M. Sowemino, 'Conservative foreign policy towards the European Union' in S. Ludlam, M.J. Smith (eds), *Contemporary British Conservatism* (Basingstoke: Macmillan, 1996) pp.244–63, M. Camps, *Britain and the European Community* (Oxford: Oxford University Press, 1964); J. Young, *Britain and European Unity* (Basingstoke: Macmillan, 1993);

D. Dutton, 'Anticipating Maastricht: The Conservative Party and Britain's First Application to join the European Community', *Contemporary Record*, Vol.7 no.3 (1993) pp.522–40, S. Onslow, *Backbench Debate within the Conservative Party and its influence on British Foreign Policy, 1948–57* (Basingstoke: Macmillan, 1997); S. Ludlam 'The spectre haunting Conservatism: Europe and backbench rebellion' in S. Ludlam and M.J. Smith (eds), *Contemporary British Conservatism*, pp.98–120, D. Baker, A. Gamble and S. Ludlam, 'The Parliamentary siege of Maastricht 1993', *Parliamentary Affairs*, Vol.47, no.1 (1994) pp.37–60; D. Baker, I. Fountain, A. Gamble and S. Ludlam, 'Conservative Backbencher Attitudes to European Integration', *Political Quarterly*, Vol.66, no.2 (1995).

2   M. Sowemimo, 'The Conservative Party and European Integration', *Party Politics*, Vol.2, no.1 (1996). pp.77–97.

3   J. Young, 'Churchill's "No" to Europe', *Historical Journal*, Vol.28, no.4 (1985) pp.923–37; Onslow, *Backbench Debate*, pp.33–54, 78–106.

4   For a 1990s Eurosceptic view on these words see M. Spicer, *A Treaty Too Far* (London: Fourth Estate/Guardian Books, 1992).

5   C[onservative] P[arty] A[rchive]: Conservative Overseas Bureau '2nd Strasbourg study-visit, 20–27 September 1953, Group Report' CC04/5/328, Bodleian Library.

6   CPA: General Director to Chairman, Conservative Central Office, 19 January 1955 memo 'External Relations' CCO4/6/364. Woolton minuted this 'I agree'.

7   J. Ramsden, *Age of Churchill and Eden* (London: Longman, 1995) p. 196.

8   P. Murphy, *Party Politics and Decolonisation* (Oxford: Clarendon Press, 1995).

9   Marten Mss: files relating to ACML and Committee on Europe, MS.Eng.hist.c.1130, Bodleian Library.

10 N. Ashford, 'EEC' in Zig Layton-Henry (ed.) *Conservative Party Politics* (Basingstoke: Macmillan, 1980) p. 103.

11 Marten Mss: Richard Wood to Marten, 12 December 1967, MS.Eng.hist.c.1137, ff. 94–5.

12 CPA: Gorell-Barnes to Michael Fraser, 14 December 1967, CRD3/10/9.

13 Marten Mss: memo. 8 March 1968: report of 7 February 1968 meeting of Committee on Europe.

14 CPA: Gordon Pears to Brian Reading, 1 March 1968, CRD3/7/8/1.

15 *Hampshire Chronicle,* 18 June 1971, James Spicer.

16 Marten Mss: Derek Walker-Smith to Tufton Beamish, 18 March 1971.

17 From November 1962 Conservative MPs were receiving advice on relevant literature on Europe as well as a weekly briefing on the Common Market courtesy of the Conservative Research Department: CPA: Common Market Topics, 7 November 1962, CRD2/42/8.

18 Chelmsford CA: finance and general purposes committee, 23 June 1961, D/Z96/11, Essex Records Office.

19 CPA: general purposes committee minutes 3 May 1962, NUA5/2/1.

20 CPA: Macleod to Macmillan, 25 January 1963, CCO20/8/6.

21 CPA: Micro Fiche Archive, annual conference 1949, resolution on European unity, card 80.

22 Martin Ball, *The Conservative Conference and Euro-sceptical Motions, 1992–5,* Bruges Group Occasional Paper, No 23.

23 *Mail on Sunday,* 8 January 1995.

24 Legge Bourke Mss: HL-B to J.E. Dagless, 19 July 1971, MS.742/ 859, Brotherton Library, Leeds University; Marten Mss: Marten to President of Banbury CA, 12 December 1973, MS.Eng.hist.c.1134 ff. 209–213; South Bucks CA, executive 19 July 1971, Finance and General purposes committee, 16 June 1975, D1631/2 and D163/ 2/3/1, Buckinghamshire Records Office.

25 Woolton Mss: Woolton to Churchill, n.d. [July 1948], box 21, Bodleian Library.

26 Chelmsford CA: finance and general purposes committee, 23 June 1961, D/Z96/11.

27 Bourke Mss: H L-B to editor, *The Times,* 22 September 1956.

28 CPA: Parliamentary Group on the Common Market, minutes 4 February 1963, CRD2/48/8. Some useful work has been done on the influence of the farming lobby in the party during the inter-war years but it is an area that needs further examination for the European issue.

29 J. Peterson, 'The European Community' in P. Marsh and R. Rhodes (eds), *Implementing Thatcherite Policies* (Milton Keynes: Open University Press, 1992) p. 162.

30 Winchester CA: press cuttings, 12 November 1960, *Hampshire Chronicle*, 73M86W/41, Hampshire Records Office.

31 Tynemouth CA: cutting from *Newcastle Weekly News*, 26 January 1962, 1633/17/5, Tyne and Wear Archive.

32 See *Yes to Europe: Conservative Campaign Notes*, No 1 19 May 1975 filed with Newcastle West CA 1579/42.

33 P. Whiteley et al., *True Blues: The Politics of Conservative Party Membership* (Oxford: Oxford University Press, 1994) p.57.

34 D. Baker, A. Gamble and S. Ludlam, '1846, 1906, 1996? Conservative splits and European Integration', *Political Quarterly* 64 (1993) pp.420–34.

35 See Spicer, *Treaty*; T. Gorman, *The Bastards: Dirty Tricks and the Challenge to Europe* (London: Pan, 1993).

36 Ludlam 'The spectre haunting Conservatism' in Ludlam and Smith (eds), *Contemporary British Conservatism*, op.cit., p.100.

37 Marten Mss: Sir Cyril Black to Neil Marten, 13 June 1975, MS.Eng.hist.c.1132 ff 134–5.

38 The whipless nine launched their own manifesto in March 1995 and drew support from Tebbit in an interview in the *Daily Telegraph*, 27 November 1994. For Major's perspective see A. Seldon *Major: A Political Life* (London: Harper Collins, 1997) pp.511–12, 520, 544–5.

39 By the end of 1996 the Positive European Group was claiming a membership of 84 MPs.

40 *The Independent*, 19 Sept 1996, 5 Jan 1998. Letters to editor.

41 *The Independent*, 19 Sept 1996.

42 J. Ramsden, *Making of Conservative Party Policy* (London: Longmans, 1980) p.3.

43 This is examined in greater detail by Baker, Gamble and Ludlam, '1846, 1906, 1996?'.

44 Sowemimo, 'The Conservative Party', pp.83–87.

45 Filed amongst the Marten Mss is a letter Gardiner wrote to Neil Marten 3 March 1975 in his capacity as editor, *Monthly News*: 'the function of *Monthly News* is to present and argue in support of the Party's official policies. [...] I'm sure you will understand, therefore, that it is not possible for us to carry a contribution from a distinguished anti-Marketeer such as yourself when the paper's task is to argue in support of our Party's official pro-Market commitment.' MS.Eng.hist.c.1141 f. 313.

46 For example see, *The Times,* 10 March 1996.

47 *The Sunday Times,* 16 March 1997.

48 For example South Buckinghamshire CA: AGM agenda 26 March
     1956, D163/1/3; Finance and General Purposes Committee 16
     June 1975, D163/2/3/1.

49 The result announced on 5 October 1998 was 84.4% Yes to
     Hague's policy of ruling out the single currency until at least the
     end of the next Parliament; 15.9% No.

50 *Daily Telegraph*, 2 October 2000 reporting on monthly Gallup poll
     for the paper.

A Problem of Synchroneity:
The Labour Party, European Integration and the Search for Modernisation

Brian Brivati

The metaphor that is usually deployed with respect to the relationship between Britain and the process of European integration is that of missing things. Boats, trains and buses have all at various times been used. But as Miriam Camps has put it: 'No boats were missed Messina, that is at the meeting held there in early June 1955. There was no reason for the British to have gone.'[1] Like Dean Acheson's famous, 'Britain has not yet found a role', when the problem was Britain had not yet shed a sufficient number of its existing roles, the problem, according to Camps, is that Britain was not trying to catch something so could not have missed it. This presupposes that what was leaving the port of Messina was not something constructed out of the political choices which faced the nations of Europe in the aftermath of the Second World War. The rise and fall of the Great Powers was superseded at Messina by the unity of some of those powers in a number of ways that produced the embryo of a new era. Therefore, Britain was faced with a fairly straightforward policy choice: belong to this process or do not belong. Given subsequent events, in terms of both the development of the European Economic Community and the history of the cold war, and the subsequent evolution of a more regional and global economy, can we still fail to see Messina in such a light? The talks were a tentative, and by no means inevitable, groping towards a new relationship between individual nation states and each other, and between groups of nation states and the rest of the world.

If this is the case, then Britain was much more than absent from Messina, Britain was out of sync with the direction of history. And, if we accept the admittedly rather grand claims for Messina, then what does the British labour movement's failure to grasp the opportunity of European unity from the earlier moves in the 1940s to the later period of the 1970s and 1980s mean? Should it be understood as a problem of discourse, of language, that was simply not understood to be inclusive or the same language that others were speaking. Did the labour movement suffer from a sort of collective dose of 'do they mean us?'

Before attempting an answer to this question the relationship between the first and last elements in the title of this essay needs some explanation. The problem of synchroneity is stated quite simply: historical actors do not always do what is in their own interests. Sometimes historical actors simply misunderstand the nature of the times they are living in, their self perceptions and what, with the benefit of hindsight, we might call their long-term objective interests, becomes out of sync. Historians, however, tend to prefer explanations of choices that reflect the fulfilment of self-interest. In the case of the Labour Party and Europe, explanations for the party's resistance to supporting the forms of European integration adopted at Messina concentrate on the extent to which these forms were against the party's interests, when there is a strong case to be made that this was not so and that the problem was one of synchroneity rather than incompatibility.

The search for 'modernisation' is rather more difficult to pin down. Labour came out of the Second World War with considerable ideological confidence. The success of the 1945–51 government used up much of this feeling and after 1951 there was a search for a new direction. This can be characterised as the search for a model for the future. Only a small group of Labour MPs adopted integration with western Europe as that model. Initially including members on both the left and the right, this faith in European integration gradually migrated from the internationalist sections to some of the revisionists. The politics of personality and factionalism came to provide much more of the explanation for Labour's European policy than objective judgements of interests. But the anti-Europeans cannot merely be dismissed as factionalists. The attempt to put flesh on alternative economic and social policies was not only about opposing the dominant ideas of the 1950s and early 1960s, it was also about profound misgivings about the nature of the European project. Here again, though there is insufficient space to unpack these ideas fully, a misunderstanding of the nature of the Community and its objectives in the mid-1960s to mid-1970s, most importantly a failure to understand the dynamic rather than passive ideological basis of the Community, seems to explain the anti-Marketeers' position better than the conventional and contemporary accounts. Finally, there was something much bigger than the Labour MPs themselves at work: British political culture. A culture that is usually portrayed as being sterile and declining, but was, for much of this period, a dynamic force which instilled a well developed sense of exceptionalism in the British political class.[2]

To explore these themes, I will first survey the history of Labour's modernisation process since the war and then summarise the evolution of the EEC, before attempting to combine the two in a final section on Labour and Europe.

Labour and modernisation

As an organisation, whether new or old, the Labour Party proved its resilience on 1 May 1997 and confounded much analysis that had suggested it was in permanent decline.[3] However, while the landslide victory in the 1997 general election may have challenged the notion of Labour's electoral decline, the ideological make-up of New Labour must also force a rethinking of the nature of democratic socialism: did an organisation with a recognisable historical connection with the party founded in 1900 win the 1997 general election or was this a new party? If there remains a clear connection then what has been the extent of the change? If this is a new party then do we need to reassess the nature of the 'historic' Labour Party? In other words, the 'declinist' literature may have been accurate because in order to win the Labour Party had to become a new political party.

Indeed, a central feature of the campaign that resulted in the election win was the claim, both in presentational and in policy terms, that Labour had become New Labour. This was labelled by the party leadership as a process of 'modernisation' and those who supported this process became known as the modernisers.[4] This notion was defined as the adaptation of the party's ideology to a new set of economic and political 'realities' with respect to the role of the state in the economy, over, for example, public ownership; a new relationship to the European Union based simultaneously on a renewal of the 'special relationship' with the United States and an acceptance of the Social Chapter, and a new internal structure designed to maximise electoral efficiency by minimising room for dissent and centralising policy making in new political forums based on new centres of power.[5]

Each of these changes has been presented as a response to a set of changes in British society and the global economy. Moreover, each element in this process of change has been historically informed, indeed, presented as being the way in which the party can escape its past to achieve greater success in the future. However, while the contemporary Labour Party deploys the term modernisation as a selective rejection of the party's past,[6] this ignores the extent to which modernisation has been a deeply contested term in the history of the Labour Party. At the outset of this period modernisation was expressed as a vision either of a planned or a mixed economy, with a substantially collectivised sector, generating a more egalitarian and cohesive society. This perception had been enshrined in the 1918 party constitution and was expressed in the debates on nationalisation at the party conference of 1944. It was not, at this stage, defined purely in terms of electoral relevance. The notion evolved through the general elections of the 1950s in the context of a sustained clash on the nature of the road forwards from 1951.

This clash came to a head in the aftermath of the 1959 general election when Hugh Gaitskell advocated a reform of the 1918 constitution and the acceptance of the revisionist notion of modernisation. In contrast to this were two positions. On the one hand there was a renewed call from groups like Victory for Socialism for a planned economy and an alternative 'left wing' perspective which was heavily supply side in emphasis, advocated planning and was to develop into the electoral strategy of Harold Wilson in 1964. It was Wilson's vision which triumphed at the general election and which formed the basis for the economic policy of the 1964–70 government. Though there were these three competing visions of the future Labour offered, each was based on the presumption of an interventionist economic and social policy. Modernisation was still defined in a way that would have been recognisable to the 1945–51 government.

On the other hand, 20 years later, initially in the policy review started by Neil Kinnock[7] and later through the series of reforms instigated by John Smith and Tony Blair, modernisation has come to mean the acceptance of the inevitability of the neo-liberal settlement in market economics, particularly in terms of state ownership and the advocating of new forms of state and collective action to renew community and reduce dependency through workfare, the state as enabler rather than as planner and the local community as the unit of action rather than the whole economy. In the process this approach to the social and economic questions of the day has been merged with electoral strategy, in effect moving away from a situation in which ideas led and informed electoral strategy, which had been conspicuously unsuccessful in the 1950s and 1980s, to a situation in which electoral strategy helped to shape the party's ideas. The move away from questions of ownership and direct intervention towards a limited state function for enforcing desired outcomes through market mechanisms has become the single operational definition of modernisation. Moreover, it is not clear quite where the notion of inevitable change in the face of shifts in the nature of capitalism, summed up in the process of globalisation ends and where electoral strategy begins.

Aside from the internal party debates, the detail of policy and the choices about the way in which policy was presented to the electorate interacted with two other kinds of conflicts. The first, was obviously, the electoral competition with the other major parties, notably the most electorally successful British political party, the Conservatives. The second is related to the straight political battle in the arena in which political ideas fight for influence and seek hegemony. At the outset of the period, a conditional form of collectivism held hegemonic sway in the political, social and economic thinking of the UK elite. This was conditional on the continuance of the war and profoundly contested once the war ended.[8] However, in peace, collectivism remained the more dominant set of ideas and informed the policy making of the postwar war government headed by Clement Attlee and the debates in opposition down to the general election of 1959. Though continuing to be a more convincing story of how the political economy of the UK worked, mixed-economy-collectivism slipped in the decade from the early 1960s to the early 1970s in the face of a onslaught from, on the one hand, planned-economy-collectivism and from, on the other, an increasingly bold restatement of economic liberalism. At some point in the mid-1970s, the hegemonic mantle shifted from mixed-economy-collectivism to an ill-defined set of alternatives that took something over a decade to be articulated as a neo-liberal free market economy. Some historical actors in these debates were aware of these shifts, while others remained, perhaps remain, convinced that nothing has or needed to change.

However the evidence suggests that the foundation of postwar modernisation had shifted. A future defined by the increasing harnessing of the state to the collectivist mixed economy had been replaced by the collapse of confidence in the efficacy of intervention amongst many democratic socialists.[9] Some took refuge in planned or siege economies, while others began the process of embracing and attempting to tame the new hegemony of the free market state. This is not to argue that political economy returned to a pre-war basis but it is to argue that the foundation on which policy was formulated in the British Labour Party had shifted substantially away from the historically informed basis of collective action and harnessing the state for redistribution towards a new basis. This new basis, the gradual acceptance of the neo-liberal settlement, of a non-mixed but welfare state economy, was enshrined in the general election manifesto of 1997.

The evolution of the European Community

As the Labour Party developed through these years with competing forces dominating the party in different periods, so the European Community, and the objectives for which it was in existence, have evolved over the period. The Rome treaty, either implicitly or explicitly, contained seven main objectives. These form the ideological framework of the Community and now Union. Put very simply these objectives were, peace and reconstruction, democratic consolidation, agricultural development/ protectionism, economic and social development in a free market framework but embracing planning, currency stability, political integration and legal and market harmonisation. Opponents of the Community frequently present the Rome treaty as a blueprint for action that was somehow fixed in time and intention. However, like all ideologies, the framework of the Union was both flexible and developing. In particular, new issues arose which the framework of the treaty was not designed to cover, such as external and foreign affairs, which were drastically altered by the ending of the cold war, migration, which became a much more central problem than envisaged in the treaty, and so on. Existing issues were supported by more powerful coalitions within the Union at some periods, and less so at others. Political integration and monetary stability being the two most obvious examples.

While it is difficult to generalise a rough picture of the competing importance of the different elements in the founding ideology of the Community, might look something like figure 1. The main additional feature of Community debates not shown being enlargement, which, roughly, follows the same trajectory as political integration, but is contested in very different kinds of ways. The three core issues at the foundation of the European movement in the ashes of 1945 were peace and reconstruction, democratic consolidation and, in rhetoric at least, political integration.

By 1965, all these concerns had been reduced and the more economic concerns of economic development and agricultural protection had come more to the forefront, with political integration stalled during the Gaullist era. By 1985, the economic and harmonisation policies of the community dominate, both in terms of the 1970s challenge of inflation and in terms of the formation of the single market. In a sense, political integration is a secondary consideration in this period because of the primacy of the single market operation. By 1995, currency stability, legal and market harmonisation, economic development and political integration are all competing at the forefront of the Community's concerns. Though this is very crude and brief picture, a general sense emerges. An evolution of the community and its priorities which alters with political balance shifts and has a periodically dynamic nature.

Figure 1 Evolving Priorities of the European Community

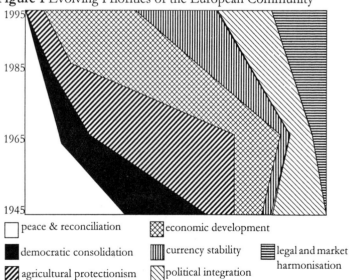

war, nevertheless the party was constitutionally, rhetorically and in its manifesto commitments at every general election of the 1950s and 1960s committed to an internationalist course. The discourse of internationalism preached by the Labour Party did not match that of the move to European integration – the content and objectives were not always the same – but the perception of the nature of engagement between nations was a common feature of Labour's general election manifestos from 1945 to 1964. In other words, though different the Labour Party and the EEC operated within the same internationalist parameters.

The second level of discourse at which there should in theory have been synchroneity was over the broad aims of social and economic policy with the possible exception of nationalisation. The EEC was protectionist, but it was protectionist to promote economic growth, ensure full employment and thereby underpin democratic consolidation and prevent a renewal of European war. The nature of the planning that the EEC envisaged was certainly less widespread than that envisaged by Clause IV of the Labour Party constitution but not that envisaged by the policy document *Industry and Society*, which was published shortly after the Rome treaty had been signed in 1957.

This general ideological development was reflected in the relationship between the Labour Party, in and out of government, and the European Community. At the latter's foundation, though Camps may have been right to question whether the UK had any place at Messina, the deeper question must be, why was the UK not part of the European Coal and Steel Community. Though Edmund Dell has suggested that the evidence for exceptionalism in the rejection of the ECSC is at best mixed, at a deeper level the message was clear: Europe would follow British democratic socialism to the future and not the other way round. This was not an unreasonable view of the future in 1945, though it looked less secure by 1947; it was actually much more meaningful by the time the Labour government fell. Though it sounds paradoxical now, the very success of the postwar government's industrial reconstruction is illustrated not only by the level of recovery in exports but in the view that Britain could sustain the rearmament programme that Gaitskell proposed to support with his 1951 budget.

What becomes curious is the length of time the dominant view in the Labour Party remained that exceptionalism was the answer. Britain's stage was the world stage: the business of Europe was small. This view held sway down to Suez and, to an extent, beyond. Because the expression of it was largely confined to the conference halls in the great debates on nuclear weapons, it is too easily assumed that it did not extend further into the way this generation of Labour politicians thought and felt. Slowly, new generations reached leadership positions, their notions of modernity different, their perception of the Labour Party's path to the future more in tune with the direction of the Six, but this took time and for much of the 1950s the Labour leadership reflected many of the norms and values of the rest of the British elite.

The irony in all this is that the community created by the Six at Messina was not an evil piece of free-market superstate, it was, if anything, already moving in a heavily protectionist and inherently corporatist direction. The level of planning, intervention, trade union and price protection built into the Rome treaty should have offered an ideal agenda for modernisation for Labour to follow. Some, indeed, did pick up this overall structure of the EEC and argue that it was a means of reforming Britain, but most argued along the lines of British involvement as part of the process of European integration or because they perceived the community as being a means of maintaining British political dominance. Bevan represented one strain, the other was found amongst the Gaitskellites who opposed their leader on the issue of Europe. In the run up to his famous '1,000 years of history' speech to the party conference of 1962, the issues of Europe was debated at length amongst the Gaitskellites in the pressure group CDS. CDS had been founded in the spring of 1960 to campaign in support of multilateralism and Gaitskell's leadership of the party. From the outset the CDS had indicated that it would support moves for further European integration. However, the manifesto, largely drafted by Tony Crosland, appeared before Macmillan's first bid for entry was in full flight.

The first public comment by the Campaign after Macmillan's approach to join appeared in the CDS newsletter, *Campaign*, in July 1961. Stressing that the most important thing was for the Labour Party to remain united, it set out to refute the charges of the anti-Marketeers. In marked contrast to Gaitskell's line which was consistently to state that the economic argument was 50–50,[10] *Campaign* rejected the notion that entry would mean higher food prices and an invasion of Italian workers and concluded: 'Indeed from an economic point of view it is scarcely open to question that Britain would benefit from membership.'[11] This pro-Market line was kept up in subsequent editions. Small pieces were published with quotations from leading party figures in favour of the Common Market.[12] These were followed up with two large articles 'Common Market Facts' (*Campaign 14*, March 1962) and 'The Common Market, More Arguments Refuted' (*Campaign 16*, May 1962). Both were in the style of questions and answers and dealt with the familiar set of objections to the Community. However, with the conference approaching, the tone of the articles became more positive. In 'Socialists and the Common Market' the case for a socialist justification for entry was made:

> There are few greater illusions than the view that an isolated Britain would be a socialist Britain. Our national record is that of only two effective left-wing governments in the 62 years of this century. And an inward-looking re-orientation would encourage the conservative and not the progressive forces in Britain. Those who are most suspicious of foreigners are most nervous of change.[13]

This was followed by a forthright attack on the possibilities of the Commonwealth being an effective world force. CDS evolved, with some loss of members, including Tony Crosland, into the Labour Committee for Europe, which in turn campaigned hard for entry and organised the rebel MPs for the crucial vote in favour of entry in October 1971.

By this stage the left which had been hostile to the Community in its 1957 form but had earlier favoured European integration, was opposed to the Community. The hope expressed in the *Campaign* article was frankly ridiculed by the anti-Marketeers who rejected the notion of the Community as a progressive force. They argued that the Common Market was a capitalist club that was interested in promoting the market through protectionism. The inherent contradictions in this position were ignored as much by the left of the party as by the framers of the Single European Act who set out to create a single market that contained the common agricultural policy. However, in terms of dominance, this anti-Market view now came to dominate the party down to the 1992 general election and the terms of the opposition, fixed in the 1950s, remained remarkably consistent, impervious to changes in either the Community or the Labour Party's own approach.

We might understand why the left of the party would reject the competition policy adopted by the Six, but the revisionists and the centre of the party, not to mention the trade unionists, who had a great deal to gain from the corporatist notions of European Christian Democracy which underpinned much of the economic and social thinking in the treaty? The language used in the respective policy debates and pronouncements and the self-perception of the British left obscured the level of compatibility between the interests and ideas of the Labour Party and that of the Community.

To put it very crudely, between 1957 and the mid-1970s, the EEC was concerned with the promoting of economic growth through reconstruction in the context of a full employment economy, full employment being in part at least an element of the democratic consolidation process. The Labour Party was looking for the same objectives for the British economy, was interested in the element of the EEC policies which promoted growth but was suspicious of industrial policies because of the question of ownership. From the mid-1970s to the mid-1990s the EEC became increasingly concerned with market harmonisation and the creation of a single European market, for elements in some states as the precursor to greater political unity, for others for the same kind of economic growth goals but with a greater awareness of and interest in the fight against inflation. The Labour Party in the same period was primarily concerned with employment policies and industrial intervention and turned directly against the Community. By the time it had come around to membership, in the 1992 election for example, this was partly positive but mostly a negative identification of Conservative opposition. In the 1997 election Labour was backing a deregulatory programme that was at odds with the French-led move to put employment creation back at the heart of European policies, though employment was also supported by Britain, so in some ways New Labour has achieved a more meaningful connection than the party has managed in previous periods.

The key question is whether or not the economic policy of the European Community was incompatible with the economic policy of the Labour Party, especially with respect to competition policy. The answer really depends on which policy of the party you are talking about. Between 1957 and the early 1970s this was based on selective public ownership through share purchase and regional industrial development. Neither policy was incompatible with the Rome treaty. But even if they had been, the inability to engage with the meaning of the treaty accepted defeat on its interpretation before even beginning the process of engagement. From the early 1970s to the 1983 election, Labour's economic policy was incompatible with the Rome treaty and the competition policy of the EEC. It was Labour that moved away from policies that were compatible with the Community rather than the Community that had become more market-orientated. After the 1983 election, and more particularly in the Labour manifesto for the 1992 election, compatibility with the European Union was a central feature of Labour's approach. The creation of the Single European Market had, arguably, shifted the ethos of

Europe's economic policy away from the goals that Labour was still advocating in the manifesto of 1987 – which still opposed membership – and that of 1992 which accepted it. The point is that the Community was not a fixed entity which the Labour Party could reject in 1957 and continue to reject, for the same reasons in 1987, any more than the Labour Party had a fixed ideology. Both actors altered position and ethos through the period and neither ever quite matched up to the other.

British exceptionalism

The British political elite of the 1940s believed in a path of exceptionalism. The argument of this essay is that while not perhaps missing buses, the British, and in particular the Labour Party, has repeatedly suffered from being out of sync with the rest of Europe. This is in part explained by Britain's political exceptionalism, which is not the same as economic or cultural exceptionalism, neither of which, the evidence suggests, have been much in evidence over the last 50 years. It is rather the history of distinctive political ideologies, and their related political cultures, which have left Britain a pace behind – or, depending on your point of view, a pace ahead – of the European Communities. The journey taking place has not been a journey to a entirely unknown destination but rather a journey towards an ill-defined modernity. What is striking over the period is the way in which the Labour Party's definition of modernity, of the society that Labour in power would create by its modernisation policies, has been out of sync with the ethos of the European Economic Community and now Union. The cost of this lack of synchroneity has been a Europe shaped largely without the active help of the Labour Party and one which today is again somewhat out of the sync with the new Labour Party.

Notes

1   Miriam Camps, 'Missing the boat at Messina and other times?', in Brian Brivati and Harriet Jones (eds), *From Reconstruction to*

Integration, Britain and Europe since 1945 (Leicester: Leicester University Press/Pinter, 1993) p.136.

2   There is a growing literature on the labour movement and the European Community but this is one of the few areas in contemporary history where considerably more has been written about the Conservatives. See Roger Broad, *Labour's European Dilemmas: from Bevin to Blair* (Basingstoke: Palgrave, 2001); N Ashford, 'The Political Parties', in Stephen George (ed.), *Britain and the European Community: The Politics of Semi-Detachment* (Oxford: Oxford University Press, 1992); D Baker, et al., '1846, 1906, 1996? Conservative Splits and European Integration', *Political Quarterly*, 64 (1993); P Daniels, and E. Ritchie, '"The Poison'd Chalice": The European Issue in British Party politics', in Peter Jones (ed.), *Party, Parliament and Personality: Essays Presented to Hugh Berrington* (London: Routledge, 1995); A Geddes, 'Labour and the European Community, 1979–1983: Pro-Europeanism, Europeanisation and Their Implications', *Contemporary Record*, 8 (1994); Stephen George, *An Awkward Partner: Britain in the European Community* (Oxford: Clarendon Press, 1990); R J Lieber, *British Politics and European Unity: Parties, Elites and Pressure Groups*, (Berkeley: University of California Press, 1970); and S Tindale, 'Learning to Love the Market: Labour and the European Community', *Political Quarterly*, 63 (1992).

3   David Coates, *The crisis of Labour*, (Oxford: Philip Allan, 1989); Ivor Crewe, 'Why Labour has lost the British elections', *Public Opinion Quarterly* (July 1983); Ivor Crewe, 'The decline of labour and the decline of Labour', *Essex Papers in Government and Politics*, No. 65, (1989); Eric Shaw, 'Before the policy review: the evolution of Labour's economic strategy 1979–1987', paper presented to the PSA, 1990 and Martin Jacques and Francis Mulhern, (eds) *The forward march of Labour halted?* (London: NLB in association with *Marxism Today*, 1981).

4   See, Peter Mandelson and Roger Liddle, *The Blair Revolution: Can New Labour Deliver* (London: Faber, 1996); John Rentoul, *Tony Blair* (London: Little, Brown, 1995), and Jon Sopel, *Tony Blair: The Moderniser* (London: Michael Joseph, 1995).

5   Tony Blair, speech to 'Passing the Torch', LSE, 1 March 1997, all but the last point were explicitly made in this speech.

6 See Tony Blair, 'Introduction', in Tony Wright and Matt Carter, *The People's Party* (London: Thames and Hudson, 1997).

7 Martin Smith and Joanna Spear (eds), *The Changing Labour Party* (London: Routledge, 1992).

8 Indeed debated within the wartime coalition, see Stephen Brooke, *Labour's War: The Labour Party During the Second World War* (Oxford: Clarendon Press, 1992) and Kevin Jefferys, *The Churchill Coalition and Wartime Politics* (Manchester: Manchester University Press, 1991). The later debates are summarised in Harriet Jones and Michael Kandiah (eds), *The Myth of Consensus, New Views on British History 1945–64* (London: Macmillan, 1996).

9 A situation not confined, of course, to the UK, see Herbert Kitschelt, *The transformation of European Social Democracy* (Cambridge: Cambridge University Press, 1994).

10 Philip Williams, *Hugh Gaitskell* (London: Cape, 1979), p.713.

11 *Campaign 7*, July 1961, 'Labour and the Common Market' unsigned but probably written by Tony King.

12 *Campaign 8*, August-September 1961, 'Opinions on the Common Market' from Lord Morrison and Bill Carron, *Campaign 11*, December 1961, 'More Common Market Views' from Sir Alan Birch and Roy Jenkins.

13 *Campaign 18*, July 1962.

The British Contribution to the European Union

Théo Junker

It is easy for a critical mind to wax ironically on this subject, and there has been no shortage of this, wherever it was mentioned. On the other hand, it is fairly difficult to deal properly with such a broad and unfocused topic. So an approach and a plan are needed to provide a framework for the following remarks, for their purpose and, above all, for their limitations.

The proposed subject covers only the second half of the period under consideration in this volume, so this chapter could be limited to the period after 1973. To do this would be to fail to do justice to the European policy of the United Kingdom and would make it impossible to understand various deeds and words which are of older – sometimes much older – vintage. This is why any study of the past quarter-century has to be based on knowledge of the evolving or successive ways of thinking, principles and traditions which underpin the attitude of the present generations of Britons to Europe in general, to the Community, and to the European Union in particular. Such knowledge can only be supplied by the British actors involved, particularly politicians, and historians of the 20th century. This is the real interest of 'contemporary history', the study of which should minimise errors of interpretation regarding the recent past and what is happening today.

For the Europeans that we all are, albeit in our different ways, it is clear from the outset that each member state contributes something to the Union, just as it takes something from it, too. This question of principle and evidence could be illustrated for each and every one of them. For some, it would then quite simply be a matter of two accounting columns, the first setting out everything that that state had contributed and the second showing what it had received. Isn't this the rather simplistic model of any political philosophy based on 'fair return'? If it were possible to operate like this, all that would be needed would be to instruct a European agency, such as the EC Statistical Office, to draw up balances, month by month and year by year, with the figures showing the credit or debit situation of each member state vis-à-vis the European Union. The limitations of such a purely quantitative exercise are manifest. Perhaps it should be carried out nonetheless, over a significant period. It has been done a few times, and the results have generally been surprising: those who thought they were creditors were themselves beneficiaries, even major beneficiaries, by one of those miracles which are simply called 'the Common Market'.

Political strategies

So let us abandon this sterile game, because it does not really take into account what each country participating in the Community adventure has contributed most. By piling up a mountain of facts and arguments, we lose sight of what is actually happening. In order to avoid this, we must step back a bit from the figures, the statistics and the tabloid headlines and consider instead the psychological aspect of political strategies, which are sometimes defective and sometimes positive. By this I mean, at one and the same time, general opinion, political awareness and, perhaps, the image of self which underpins and provides a vehicle for different European or anti-European policies. However, it also covers the image conveyed by and thus received from outside: the way in which a country is viewed, perceived and, ultimately, judged by others. In these perceptions of national and international, political, social and cultural psychology, states 'win' or 'lose' more than is generally admitted, whether this is in terms of confidence and credibility, or as regards authority and influence. It is interesting to note that the world of economics, money and finance has long since discovered and recognised the key part played by the psychology of individuals in everything to do with steering and then preparing, managing and controlling day-today operations in their sphere of responsibility. By contrast, it is curious to realise that political circles are by and large not so advanced. Even though they consume opinion polls greedily, it is surprising to find that possible psychological effects are not always incorporated into their forecasts, calculations or decisions. (Of course, it would be easy to cite against this analysis all those cases in which a government has abandoned or adjusted its line *after* testing the contrary winds of public opinion. However, that is not the question). What is at issue, instead, is the capacity to see, simultaneously and together, the psychological element which is inherent in any policy and the 'ideological' element, whether this is constituted by fundamental political or economic interests, programming priorities, traditional principles, etc. This is probably the level at which the question of the British contribution to Europe and the European Union needs to be put and discussed.

In any event, that is the choice that has been made for this chapter. It will not be concerned simply with listing the various kinds of contribution, or the shortfall in contributions in this or that area, that the United Kingdom has made since accession; it will be instead a search for the meaning to be ascribed to the successive European policies of British governments. It will be a modest attempt to interpret words and deeds as they have evolved since 1972, to discern possible structures or constants therein, probably to encounter certain blockages and persistent misunderstandings, and finally to end with a few practical questions arising from our findings.

We might jokingly say that 'in the beginning was Winston Churchill', because for many people his considerable stature constitutes the foundation stone of European integration, stemming from his post-war call on Europe to pick itself up and unite. Good historians find that he himself had British predecessors. Jean Monnet, for his part, recognised Churchill's merits, but also his limitations: 'Churchill ... Did he see beyond the interests of Great Britain? I think not – but for him, as for many of his compatriots, British interests were those of vast areas of the world. Wherever the Union Jack flew, Britons ruled the waves.'[1]

We should not forget the part played by Ernest Bevin, the Foreign Secretary in the immediate post-war period, who was involved in setting up the Council of Europe and who proposed that its seat should be in Strasbourg, as a city symbolic of a peaceful, democratic Europe engaged in uniting its peoples, notably through elected representatives.[2]

Then came the years of diverging paths. The United Kingdom did not join the six other states who came together in the ECSC, although it maintained a liaison office with it. However, when preparations for the Rome treaty and the European Economic Community were under way, the United Kingdom launched what was intended and/or understood to be a major spoiling operation, namely the FTA; this was conceived as an alternative, as a competitor offering the same advantages but without the same constraints.[3] The smaller scale EFTA which emerged brought together with the United Kingdom states which were not in a position to join the Community; it never constituted a serious alternative. At the time, admittedly, some countries were content with it: I well remember the distinguished ambassador of a neutral country who explained in all seriousness that his country, as a member of the Council of Europe and EFTA, would never see either the benefit of joining the Community or the need to do so. How true it is that credos, which are undoubtedly valid at some point, need to be revised from time to time. Britain, which had thought again about where its interests lay, subsequently presented and then renewed an application to join, which produced results only after President de Gaulle had left the scene.

After accession

We should therefore consider the question of the United Kingdom's contribution to the Community and the Union since its accession, because previously it was simply adopting external positions. In the context of this chapter, I shall indicate a few avenues to be explored, in no particular order.

It is agreed that the United Kingdom made a major contribution to the Single European Act and thus to the single market. It has pushed for the deregulation and liberalisation of markets in many areas. While the debate on this subject may be renewed in terms of the economic and social outcome of the various operations, it has to be acknowledged that this new economic dynamic was an inevitable result of the establishment of a large, unified internal market for all the Twelve (later the Fifteen).

The British contribution regarding greater transparency in the use of public funds, in the sense of value for money, also has to be acknowledged. It is easy to discern British influence in the attention paid to accountability, to budgetary control, the control of public funds, investigations into fraud and the role of the European Parliament and, more recently, the Court of Auditors, etc., which now characterise all the Community institutions. These efforts are widely supported by other member states, but the know-how and expertise undeniably bear the stamp of the United Kingdom.

The same applies where the budget of the European Union is concerned. This matter is of particular interest to the European Parliament, which has fought hard gradually to secure budgetary power, without which a parliament has no clout. British parliamentary example and practice have undoubtedly had an influence.

This positive appraisal needs to be accompanied by certain reservations, however. When the United Kingdom fails to get what it wants in the Union by political means (reform of the CAP, for example), it tries to use the budgetary procedure to achieve its ends. A classic modus operandi, some will say, but one which shows little respect for democratic decision-making or for that legendary sense of fair play... Without returning to the episodes of the demand for a 'fair return' or of that for a reduction in own-resource payments from VAT receipts, let us just note (as do the experts) that the per capita contribution to the

European Union budget (as a percentage of GDP per inhabitant and per member state) is particularly low for the British citizen. Only Irish citizens contribute a smaller percentage of their income to the EU budget, while in absolute terms Danes, Germans, Frenchmen, Italians, Luxemburgers and Dutchmen all pay about twice as much individually to the EC as their British counterparts.[4]

Talking of the CAP, it is worth pointing out that British criticisms of around 20 years ago have borne fruit to some extent. They called for price support for farm incomes to be abandoned and replaced by direct income subsidies, while the prices of agricultural products should adjust to world prices. They were right, ahead of their time. Community prices have now moved closer to world prices. Moreover, there is a whole system of income support based on subsidies related to farming activity (depending on the region). Finally, production in several sectors (milk, cereals, wine) has been made subject to quotas. Similarly, the United Kingdom has introduced several innovations in the fisheries sector, such as fishing licences and boxes – areas in which fishing is restricted.

Legal experts point to an interesting element, which has as yet been under-reported and not explained, characterising the jurisprudence of the European Court of Justice. It appears to be developing European case law, heavily based on precedent and showing a striking similarity to the style of English common law.

In all these examples it can be seen that an important member state has managed to exercise its influence on certain aspects of Community policy and has been able to initiate reforms in certain areas. On the other hand, it has not managed either to reshape the overall project or to any significant degree reorientate what other member states held dear. In other areas of Community activity, the United Kingdom has not even managed to get its arguments across with its partners.

The social aspects and the Social Chapter undoubtedly ought to be considered in detail. Such an examination would show, first, the ability of a single government to resist changes that everyone else wanted. It would then reveal the retrograde image that this refusal is bound to generate. It would, perhaps, explain how this refusal helped to bring about the doctrines of 'flexibility' and 'enhanced cooperation' (the latter is already present in the treaty on European Union). It should be noted here, however, that in the area of Community social legislation which has been adopted, the United Kingdom does enjoy a degree of credit where its transposition into national law and implementation are concerned.

Monetary union

Turning to monetary union, we are forced to admit that the United Kingdom is not absent from the debate, but that its participation is more difficult than it is for others. The first attempts to combine the member states' limited monetary strength date back to the Werner and Barre Plans, i.e. before British accession.[5] This monetary awareness and philosophy never seem to have been accepted by the United Kingdom, despite the fact that they undoubtedly formed part of the *acquis communautaire*.[6] Maybe monetary affairs should not have been put into brackets during the United Kingdom's accession negotiations?

During the penultimate year of Mrs Thatcher's government (1979–90) Roy Jenkins, the former President of the European Commission (1977–81) and since 1987 Chancellor of Oxford University, expressed repeatedly his concern about how the Conservative Party's attitude in this connection might affect his country. He feared that British national interests might be damaged by lack of action on the part of the United Kingdom. If it did have reasons for viewing monetary issues differently from its partners, it has not succeeded in making them give up their objectives and timetables in this respect. By and large, monetary union and the introduction of the ecu or the euro are the logical development of a process of integration which dates back 40 years; that process is now seen as the only thing which can give it the stability and strength that it needs to continue towards a political Europe. Here again, opting-out prompts an adverse reaction among Britain's partners.[7] However, significant voices can be heard in Britain itself calling for a solid and lasting economic and monetary union.[8]

In 1990, when John Major replaced Margaret Thatcher, he wanted Britain to occupy 'a place at the heart of Europe'. He added that in this way the United Kingdom should pull the Community in the direction that it wanted it to take. We have already seen that this great ambition has not been fulfilled. However, the United Kingdom has got across a number of arguments, drawn from its wealth of diplomatic, commercial, military and cultural experience, to clarify various common policies (mainly those provided for by the Maastricht treaty on the European Union).

These British arguments had been signalled in March 1991.[9] They hold that national policies on foreign affairs and security are the fruit of specific historic experiences and take account of the national interests brought into play by events. They cannot be modified by recourse to majority voting. No member state would let itself end up in a minority. They all have their own national interests which are deemed to be more important than an artificial, imposed common policy. In the sphere of security, cooperation should gradually be extended while waiting for a EU defence and security policy; WEU should for a limited time continue to be a bridge between its member states and NATO. The future of European security and defence calls for debates, in accordance with their substance, within the European Union, WEU and NATO and between them.

Evaluating the UK contribution

How should we now evaluate this 'contribution'? It contains both centrifugal and centripetal elements. As we have seen, the purely intergovernmental stance refuses to see the Union as a superior common good; it sees it simply as a means of safeguarding and promoting national interests. For the United Kingdom, might not Europe be merely a partnership of nations, rather than a grouping with federal ambitions or even a federal system? So when Britain expresses support for the early enlargement of the Union to embrace the countries of central and eastern Europe, its partners ask it 'hard' questions. Is it with the aim of diluting the Union, without establishing an effective decision-making mechanism, without any extension of majority voting, and without any appropriate operating rules? Is it on account of a purely economic vision, simply in order to create an even bigger market, a new EFTA? The suspicions regarding social and monetary matters clearly coalesce here with the doubts that may be felt about deep-seated British convictions about the Community of will and destiny which defines Community Europe.

The realism that informs the British attitude cannot be denied. The British are cautious about a common foreign and security policy (CFSP) which runs counter to what are claimed to be national interests. There is probably a need to consider the interests of all the various member states more closely, to ensure that others get to know and understand and to rate them; why not bring the subsidiarity principle into play where the CFSP is concerned? Bearing in mind the history of the countries of Europe, it would undoubtedly be appropriate – for a while – to draw a distinction, agreed in advance, between what can be decided by a majority and what requires unanimity, in order to take account of legitimate minority reservations.

Despite everything, significant developments in the direction of the provisions and spirit of the European Union treaty should already be noted. For example, there have been many instances of rapprochement between Britain and France, particularly on the basis of their experiences in the former Yugoslavia (or their experiences as nuclear powers).

Do other areas reveal a comparable rapprochement which, albeit limited to two players, is nonetheless of wider European interest? One example which may spring to mind is development cooperation, particularly with the countries of Africa. Following a period in which the African, Caribbean and Pacific (ACP) states were primarily of interest to France and Belgium, as a result of their traditional links with their former colonies, the enlargements of the Community introduced new post-colonial sensibilities, with the accessions of Portugal and, above all, the United Kingdom. The arrival of the United Kingdom and of the English-speaking African countries markedly changed the character of this major international forum, and not just from the linguistic point of view. Here again, the experience gained by the former colonial powers has worked to give development cooperation policy a more European dimension. Not all the colonial and post-colonial dominant positions and illusions disappeared overnight, but the ACP partners found that they gained by dealing with a greater number of European capitals. This diversification of relations, while leading to a reduced share of ACP markets for some, has indubitably helped to clarify political relations and to further progress, which is sometimes very laborious, along the path to independence. If development cooperation for Africa appears regularly to be assigned to Europe by the geopolitical division of labour among the world powers, this association is to the credit of both the African ACP states and their European partners, who have demonstrated their ability to emerge from the colonial period, and virtually from the post-colonial period, and to open a new chapter in north-south international relations. This plus point obviously cannot disguise the enormous and sometimes desperate difficulty of the task. It perhaps allows the hope of decisive action by the European Union in favour of the poorest and least-developed continent. It would be a matter of course for London and Paris to involve the other capitals of Europe in such a political vision, which would now be less popular than ever, at a time when skills, investments and finance are scouring the world for short-term returns, fascinated by 'young tigers' and 'new dragons'.

From the institutional point of view, and particularly that of the intergovernmental conferences (IGC), the United Kingdom has certainly been involved actively, but in a manner which is generally regarded as being unconvincing, at least until the late 1990s. The areas in which British initiatives and contributions are traditionally expected have unfortunately not produced the expected encouragement or support from London. I am referring here to parliamentary democratisation and parliamentary control at European level.

It was a long time ago that the much-regretted Sir Peter Kirk managed, almost single-handedly, to introduce the concept and a certain practice of a British-style question time into the European Parliament's rules of procedure and the business of plenary sittings. Happily, the newly-created parliamentary committee of inquiry foreseen by the European Union treaty has added a valuable instrument (it has already been used a number of times by the European Parliament[10]) which enables MEPs to pursue their investigations further and hence along the lines of true parliamentarism.

In the often delicate relations between the member states' national parliaments and the European Parliament it has long been clear that it is not a question of removing powers from the European Parliament and giving (returning?) them to the national parliaments, but of enhancing at national level the control by national parliaments over the European policy of their national governments. In this connection, the British Parliament and the United Kingdom government might have played, and might still play, a leading role which would be convincing, given its place and its active part in parliamentary history. The democratic deficit of the European institutions, and thus of the European Union, cannot be made good by national control, 15 times over, of European affairs, but by a European Parliament which has the requisite parliamentary powers. It is therefore not a question of weakening the democratically elected Union institution which represents all the peoples of the Community, but of developing the Union dimension of the national parliaments and of involving them, in each national capital, in the common endeavour. There is still a great deal to do in this respect.

A worthy contribution

Each of the many avenues which have been mentioned, outlined and explored too briefly here should be the object of systematic study by legal and institutional experts, political scientists and historians. While some work has been carried out, there is still work to be done before we are in a position to give an adequate response to the following questions:

- As we have seen, the contributions made by the United Kingdom exist, are genuine and can be illustrated, but is the contribution adequate as a whole?

- Even if some people regard this contribution as being adequate, the following question arises: is it comparable to that of other member states, say, the three other 'big' member states (Germany, France and Italy)?

- If this question is disliked, the following questions nonetheless arise: does this contribution
  i) do justice to British ambitions?
  ii) do justice to British capabilities?

- If one prefers not to answer these questions, we come to the real political question: has the British contribution to the European Union to date really served British interests? In the short term, perhaps, but in the long term?

- At certain points I have mentioned the expectations of Britain's partners since its participation in the European Union. The following question should be explored on a more systematic basis: what is expected of the United Kingdom within the European Union?

This *tour d'horizon* has revealed certain facts, interpretations, expectations, disappointments and instances of satisfaction. Putting it in a nutshell, the findings – the balance-sheet – are not glorious. But they are not disastrous, either. We have been able to see that not everything has been done as it could have been done, and also how much remains to be done. But we have also seen that the United Kingdom knows how to acknowledge facts and often knows how to adapt itself to them, albeit at its own speed, which is often too slow, and sometimes exasperating, for others. Let me leave almost the last word to Jean Monnet, who wrote that 'one can afford to be patient when certain of the outcome.'[11]

Many people thus hope for a clearer and more determined British presence in the European Union.[12] Not in terms of a sectoral and selective approach, but with a global imagination and strategic vision about the place which Great Britain can and should occupy in the world of tomorrow which also means, in Europe, uniting.

Notes

1   Jean Monnet, *Mémoires* (Paris: Fayard, 1976; Livre de poche 6506 (LP 15), ed. 1988), p.196; English edition (tr. R. Mayne), *Memoirs* (London: Collins, 1989).

2   Following the advice of the future Lord Gladwyn, January 1949.

3   Jean Monnet saw this clearly (op. cit,. pp. 666–7): 'The best thing they (the Six) could do, in the face of the British initiative, was to make faster progress themselves ... The Communities had to exist in themselves and affirm their own identity as distinct from the Free Trade Area project, whose structure remained vague and whose aims were essentially commercial.'

4   See the report on the management of own resources, Rapporteur: Mr Otto Bardong MEP, for the Committee on Budgetary Control of the European Parliament (PE 213 380 and A4-0000/95) of 1 June 1995, which quotes from the Court of Auditors annual report for the 1993 financial year giving inter alia a breakdown of the revenue paid by each member state. The table below eliminates the impact of where customs duties are collected (for instance Rotterdam v. others customs offices) but takes into account the rebate on VAT resource payments granted since 1984 to the UK. See also EC, Euratom, CECA, Draft supplementary and amending Budget No.1 for the financial year 1997, Section III – Commission, established by the Council on 19 June 1997 in Doc 9210/97.

Table 1: per capita contribution to the European Union budget

Member state	Percentage of GDP per inhabitant
Belgium	0.89
Denmark	1.10
Germany	1.12
Greece	1.01
Spain	0.98
France	1.01
Ireland	0.31
Italy	0.96
Luxembourg	1.82
Netherlands	1.05
Portugal	0.75
United Kingdom	0.57

5   Pierre Werner, former Deputy Prime Minister of Luxembourg, and Raymond Barre, former French Prime Minister.

6   Monnet, op. cit., pp.742–3: 'My letter to (then) German Chancellor Willy Brandt went on: "As for the limited pooling of national sovereignty that such a monetary organisation would require, it becomes clearer every day that this would be a great deal more modest than the blind and total abandonment of sovereignty which is involved today in the continuing drift towards a dollar zone, and the continuing and uncontrollable financing of the deficits run up by the so-called reserve currency countries – the United States and Britain – either through our own central bank issues or through their merchant banks and the Eurodollar market." This same phenomenon of receding national sovereignty by trying to protect it too jealously is not confined to the monetary field. It runs through the whole history of European countries in the past twenty years, delaying and jeopardising the collective action needed to make them genuinely independent. Brandt took the point; and he persuaded the Hague summit to adopt the plan for economic and monetary union, with a European Reserve Fund, as the Action Committee had proposed.'

7   See Etienne Davignon, Chairman of Société Générale de Belgique, former Vice-President of the Commission, interviewed in *Le Monde*, 25 February 1997:

'– Wouldn't the German concept of a 'hard core' be aimed at creating a club of serious-minded people – Germanic, Scandinavian – generously enlarged to embrace France?

– I don't think so. As is always the case, you need to look at the origin of ideas and then see how they develop. Initially, there was the feeling that the malfunctioning of the Union caused by British obstruction had to be brought to an end ...

– Don't the Germans take a softer line with Britain than they do vis-à-vis Italy or Spain?

– If I were British I would be really worried. The British no longer count. First of all, it was decided that they were not going to influence us; then, in view of the inextricable situation that they had got themselves into, that we were not going to influence them, either. Consequently, what Britain does or doesn't do no longer matters in relation to what we are undertaking. In all the world's languages, this means that it has lost its place.'

8   Cf. Niall Fitzgerald, Chairman of Unilever, in *The World Today* (December 1996): 'What Europe cannot afford is the failure of EMU ... We need a successful EMU that is *built to last*. The tragedy of British policy is that, while we should be taking a lead to secure that lasting success, we are seen as spoilers whose motivations are suspect and whose hesitations are dismissed as pathetic.' See also Sir Roy Denman in the *Independent on Sunday*, 23 March 1997.

9   Mark Lyall Grant (then First Secretary at the British Embassy in Paris), 'The European Union: a British point of view', *Défense Nationale* (June 1991) pp.97–102.

10 The first two on BSE and on fraud in Community transit (the latter committee of inquiry was chaired by a British MEP, John Tomlinson, and its rapporteur was another Briton, Edward Kellett-Bowman).

11 Monnet, op. cit., p.666.

12 Sir Nicholas Henderson, 'Mad John Bull disease', *The Economist*, 23 November 1996.

Missing the Bus, Missing the Point: Britain's Place in the World since 1945

Ian Davidson

Britain's place in the world, over the past 50 years, has, it seems to me, been largely determined by two objective external factors: the rise and fall of the cold war; and the strength and policies of the United States. British politicians have loved to give us the business, about how Britain has a leading role on the international stage. But the reality is that Britain has not been master of its fate this past half century; its place, and its role, have been essentially framed by factors over which it has had no control, and precious little influence.

You could say: why pick on Britain? After all, the whole world has been subject to these two overwhelmingly important factors. The French, for example, tried on many occasions to contest the massive power of the United States; at one period, they also tried to assert a distinctive and different policy towards the cold war. On both fronts, they failed.

The difference between Britain and France, or rather the difference between Britain and most of its partners in western Europe, is that the European countries have devoted long-term efforts to trying to shape those areas of their strategic environment which they could control, and which were not determined by the two mega-factors. By which, of course, I mean that they pursued economic and political integration in Europe.

Now the purpose and function of European integration can be explained in many different ways, and the fact that it can be explained in so many ways, is one of the reasons why it has proved so strong and so durable. But one of the ways it can be explained, is that it is a strategic response to a world determined by others: a way of creating space and options for independent action.

The British, by contrast, have been unable to find any means of coming to terms with the European integration agenda, as an instrument of grand strategy. As a result they have, whether consciously or unconsciously, effectively limited their strategic options to reacting inside a context and an agenda set by the two mega-factors. What this means is that this post-war period marks a fundamental paradigm shift in British foreign policy: for the first time in many centuries, Britain has effectively opted out of any significant national grand strategy.

I will come back to this question of Britain's lack of a European strategy, or indeed of any distinctive national strategy. But first I shall consider a little more in detail how I see Britain's place in the world since 1945.

The past 50 years can be conveniently divided into five periods, the first four of which each ends with one or more turning points, or some fundamental shift in the international strategic situation. Let us give these periods descriptive titles.

Period One: 1945 to the mid-1950s: *Victory.*
Period Two: mid-1950s to early 1970s: *Follow My Leader.*
Period Three: early 1970s to 1979: *European Interlude.*
Period Four: 1979 to 1991: *The Empire Strikes Back.*
Period Five: 1991 onwards: *The Strategic Dilemma.*

In Period One, Britain claimed the glory of *Victory* and the privilege of Empire. Britain was a permanent member of the UN Security Council, NATO was formed, and Britain developed its own nuclear weapons. But Britain's delusions of grandeur ended abruptly and without recall at Suez in 1956, not because it was a stupid adventure (which of course it was), but because the Americans put a stop to it. Thereafter, Britain never again risked offending US strategic choices.

In the next period, *Follow My Leader*, from the mid-1950s to the early 1970s, Britain adopted the role of the faithful acolyte of the US, because it could not afford, and did not dare, to pursue any alternative options. One of the central events of this period was Macmillan's belated attempt to take Britain into the European Community. But it is fairly clear that Macmillan had not really made a strategic conversion to the full implications of Community membership, on the contrary he saw it primarily as an instrumental device for staying in with the Americans. Britain could only afford to remain a nuclear power with the help of the Americans; and with the Nassau agreement for the purchase of Polaris, Macmillan publicly demonstrated to de Gaulle where his real priorities lay. He thus fatally jeopardised his European tactic, and de Gaulle brought down his veto. Yet loyalty to the US brought few benefits. Britain did not dare to dissent from the US over the damaging strategic implications of the Vietnam war, or to criticise the balance-of-payments consequences of the war.

With hindsight, Britain's chosen role as the unswervingly faithful lieutenant of the US only seems to make sense on two assumptions. First, that the US could be counted on to carry out its role as the superpower leader of the west, with wisdom and with consideration for its allies., and second, that the confrontation with the Soviet Union would be permanent and unchanging. By the end of this period, America's Vietnam strategy was in ruins, and the financial cost of the war had brought the Bretton Woods international monetary system crashing down. At the same time, the US had been forced, partly by the wreck of the Vietnam war, but mainly because the Soviet Union had now secured a nuclear balance of terror, to negotiate the beginnings of a strategic detente with the Russians, in the ABM and SALT-1 treaties.

In Period Three, spanning most of the 1970s, Edward Heath took Britain into the European Community, and after the 1975 referendum, Harold Wilson just about managed to keep Britain in the Community. I call this period a *European Interlude*, because (as is now clear) Britain secured membership of the Community without any strategic shift in attitudes towards the European project.

Period Four, from 1979 to 1991, I call the *Empire Strikes Back*, because, during the partnership of Ronald Reagan and Margaret Thatcher, the dual premise of Britain's 'special relationship' – American leadership, and the cold war confrontation - were restored in all their former vigour. The crisis over the stationing of medium-range missiles in Europe, which started in 1979, gathered speed and momentum under Reagan, and the intensity of the accompanying east-west confrontation was further increased both by his denunciations of the Soviet Union's Evil Empire, and by his programme for Star Wars. Amidst so much bellicosity, the Falklands war was a happy accident, further cementing the Anglo-American partnership.

Unfortunately, the dual premise proved as unreliable and impermanent this time round as it had before. George Bush and John Major were no match for Reagan and Thatcher, and they could not keep the cold war going. By 1991, the Berlin Wall had fallen, Germany was united, eastern Europe was free, and the Soviet Union had collapsed. And the fleeting triumph of the Gulf war could not prevent everyone from seeing that the bitter four-year conflict between Europe and the US over the war in former Yugoslavia, was reaching the point where it could cause serious damage to the Atlantic alliance.

Period Five started in 1991. I have called it *Strategic Dilemma*, because the dual premise has now disappeared for ever without hope of recall. The Soviet Union has vanished, and with it the life-and-death polarisation which made Britain a very desirable, though not absolutely essential, adjunct for US strategy. NATO has been enlarged to eastern Europe, partly to satisfy the east European lobby, but primarily to gain extended legitimacy for America's continued role in Europe. Yet America is still likely to disengage from Europe in time, as well no doubt as from other foreign commitments. But even if America remains committed to Europe, it is now clear that Britain has been displaced as America's principal ally in Europe by the reunited Germany. Meanwhile it has also become clear, ever since the Maastricht treaty of 1991, that Britain's refusal since 1973 to develop a viable strategy in the European context, is beginning to reach the limits of sustainability. Saying 'no', even very loudly, is not a serious strategy.

No British strategy at all

Needless to say, the Foreign Office would not agree with anything I have said. They would no doubt claim that Britain is doing splendidly. But the rhetoric of official productions may sometimes reveal an underlying message which is different from the official text. Douglas Hurd, the former Conservative Foreign Secretary, was given to claiming that Britain was 'punching above its weight'; and his successors frequently cried that Britain is 'winning the argument'. Now from the point of view of professional taste, let alone the national interest, Douglas Hurd's choice of a pugilistic image was really quite strange. Did he seriously wish to project the picture of Britain as a pugnacious little runt, permanently on its toes, for the explicit purpose of inflicting blows on others? It seems eccentric, to say the least. But the problem goes beyond mere taste. On the face of it, these are triumphalist phrases, implying national strength, success and victory. But the deeper implication is the idea that Britain is, and perhaps must be, at odds with, in conflict with others.

But where have we found Britain in a posture of systematic conflict? Only in relation to Europe. In relation to Europe, Britain has been in a posture of unresolved, systematic conflict for half a century. It is as if, first, what is in the interests of the other countries of Europe, is bound to be against our interests; second, it is as if any system of government that they might want is bound to be incompatible with our system of government; and third, consequently, it is as if 'Europe' was something being imposed on us against our will. You might think that such prolonged conflict implies that Britain has a European strategy which is at odds with that of other European countries. This would be a mistake. The paradox is that Britain does not have a European strategy, and for the purposes of this discussion, it never has had a European strategy.

When I say that Britain does not have a European strategy, I do not mean that Britain has a reprehensible European strategy, or one that I disagree with. I certainly do not mean that Britain has some kind of moral duty to follow a federalist strategy, or anything like that. Far from it. If the British want a non-federalist strategy, or an anti-federalist strategy, or an isolationist strategy, or any other kind of strategy, that's fine by me. The problem is that they do not now have, and have never had, any kind of strategy at all for dealing with the central strategic problem in Europe. If you look at Britain's history in the past 50 years in relation to Europe, you will find plenty of reflexes and emotions, you will find anger, paranoia, and nostalgia; you will find resentment, reluctance and resistance; and you will certainly find an enormous amount of ignorance and misunderstanding. But you will not find a shred of anything remotely resembling a European strategy.

Let me pose the question in concrete terms. What is the central strategic problem in Europe? Well, you could say that there are two central strategic problems. The first is structural and permanent, and it is called Germany. The second is somewhat more distant, circumstantial and conditional, and is called Russia or the Soviet Union. If you were feeling politically incorrect, you could even add that there is a third central strategic problem for Europe: and it is the United States. These are Europe's three central strategic problems. Germany, Russia, and the United States. But it is obvious that the top priority is Germany. Because until Europe has dealt with and solved the German problem, it cannot deal with either the Russian or the American problem.

For 40 years after the end of the Second World War, the second or Soviet problem loomed so large that it entirely over-shadowed the first or German problem. But the German problem existed long before the Soviet problem became a real problem at all; and in fact it is so central to the history of Europe, that it precipitated two world wars inside 30 years. For the moment, the Soviet problem has somewhat receded, at least as an immediate threat; though what the future will hold, is anyone's guess.

The German problem remains. And unless it is solved, no other problem can be solved. You would not guess that the British have ever understood any of these rather simple ideas. What is the German problem? It is simply that Germany is much larger, much stronger, much richer, much more powerful, than any of its neighbours. This is a problem for all of Germany's neighbours; so they all need a strategy for containing Germany's strength. Now there are, it seems to me, broadly three possible ways to contain an over-powerful state. First, you can conquer it, occupy it, and divide it up. Second, you can form an alliance against it; a sort of balance-of-power or deterrence strategy. Or third, you can build treaty-based relations with it.

Immediately after the Second World War, the victors followed the first of these strategies. They conquered Germany, they occupied it, they divided it up, and they limited its independence. At the same time, Britain and France also set in motion, in parallel, the second strategy, of a balance-of-power alliance against Germany, in the 1947 Dunkirk treaty between Britain and France. But it was very quickly obvious that neither of these two strategies was going to be a long-term or complete solution to the German problem. In the case of the first, repressive strategy, the victorious allies were determined to avoid the horrendous policy errors they had made 30 years earlier, in relation to Germany after the First World War. In the case of the second, the balance-of-power strategy, Britain and France had twice learned to their cost, this century, that an alliance between them was not enough to contain German expansion.

Both strategies had in effect to be abandoned, mainly because the allies needed to co-opt Germany's growing strength to help deal with Europe's other strategic problem, the threat from the Soviet Union. In response to the Communist takeover of Czechoslovakia, the Dunkirk treaty was expanded to include the Benelux countries, and in 1954 this Brussels treaty was reformed again as the Western European Union, and made the vehicle for the incorporation of West Germany as a full member of NATO.

French and British policies

It is instructive to compare the different policies of Britain and France towards the German problem. British policy towards the German problem seems to have consisted of two strands, based on the vestigial remnants of the first strategy, and a half-baked version of the third strategy. On the one hand (Strategy One), the British acted as if the German problem could be dealt with as a cost-free by-product of western strategy towards the Soviet Union. Germany would be divided and its sovereignty limited, whereas Britain and France would be nuclear powers with permanent seats on the UN Security Council. In other words (in the immortal phrase), NATO would perform the triple function of keeping the Americans in, the Germans down, and the Russians out. On the other hand (Strategy Three, binding treaty relationships), the British promoted intergovernmental institutional arrangements of an unambitious and unconstraining kind, run on a basis of consensus or unanimity; for example, the OEEC (which subsequently became the OECD) and the Council of Europe. Unfortunately, the first half of this two-pronged policy was of no long-term use in dealing with the German problem, and the second half was of no use at all.

The first half was of no long-term use, because the Germans were rapidly rehabilitated into the company of nations, and grew strong and rich again. And since 1990, of course, with reunification and the recovery of full German sovereignty, this strand of British policy has simply evaporated. The second half was of no use at all, because institutions operated on a basis of unanimity do not deal with the problems created by over-mighty states. Some people believe that consensus means that every member state has an equal vote and therefore a veto, and thus strengthens the position of the weak or reluctant. This was apparently, the view of the Major government, which resisted any increase in majority voting in the European Union.

This view is based on a profound mistake. The central characteristic of consensus institutions is that they strengthen the position of the strong. For example: NATO is run by consensus. Does this mean that Luxembourg has an equal voice with every other member, and therefore a veto? No, it means that NATO is run by the Americans. And in any case, the political utility of this strand of the policy was rendered null and void by the determination of the British that these inter-governmental institutions should be unambitious and unconstraining. For if they were to be unconstraining on the British, then they must also be unconstraining on the Germans.

Very early on, the British considered the question of more ambitious economic co-operation with Europe; but having considered it, they rejected it. This is what the Bridges committee said in January 1949:

> On merits, there is no attraction for us in long-term economic
> co-operation with Europe. At best it will be a drain on our
> resources. At worst, it can seriously damage our economy.[1]

The French came to quite different conclusions. They knew, from their national history, that they had to find a solution to the German problem. They quickly lost interest in Strategy One (divide and rule), as the instrument for dealing with Germany, since NATO was run by the Americans. They tried Strategy Two (a balance-of power alliance), but soon found they had to fold it into NATO (Strategy One). They therefore concluded that there was no alternative to Strategy Three, the negotiation of close, treaty-based relations with Germany (and with such other neighbours of Germany as were willing to see the problem in the same way). That is why, in May 1950, Robert Schuman proposed the creation of a Franco-German Coal and Steel Community.

British reactions to the Schuman Plan were suspicious, angry, and violent. It is instructive to read what they said then, for two reasons. First, because we can see that they really did not understand what the French were about. And second, because we can also see that British understanding of what the French and the others are about today, has not advanced much in the past half century.

Here is an excerpt of the minutes of a British Cabinet meeting on 10 May 1950:

> Mr Morrison said that the proposal might have been primarily economic in its origins, but it clearly had most important political implications. Sir Stafford Cripps agreed that these were the most alarming features of the proposal. It looked like a challenge to the United States and the United Kingdom. It was agreed that it showed a regrettable tendency to move away from the concept of the Atlantic Community and in the direction of a European Federation.
>
> There was general agreement that the French Government had behaved extremely badly in springing this proposal on the world at this juncture without any attempt at consultation with His Majesty's Government or the US Government.[2]

Herbert Morrison was, of course, quite wrong in his analysis. The Schuman Plan was not 'primarily economic in its origins' but explicitly political, as Robert Schuman had carefully explained in his statement in the *Salon de l'Horloge*. The purpose of the plan was not to promote free trade, but to bind France and Germany together, so as to ensure that war could never recur between them. Today, there are many people in Britain who still think that the primary *raison d'être* of the European Union is the promotion of trade liberalisation and economic prosperity. This is not now, and never has been, the central purpose of the process of European integration.

Even where the British perceived the political implications of the Schuman Plan, they misunderstood them. Here is part of a memo from Sir Roger Makins to Ernest Bevin in June 1950:

> It is essentially a question whether European countries should proceed to closer unity by means of intergovernmental arrangements or by steps leading to federation ... His Majesty's Government are not prepared to contemplate entering a federal system composed of western European states.[3]

What this passage shows is that the view in London at that time was that there were only two possible approaches to European problems, the federal and the intergovernmental. There was nothing in between.

Of course, on this question, as on so much else, Sir Roger Makins was totally mistaken. The evidence of the European Community during the past half century proves clearly that there is substantial middle ground between the intergovernmental and the federal. But what makes the Makins passage so spooky is that members of the Major government were still arguing, decades later, in the face of all the evidence, that there was only a stark binomial choice, between intergovernmentalism and federalism. Such a slow learning process does not bode well for the prospects of Britain being able to think through its European dilemma.

British leadership?

Many people have asserted that Britain could, at the beginning, have had the leadership of the new Europe for the asking, so great was its fund of goodwill after the war. And some of them have gone on to assert that Britain could, in those circumstances, have prevented the integrationist urges of other European countries. Russell Bretherton, the notorious Board of Trade official who observed, and then walked out of, the original common market treaty negotiations, was later quoted as saying that: 'If we had taken a firm line, that we wanted to come in and be a part of this, we could have made that body more or less into whatever we liked.' To some people, this may seem a very appealing form of nostalgia, as if to say that, if only Britain had been just a little bit less standoffish in 1949, we could have prevented all this silly integration, and could have insisted on a nice, sensible, intergovemmental, free-trade area.

It seems to me clear that anyone who thinks that this is the answer has not understood the question. The other European countries, starting with France, were not interested in creating a nice, sensible, intergovernmental, free-trade area. What they wanted, was to deal with the German problem, and that required a politically charged treaty with politically constraining institutions. You could add that a politically charged European treaty with politically constraining institutions becomes even more essential, if the Europeans want to be able to move on to deal with their second and third strategic problems: Russia and America. But the German problem has to be solved first. What I am saying here, is that a resolution of Europe's first strategic problem, Germany, is the precondition for Europe breaking out of its victim-submission to the two mega-factors I mentioned at the beginning: the threat of the Russians, and the dominance of the United States.

But even if Britain should come round to the view that it needed a strategy to deal with Europe's central problem, its options would be severely constrained by the views of other European countries. For a strategy of a treaty-based relationship with Germany requires, first, the agreement of the Germans, and second, the agreement of all the other European countries that want to deal with the German problem through a treaty-based relationship with Germany.

German attitudes

The key development of the past 50 years is that the Germans themselves have concluded that Germany is a central strategic problem for Europe; and they have further concluded that this problem must be settled by a treaty-based relationship between Germany and its main European neighbours. This conclusion sets the parameters for everyone else.

If the Germans and the main core countries in Europe want a treaty-based system which tends in a federalising direction, that is the kind of system there will be. Whether it pleases Whitehall or the House of Commons is by now completely immaterial. After all these many years of foot-dragging, Britain's options are now so severely constrained, that it faces a stark choice: fall in with the strategic preferences of the leading core countries (starting with Germany and France), or drop out.

From time to time, over the years, people have canvassed the idea of alternatives to the integrationist agenda. There have been suggestions, for example, that Britain might be able to form alternative alliances by-passing (and therefore neutralising) the core countries; for example with the EFTA countries in the 1950s, or with Italy since then. This could be construed as a resuscitation of the second of the three strategies outlined above, a balance-of-power or deterrence strategy. With hindsight, these attempts look quite stupid; but they always were.

For a while, the Conservative government of John Major adopted a revivalist or evangelical approach, in the hope of dissuading the core European countries from their chosen path. Malcolm Rifkind, when Foreign Secretary, made a series of speeches in a number of European capitals, with the ostensible hope of persuading the Germans, French and others to give up their integrationist agenda, and instead convert to the British government's belief in inter-governmentalism. The self-deception of his proposals was compounded by their tastelessness: in Bonn, Mr Rifkind dared to compare himself to Martin Luther, a piece of impertinent vulgarity which gave new meaning to the word chutzpah. But in any case, his proposals were not adopted, because the leading European governments had worked out that inter-governmentalism could not provide a solution to the strategic problem, which is Germany.

Britain's dilemmas unchanged

In the four years since 1997, much has happened in the European arena, but very little has changed in terms of Britain's relationship to its European dilemma. In the European Union, after the negotiation of the Maastricht treaty of 1991–2, most member states moved decisively towards the launching of the single currency. In the spring of 1997, in Britain, the Conservative government of John Major was replaced by the New Labour government of Tony Blair, who claimed to be, and who may be, a committed pro-European. But in practice his government remained impaled on most of the same dysfunctional anti-European obsessions as its Conservative predecessor, so that when, in January 1999, the single currency was duly launched with the participation of 11 member states, Britain remained, as usual, on the sidelines, a rebel without a cause.

Ostensibly, Britain could join any time soon, since it already fulfils most of the technical economic requirements of the Maastricht treaty, with the notable exception of a stable and sustainable exchange rate. Ostensibly, again, a convenient moment for getting ready to join might come early in a Labour government's second term. However, it is just beginning to occur to some observers that British membership of the euro is not just uncertain, but may be virtually impossible. The government has promised a referendum on euro entry; but public opinion is overwhelmingly hostile to euro membership. The government has presented the euro membership issue as a purely economic choice; but almost everyone can see that a referendum cannot be won on the economic arguments.

Most of the obvious claimed advantages of euro membership (low inflation, low deficits, low unemployment, high growth) are also the pre-conditions for membership: unless you can prove that you can achieve the benefits of monetary stability outside the euro-zone, you will not be allowed inside the zone. But in that case, what arguments will a British government be able to deploy, if it is to persuade a reluctant electorate?

The moral is simple: those other member states which joined the euro-zone, did not do so because they needed it for economic stability, but because they regarded it as an important building block in the construction of a more politically integrated Europe. By the same token, a British government is unlikely to be able to join the euro, unless it can persuade itself, and then the electorate, that Britain's strategic interest lies in being part of a more politically integrated Europe. But by the beginning of 2001 these are ideas which have not yet entered the vocabulary of Tony Blair and his New Labour government.

Apart from the euro, the Blair government has taken two substantial initiatives of European policy; both are designed to side-step or circumvent the mainstream or integrationist channel of European integration. The first was the joint Franco-British declaration at Saint Malo in December 1998, which called for stronger European defence capabilities. This corresponded to a real European need, notably in the light of successive European weaknesses in the wars in Bosnia and Kosovo, and may well lead to the formation of significant European forces for projection overseas. The trouble lies with the pretence that effective defence cooperation between European countries can be conducted on a purely voluntary, inter-governmental basis. This may be possible at the level of war games, but not when it comes to real military action.

The second Blair initiative was his speech on the future of the European Union, which he gave to the Warsaw Stock Exchange in October 2000. This followed spectacular speeches on the future of the European Union, earlier in the year, by Joschka Fischer, the German Foreign Minister, and by Jacques Chirac, the French President, and these in turn prompted quite a rush of speeches from other European leaders. What distinguished the Fischer and Chirac texts, was that they both called for far-reaching steps in further political integration, building on the received Community model. What distinguished the Blair speech, was that he claimed to be seeking a stronger Europe, but in fact advocated measures which would strengthen the element of inter-governmentalism in Europe, at the expense of the received Community model.

So the Blair government's attitudes and actions seem only to have confirmed my central thesis: that the British appear incapable of thinking strategically about their relationship with the rest of Europe. If there was a time when it seemed possible that this fundamental disability might have been a unique idiosyncrasy of the Conservative Party, that hope has been disposed of by New Labour rule. Whether any British government can ever rise to the challenge of grappling effectively with strategic reality, by starting to think seriously about Europe, is one of the biggest conundrums of the new millennium.

Notes

1   5 January 1949, quoted in Edmund Dell, *The Schuman Plan and the British Abdication of Leadership in Europe* (Oxford: Oxford University Press, 1995) p.70.
2   R. Bullen and M E Pelly (eds), *Documents on British Policy Overseas*, series ii, vol. I, *The Schuman Plan, the Council of Europe and Western Eureopan Integration 1950–1952* (London: HMSO, 1986) p.3.
3   Makins to Bevin, 17 June 1950, quoted in Dell, op.cit., p.153.

Index